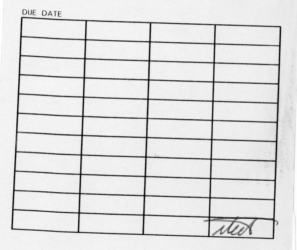

JUL   1991

299.16
E11   Ellis, Peter Ber-
              resford

           A dictionary of
           Irish mythology

DUE DATE

A Dictionary of Irish Mythology

Peter Berresford Ellis

A DICTIONARY OF IRISH MYTHOLOGY

ABC-CLIO

Santa Barbara, California

For EDWARD CARDIFF—last but not least—
who completes the circle

First published in Great Britain 1987
by Constable and Company Limited
10 Orange Street, London WC2H 7EG

Published in the United States by ABC-CLIO, Inc.

Library of Congress Cataloging-in-Publication Data

Ellis, Peter Berresford.
　　A dictionary of Irish mythology / Peter Berresford Ellis.
　　　　p.　　cm.
　　Bibliography: p.
　　1. Mythology, Celtic—Dictionaries. 2. Ireland—Religion—
Dictionaries. 3. Northern Ireland—Religion—Dictionaries.
I. Title.
BL980.I7E45　1989　　299'. 16—dc19　　　89-160

ISBN 0-87436-553-8

96 95 94 93 92 91　　　　　10 9 8 7 6 5 4 3 2

ABC-CLIO, Inc.
Santa Barbara, California

Introduction

T HE Irish language contains one of Europe's oldest and most vibrant mythologies. The language is the vehicle of Europe's third oldest literature being predated only by Greek and Latin. It is a Celtic language, a branch of Goidelic Celtic closely related to Manx and Scottish Gaelic and less closely to the Brythonic Celtic group of Welsh, Cornish and Manx. The Celts were the first transalpine people to emerge into recorded history. It was the Greek chroniclers who first designated them as *Keltoi*. It has been suggested that the word means 'hidden people' because of their reluctance to commit their vast store of scholarship and knowledge to written records until the turn of the Christian era. The etymology of the word may well be the same root which gives us *ceilt*, an act of concealment, and also the word *kilt*, the short male skirt of traditional Celtic dress.

At the start of the first millennium BC the Celts were possessed of great skill in metal work, especially in the use of iron, a metal only then becoming known to the craftsmen of the 'Classical' world. By the end of the sixth century BC their formidable armaments, spears, swords, axes and agricultural implements rendered them superior to their neighbours. Their axes and billhooks enabled them to open roadways through the previously impenetrable forests of Europe and to make extensive clearances. An ancient Irish word for road, avenue or pathway, which is still in use, is *slighe* from the word *sligim* – 'I hew'. It was the Celts, not the Romans, who were the original road-builders of the ancient world, a fact slowly being accepted by scholars in the light of new archaeological finds. To the discerning historian the evidence has always been there, especially in the writings of Julius Caesar. In 1985 a 1000 yard long stretch of road was found preserved in a bog in Co. Longford, demonstrating Celtic skill in road-building. It had a foundation of oak beams, placed side by side on thin rails of oak, ash and alder. The road is dated to about 200BC. What is particularly fascinating is the fact that such a road is mentioned in the area in which it was found in the story of 'The Marriage of Étain', when Eochaidh Airemh the High King imposed the task of building the road, across the bog, on the tribes of Tethbae (a district comprising parts of Co. Westmeath and Co. Longford). The story tells how the task was accomplished with trees used as foundations. The Latin language adopted many Celtic loan-words which were connected with roads and transport, for example the names of various vehicles: *carpentum* (from which both car and carpenter derive), *carruca*, *currus* and *essendum*.

By the ninth century BC the Celts had settled extensively in southern France; they moved into the Iberian peninsula and by the sixth century crossed the Alps into the Italian peninsula. They achieved their greatest expansion from Ireland in the west to Asia Minor in the east in the third century BC. It is generally thought that the first Celtic migrations to the British Isles took place during this period but some modern scholarship suggests that the first Celtic peoples may well have arrived as early as 2000BC and definitely not later than 1000BC. The last series of Celtic migrations to Britain occurred in the second century BC when the Belgic tribes crossed from the country which still bears their name (Belgium) to southern Britain.

Although the Irish were firmly established in Ireland, distinct from the rest of the Celtic peoples by this time, there was a great sense of unity within the Celtic world. The Irish traded extensively with their fellow Celts in Britain and Gaul and the Gauls were in regular contact with all parts of the Celtic world – even with the Galatians in what is now Turkey. This Celtic kingdom had been established in the third century BC and its people were still clinging tenaciously to their language and culture as late as the fifth century AD. So close were the contacts between the Celts that the Senate of Marseilles asked the Gaulish druids to persuade the Galatians not to aid Antiochus III of Syria in his war against Rome in 197BC. In fact, it was the druidic religion and the institution of the druids which was the corner-stone of the Celtic world, linking the Celts of Ireland with their fellow Celts in Britain and on the Continent in a common heritage.

It is natural, therefore, that Irish mythology should have its closest parallels in the mythology of Wales, representing the Brythonic Celtic culture. The old gods of Ireland are to be found in counterpart in the old gods of Wales. Bilé, for example, is Bel or Beli; Nuada occurs as Nudd and sometimes Ludd; Lir is easily recognisable as Llyr; Manannán, his son, is Manawyddan; Lugh Lámhfada is Llew Law Gyffes; while Dana, the mother of the gods, is Don. It is even argued that Fionn Mac Cumhail has a Welsh equivalent in Gwyn ap Nudd. It is significant that both Fionn and Gwyn have the same meaning – 'fair'.

However, the Welsh material is nowhere near as extensive or so old as the Irish tales and sagas. Welsh mythology's earliest survivals are from the fourteenth century AD, mainly in the *Red Book of Hergest* and the *White Book of Rhydderch*. Today we tend to speak of this corpus of mythology under the collective name 'The Mabinogion' which was the title given by Lady Charlotte Guest to her translations from the *Red Book of Hergest* in 1838. There are other mythological tales and romances to be found outside 'The Mabinogion'.

The fact that one can see relationships and counterparts demonstrates that Irish mythology is not a separate entity from the rest of the Celtic world. In it we find echoes of a common Celtic mythological, religious and, perhaps, historical experience.

It was unfortunate that after the long centuries of oral tradition, by which the tales and sagas were handed down, when they came to be written a new and demanding religion had replaced the one which the original stories reflected. The Christian scribes, in setting down the stories, were conscious of their new dogma and their transcriptions often bowdlerised the concepts and themes of the original versions, giving the tales an odd Christian veneer and, quite often, introducing improbable Christian appendages. The sea-god Manannán Mac Lir, in one story, foretells the coming of Christ to save the world. In another tale, the great champion Cúchulainn pleads with St. Patrick to intercede with Christ to save him from the fires of Hell, out of which the saint has summoned him to prove a point to a pagan Irish monarch. Thankfully, the scribes were only human and the stories were set down by individuals, working at varying times and copying more often than not from older books. Therefore much of the pre-Christian vitality survives.

According to the Celtic scholar Georges Dottin, 'it is probable that the most ancient pieces of the epic literature of Ireland were written before the middle of the seventh century; but how long previously they had been preserved by oral tradition – this is a point that is difficult to estimate'. It is sad that most of the early books have not survived. During the so-called Dark Ages, an age of golden enlightenment for Ireland, when Ireland was famous for her centres of learning throughout Europe, there were numerous *Tech Screpta*, or great libraries, in the country. There are frequent references to the enormous amount of Irish manuscript books and the 'host of books' in Ireland became proverbial. At the end of the eighth century, however, the Vikings began their raids on the country. Entire libraries were looted or destroyed. The years of book destruction continued until the Norse were finally defeated by the High King Brían Bóramha at Clontarf in AD1014. So the main surviving manuscript sources date only from the late eleventh century.

The oldest surviving books which provide the richest sources are the *Leabhar na hUidre*, known as the Book of the Dun Cow, the *Leabhar Laignech* or Book of Leinster and a book known by its Bodleian Library reference – Rawlinson Manuscript B 502. The *Leabhar na hUidre* was compiled under the supervision of Mael Muire mac Céilechair, who was killed by marauders at the monastery of Clonmacnoise in AD1106. The *Leabhar Laignech* was originally called *Leabhar na Nuachongbála*, after Noughaval in Leix, and was compiled by Aed Mac Crimthainn, head of the monastery at Tír-dá-ghlas (Terryglass in Tipperary). The Rawlinson Manuscript appears to have been compiled at Clonmacnoise.

Professor Kuno Meyer, in his introduction to *Liadain and Curithir: A Love Story* (1900) listed four hundred sagas and tales in manuscript. He added the figure of a further hundred which had been brought to light since he had compiled his list and mentioned an estimated further fifty to a hundred tales which could lie in libraries still undiscovered. He believed, therefore, that there were some five to six hundred tales of which only one hundred and fifty had been translated and annotated when he was writing. Eleanor Hull, in the introduction to her work *The Cuchullin Saga in Irish Literature* (1898), made a similar estimation. It is surprising that the bulk of these manuscripts still remain unedited and untranslated (even into modern Irish).

Modern scholarship has made its own categorisation of the sagas and romances.

1. The Mythological Cycle; that is the stories relating to the various invasions of Ireland from Cesair to the sons of Milesius and mainly concerned with the activities of the Tuatha Dé Danaan.
2. The Ulster Cycle, or deeds of the Red Branch which include the Cúchulainn tales.
3. The Cycle of the Kings, stories relating to the adventures of semi-mythical rulers.
4. The Fenian Cycle, the adventures of Fionn Mac Cumhail and the warriors of the Fianna.

While this categorisation is generally accepted I believe it is confusing and certainly misleading to entitle the first section of tales 'The *Mythological* Cycle', as being apart from the others. All the tales are myths to a greater or lesser degree. Characters from one cycle will turn up in another while the gods are all-pervasive. Although scholars are quite right to attempt a useful category system, I see nothing wrong in the system adopted in ancient times.

According to the old chroniclers of Ireland, the stories were classified into *prim-scéil* (chief tales) and *fo-scéil* (minor tales). These were sub-divided. The *prim-scéil* were: 1. battles; 2. voyages; 3. tragedies; 4. adventures; 5. cattle-raids; 6. military expeditions; 7. courtships; 8. elopements; 9. concealments; 10. destructions; 11. sieges; 12. feasts; 13. slaughters. The *fo-scéil* were: 1. pursuits; 2. visions; 3. exiles or banishments; 4. lake eruptions.

The Brehon Laws, the ancient law system of Ireland, stipulated that only qualified story-tellers could recite these sagas and tales. To be able to tell both chief and minor tales one had to have achieved the four top degrees available at the bardic schools. These corresponded to the classifications which we use at our modern universities such as fresh-man, sophomore, bachelor, master and doctor. The four top Irish degrees were *Cana* (fifth year of study), *Cli* (sixth year of study), *Anruth* (seventh to ninth year of study) and *Ollamh* (tenth to twelfth year of study). The *Ollamh* was the equivalent to 'professor' and, indeed, remains the modern Irish word for a professor. Therefore, only the *Cana*, *Cli*, *Anruth* and *Ollamh* could recite all the stories. With the suppression of the bardic schools in the seventeenth century by the English, the old oral tradition of story-telling was taken up by *seanchaí*, which word has come down in English as seannachie. It was stipulated in ancient law that a qualified story-teller should know at least two hundred *prim-scéil* and one hundred *fo-scéil*.

In Irish mythology one enters a fascinating world of fantasy which is remote from the Classical world of Greek and Latin myth. Yet, at the same time, one is constantly surprised by the fact that Irish mythology seems to share a curious Mediterranean warmth with the Classical myths rather than falling under the brooding bleakness that permeates Nordic myth. At times it is difficult to realise that we are talking of a north-west European culture. A happy spirit pervades the majority of tales, even in the tragedies such as 'The Fate of the Sons of Usna' or 'The Pursuit of Diarmuid and Gráinne'. There is an eternal spirit of optimism. Death is never the conqueror and we are reminded, of course, that the Celts were one of the first cultures to evolve a doctrine of immortality of the soul. The druids taught that death is only a changing of place and that life goes on with all its forms and goods in another world. The similarity of druidic ideas on immortality and the Pythagorean philosophy has frequently been remarked upon. Clement of Alexandria has written that Pythagoras had a slave who was a Celt and who introduced the Greek philosopher to the druidic concepts. Celtic philosophy was highly regarded among the Greeks. Aristotle, Sotion and Clement all state that early Greek philosophers borrowed many of their doctrines from the Celts.

To say that a happy spirit pervades the Irish myths is not to say that evil is never encountered. Indeed, as in the real world, good and evil are constantly rubbing shoulders and the malevolent forms of the Fomorii, lords of darkness and death, are constantly hovering on the edge of the northern ocean.

To those imbued with later folkloric developments in Ireland, it may come as a surprise to know that the old Irish gods are neither 'little people' nor 'fairies'. They are tall, beautiful and fair. They are superior to humans in their physical strength, power and handsomeness. They are somewhat reminiscent of the descriptions of the ancient Celts which survive in the writings of the Greeks and Romans. The gods also have the ability to shape-change. They appear basically as the ancestors of the people rather than their creators.

Both the gods and human heroes and heroines are no mere physical beauties with empty heads. Their intellectual attributes are equal to their physical capabilities. And they are totally human in that they are subject to all the natural virtues and vices. No sin out of the seven deadly ones is exempt from practice either by gods or humans. Their world, both this one and the Otherworld, is one of rural happiness, a world in which they indulge in all the pleasures of life in an idealised form: love of nature, art, games, feasting and heroic single combat. It was sometimes hard for the Christian scribes to admit to the old gods and often they appeared as merely mortals or, at best, evil spirits. Eochaidh Ó Fláinn (d. AD1003), an Irish poet, wrote a discourse in which he examined the ancient gods, debating whether they were demons or devils, but, conscious of the dogmas of his religion, suggested that they were merely humans without supernatural powers, heroes and heroines made into gods by his ancestors. This view also tends to be the modern view of all the world mythologies. Certainly Irish mythology is essentially an heroic one and the Irish do appear to have made their heroes into gods and their gods into heroes. In the lives of these gods and heroes, the lives of the people and the essence of their religious traditions are mirrored.

Before the eleventh century it was Cúchulainn, the Hound of Ulster, who was undoubtedly the national hero of Ireland. He has been equated with the Greek hero Achilles. The stories of the Ulster Cycle, in which he features, were popular, but particuarly so among the élite of society. The stories are an heroic literature *par excellence*, concerning themselves with the activities and virtues which typify heroic society. The scholar Alfred Nutt estimated that the entire literature of the Ulster Cycle known to contemporary scholarship would occupy a volume of two thousand pages, if all repetitions were edited out. The Ulster Cycle was considered literature of great prestige.

However, after the eleventh century, the hero Fionn Mac Cumhail, the warrior and leader of the High King's élite bodyguard, the Fianna, took Cúchulainn's place as the national hero. The Fenian Cycle became more popular among the ordinary people of Ireland in medieval times. The surviving stories, mainly told in poetic and ballad form, remain far less in number than the surviving Ulster Cycle tales.

In more recent centuries, linguistic changes in Ireland nearly destroyed the continuity of the mythological tradition. Although the vast majority of people in Ireland spoke Irish until the early nineteenth century, it should be recalled that the English conquests of the seventeenth century had all but destroyed the native intelligentsia. The learned classes of society had been especially singled out and had been killed or sent into exile as part of the conquests. As one poet, Aindrias Mac Marcais, writing in the mid-seventeenth century, put it:

Gan gaire fa ghniomhradh leinbh

There is no laughter at children's doings.
Music is prohibited, the Irish language is in chains.

Through the seventeenth and eighteenth centuries, the years of the English Penal Laws in Ireland, serious attempts were made to eradicate the language and culture, and many manuscripts and books were destroyed. Most books written in Irish during this period were actually printed in Europe. Antwerp, Brussels, Paris and Louvain became the principal centres for Irish publishing and the works, ranging from dictionaries and grammars to historical and religious tracts,

were smuggled into Ireland in an attempt to keep up a literary
continuity.

For most of the population, however, Irish mythology had become a
mere folkloric tradition, tales recited by the village story-teller (the
seanchaí) around the hearth at night, their origin and symbolism
forgotten. Few were even aware that the ancient tales had written form.
Yet while 'official' Ireland, through its English and English-speaking
administrators, presented an Anglicised face to the world, a hidden
Ireland, an *Irish* Ireland, co-existed, as has been excellently demonstrated in Daniel Corkery's study *The Hidden Ireland* (1924). Among
the Irish writers and poets who were still creating new versions of the
old myths was the Protestant Irish writer Micheál Coimín (1688–1760)
of Co. Clare. Among his surviving works was *Laoi Oisín ar Thír na nÓg*
(Lay of Oisín in the Land of Youth).

Yet the fate of the bulk of Micheál Coimín's work reflected what was
generally happening in Ireland. Coimín's son, Edward, had become
Anglicised, which also meant an acceptance that everything Irish was
worthless and something to be ashamed of, particularly the language.
Edward was so embarrassed at being the son of an Irish poet that after
his father's death he burnt all the manuscripts he could find in the
house, therefore little survives of Coimín's works.

Ironically, towards the end of the eighteenth century, Anglicised
antiquarians and folklorists were making strenuous efforts to record
and translate native traditions in English and some were trying to
preserve the language. Among the first societies formed about this time
to 'preserve' Irish was Cuideacht Gaedhilge Uladh (Ulster Gaelic
Society), founded by Belfast Presbyterians in 1830. One of its aims was
to secure 'education through the medium of the Irish language, whether
by means of Stationary or of Circulating Schools'. The president of the
Ulster Gaelic Society was the Marquis of Downshire, who wrote: 'The
Ancient Irish Literature ought no longer to remain in the obscurity
in which it has been laid.' The Ulster Presbyterian, Christopher
Anderson, author of *Historical Sketches of the Ancient Irish* (1826), had a
profound effect in the move to 'rescue' Irish and its literature. He not
only pointed to the literary wealth in Irish but denounced the English
policy of Anglicisation and the wrong being done by keeping people
illiterate in their own language. Anderson was extremely active in the
move to reprint the Bible in Irish and use it as a means of teaching the
language. It was Anderson who translated into Irish John Bunyan's
Pilgrim's Progress, published in 1835.

While some laboured to preserve the language, others worked at collecting the new oral tradition. Among the first to record the myths in English as they had come down in this new tradition was William Carleton (1794–1869) with works such as *Traits and Stories of the Irish Peasantry* (1830) and *Tales of Ireland* (1834) which became very popular. T. Crofton Croker (1798–1854), with his *The Fairy Legend and Tradition of the South of Ireland* (1825) and *Legends of the Lakes* (1829), made this folkloric research fashionable. The Brothers Grimm became interested in Irish legends and translated *The Fairy Legend* into German. Oscar Wilde's mother, Lady Jane Francesca Wilde, was also fascinated in collecting the tales which she published in *Ancient Legends, Mystic Charms and Superstitions of Ireland* (1888).

The first writer to seize upon the written tradition of Irish mythology and attempt to popularise it again was Standish James O'Grady (1846–1928). He must not be confused with his cousin Standish Hayes O'Grady (1832–1915) who was an Irish scholar, president of the Ossianic Society in 1856, and whose *Silva Gadelica* (1892) was a valuable translation of mythological tales from some of the old Irish manuscripts. Standish *James* O'Grady has been called the 'Father of the Irish Literary Revival'. It must be pointed out that the 'Irish Literary Revival' of the late nineteenth century meant the creation of a literature written in English. O'Grady discovered the fascination of Irish mythology by reading the work of Eugene O'Curry (1796–1862). *Manners and Customs of the Ancient Irish* (1873) was a collection of a series of lectures O'Curry had given, forming a comprehensive account of the principal Irish medieval manuscripts, chronicles, tales and poems. O'Grady's interest caused him to write *The History of Ireland: The Heroic Period* (1878–80). He then began to publish a series of novels based on mythological themes such as *Finn and His Companions* (1892) and *The Coming of Cuchulain* (1894). It is acknowledged that he awoke his contemporaries to the existence of Ireland's epic literature.

Lady Isabella Gregory (1852–1932) took the work further by publishing new English versions of the heroic sagas under the titles of *Cuchulain of Muirthemne* (1902), a book which Theodore Roosevelt is said to have carried with him on his travels, and *Gods and Fighting Men* (1904). Also working at this time on Ireland's ancient literature was the scholar Douglas Hyde (1860–1949), who became the first President of the Irish State in 1937. A Protestant from Co. Roscommon, he used the pen-name *An Craoibhín Aoibhinn* ('the delightful little branch') to publish re-tellings of folktales and myths which kindled the imagination of Lady Gregory and W. B. Yeats and others in the Irish Literary Revival movement. His study of the literature in the Irish language, *A Literary History of Ireland* (1899), remains a classic textbook.

Among all the people working in this field, scholars, novelists and poets, during this time, it is the poet William Butler Yeats (1865–1935) who remains the most internationally known figure of the Irish Literary Revival. In 1923 Yeats was awarded the Nobel Prize for Literature. He first fell under the spell of Standish James O'Grady and then John O'Leary (1830–1907). O'Leary was a Fenian leader and journalist who had served nine years' imprisonment for his political activities. Yeats helped O'Leary found the National Literary Society in Dublin in 1891 whose immediate object was to publicise and promote Irish mythology and folklore. In 1889 Yeats had published *The Wandering of Oisín*. Soon numerous poems and plays on mythological themes were to follow from his pen.

In recent years Irish mythology has been undergoing a new wave of popularity in modern fantasy writing with numerous re-tellings and fantasy novels based loosely on the Irish sagas. A curious impetus was given to the development of Irish mythology as a vehicle of modern fantasy by an American 'pulp' magazine writer, Robert E. Howard (1906–36). A Texan, Howard managed to achieve an enviably productive writing career before, at the age of thirty, he committed suicide in a fit of depression. He was an eager student of Irish mythology and, while he did not have any Irish ancestry, he claimed to be 'four-fifths' Irish to the extent that he sometimes Gaelicised his name. His most famous creation was Conan the Barbarian, now the hero of numerous books, comics and a recent major film production. Howard's literary executor Glenn Lord has written: 'Conan was a literary descendant of Conan from the Fenian, or Ossianic myth cycle.' Conan became so popular that the series of Conan books has been continued by a new generation of writers such as L. Sprague de Camp, Lin Carter, Björn Nyberg and Andrew Offutt. Another creation of Howard's was his hero Bran Mak Morn, who has also achieved a lasting literary popularity amongst devotees of fantasy literature.

Today's generation of fantasy writers are certainly conscious of the scope and possibility in the use of Irish mythology as a fertile ground for ideas and background. Works range from stories inspired by the myths, such as Patricia Finney's *A Shadow of Gulls* (1977) and *The Crow Goddess* (1978) and Patricia Keneally's *The Copper Crown* (1984), to

Lord Tennyson. This was later set to music by the Irish composer, Charles Vivian Standford (1852–1924).

Like Greek mythology, Irish mythology has not confined its influence simply to literary expression. It has inspired a great deal of musical composition. This would be the subject of a study in itself, even if one confined oneself to Irish composers and went no further back than Turlough Carolan. Yet Irish mythological themes have been used by American, Australian, British, German, Russian and Swiss composers. Sir Arnold Bax (1883–1953), a naturalised Irish citizen, regarded as the leading composer of the 'Celtic Revival', used such themes for many of his symphonic poems (as in 'The Garden of Fand') and his symphonies. Fiona MacLeod's drama 'The Immortal Hour' was given an operatic setting by Rutland Boughton (1878–1960) which had the longest consecutive run of any opera anywhere in the world. The first symphony of importance produced in America was the 'Gaelic Symphony' by A. M. Beach (1867–1944). Here it must be mentioned that it is sometimes thought that Mendelssohn's overture 'Fingal's Cave', first performed in London in 1832, was inspired by MacPherson's *Ossian*. However, it is generally accepted that the music was written after a visit to the cave, in Scotland.

In summary, Irish mythology is one of the bright gems of European cultural inheritance. As Professor Kenneth Jackson once put it (in *The Oldest Irish Tradition: A Window on the Iron Age*, Cambridge, 1964), Irish myth presents a fascinating window on society in Iron Age Europe. He also points out that the myths differ from the early epics of other peoples in that 'they are inclined to desert the natural and possible for the impossible and supernatural, chiefly in the form of fantastic exaggeration. One should not misunderstand this, however; it was not done in all seriousness, but for its own sake, for the fun of the thing' (*A Celtic Miscellany*, London, 1951). Irish mythology is both unique and dynamic, a mythology which ought to be as well known and as valued as those of ancient Greece and Rome.

In endeavouring to present a work for the lay reader there are some problems which need comment. The major one is that of obtaining a consistency in the spelling of names. In this respect we are not simply dealing with the natural orthographical changes of a language over the centuries. Irish, in respect of natural orthographical change, can be divided into Old Irish (AD700–950); Middle Irish (950–1350); Early Modern (1350–1650) and Late Modern (1650 to date). It should also be pointed out that some new spellings were introduced in the mid-1950s and these achieved standard recognition with the publication of the De Bhaldraithe dictionary in June 1959. As a language, Irish achieved a standard orthography at a very early stage with a much more consistent grammar and spelling standard than, for example, English.

The main problem lies in the displacement of Irish by English as the more widely used language in Ireland and, from that position, in presenting a dictionary for the English reader. Because of the linguistic changes in Ireland, the nineteenth-century interpreters of the myths tried to make things easier on English readers by inventing their own varied systems of Anglicised spellings. Instead of making things easier, they merely caused greater confusion. For example, the High King Eterscél can appear as Eterscelae, Etterskel, Eidirskeal, Edersceal and even Aedarscal. Some interpreters were unsure of names given in dative, genitive and vocative form. An easy example of 'sound difference' can be demonstrated with the common name Séamas. In vocative form, this becomes Shéamais, pronounced 'Hamish' in English phonetics. Thus Hamish has become an accepted fore-name in English without it being generally realised that this is simply a vocative form.

To overcome this difficulty, Jeffrey Gantz, in *Early Irish Myths and Sagas* (Penguin Classics, 1981), decided to leave all proper names in their Old Irish spelling 'which seemed preferable to Anglicization and modernizations'. Yet the hero Cúchulainn is more popularly recognised by that form than by Cú Chulaind. While in many ways I agree with Dr Gantz's motives, my aim is to present a work for English readers and therefore it has been impossible to agree on a spelling standard. I have attempted to resolve this problem by putting down the most popular form encountered, often with cross-references to other spellings.

Another difficulty has been the confusion of the variation in versions of the tales. Because the manuscript sources were written down by diverse hands at various times over the centuries, the names of many minor characters have become confused and events accredited to one person in one version may be accredited to another in a second account. For example, Naoise, the son of Usna, is killed by a Norse prince called Maine in one account, and by Eoghan Mac Duthacht in another. Gelban is named as Conchobhar Mac Nessa's spy in one version of 'The Fate of the Sons of Usna' while he becomes Trendorm in another version. Tuireann, in the Fenian Cycle, is variously given as the sister, sister-in-law and even aunt of Fionn Mac Cumhail. Where this confusion applies I have given the differing versions and cross-references.

The difficulties caused by both spelling and the differing versions should have been tackled by Irish scholars before now. The fact that so many Irish manuscripts remain untouched by the academic world is rather surprising. It is my sincere wish that before long, with the backing of the Irish state and its academic resources, a complete and careful study and synthesis of all the manuscript sources of Irish mythology could be made with the purpose of producing an exhaustive academic reference dictionary, containing all the names, major and minor, with their variants and manuscript references with modern acceptable forms: a reference work, for example, on the model of the five-volume study *Greek Mythology*, compiled under the editorship of I. T. Cacridis (Ekdotiki, Athens, 1986).

Before moving from the difficulties of handling the material, I must also point out the problem of delineating where Irish myth ends and history begins. The Celts frequently embellished their historical accounts with allegories, supernatural happenings and meaningful fantasy. Newcomers to the myths may therefore be surprised to find historical High Kings and personages given reference in this work. The accounts of their reigns and stories related to them were often mythologised by the medieval writers and therefore they become part of mythology itself rather than history. One could, of course, move from this point into a deeper discourse as to what is mythology and what is history. As Napoleon Bonaparte once said: 'What is history but a myth agreed upon?'

In compiling this dictionary, I must stress again that I do not pretend that I am producing an all-embracing guide for academic reference nor am I qualified to do so. This work is essentially for the lay reader; a guide for enthusiasts by which they may pick their way through the fascinating labyrinth of one of Europe's oldest mythologies. It is simply a who's who and what's what of the epic sagas and tales; an accessible, easy-to-use handbook, giving an immediate reference to the gods and goddesses, the heroes and heroines, the magical weapons, fabulous beasts and Otherworld entities that populate the stories.

Peter Berresford Ellis
'Lios na nAislingí'

A. *Ailm* (pine) in the Ogham alphabet.

Abarta. Also known as Giolla Deacair (the Hard Servant), Abarta was a mischievous member of the Tuatha Dé Danaan. The name signifies 'The performer of feats'. He sought to become the servant of Fionn Mac Cumhail. He came to the Fianna with an ugly, grey horse which was of a nasty temper and which attacked the horses of the warriors. Conan Maol managed to put a halter on it and tried to ride it but the horse refused to move. The other members of the Fianna suggested that Conan was not heavy enough and no fewer than fourteen warriors mounted the beast. Abarta then mounted behind them and the horse galloped away with a fifteenth member of the Fianna, Liagan, running behind and holding its tail, unable to let go. In this fashion Abarta returned to the Otherworld with his captives. Fionn sought the aid of Faruach, who could make a ship by magic, and Foltor, the best tracker in Ireland, and, together with the rest of the Fianna, they tracked Abarta to the Otherworld. Abarta agreed to release his prisoners but Conan Maol demanded reparation, suggesting that fourteen of Abarta's servants should ride the horse back to Ireland while Abarta himself should run behind holding on to its tail. Abarta agreed and there was a peace between him and the Fianna.

Abhean. A harper of the Tuatha Dé Danaan who came to them from the hills; in some versions he appears as a mysterious Fomorii.

Accasbel. A follower of Partholón who is said to have built the first tavern in Ireland.

Acéin. See **Ochain**.

Adhnuall. One of the hounds belonging to Fionn Mac Cumhaill which was stolen by Arthur, son of the King of Britain. The Fianna chased Arthur and recovered the hound. Later, after a battle in Leinster, Adhnuall strayed and circled Ireland three times until he returned to

the battlefield. The hound came to a hill where three of the
Fianna were buried. At this spot the hound gave three howls and
died.

Adna. 1. Chief poet of Ireland during the early days of Conchobhar
Mac Nessa and the champions of the Red Branch. He was father of
the poet Neide.

2. An explorer sent by Ninus, King of Assyria, to report on conditions in Ireland.

Aedan. The warrior who slew Mael Fhothartaig, son of Ronán, King of
Leinster, on the orders of Ronán himself because the king was made
jealous of his own son by his young bride. Aedan was slain by Mael
Fhothartaig's sons. See **Mael Fhothartaig**.

Aedh. Sometimes given as Aed.

1. The father of Macha Mong Ruadh (see **Macha** 4). He is said to
have been King of Ireland in the fourth century BC, ruling alternately
with his brothers Dithorba and Cimbaeth, sometimes referred to as
his cousins.

2. A son of Fionn Mac Cumhail.

3. A king of Oriel (Airgialla) who carried a shield called Dubhghiolla
(Black Servant) on whose rim Badb, one of the goddesses of war,
perched in the form of a crow.

4. Original name of Goll Mac Morna, the leader of the Fianna who
slew Fionn's father.

5. The dwarf of Fergus Mac Léide of Ulster who accompanied the
poet Eisirt to the Otherworld kingdom of the Faylinn, a land of little
people ruled by Iubdan.

6. A son of the god Bodb Dearg.

7. The son of Ainmire. Aedh was High King and made war on the
wily Brandubh, King of Leinster. Aedh was defeated and perished at
Brandubh's hands because he lost a magic cowl which protected him
from being wounded or slain in battle. Another version of this story
has him slain by Brandubh's spy, Ron Cerr, while a Christian
appendage has the magic cowl given as a present from St. Colmcille
(Columba).

8. One of the four children of the ocean-god, Lir, who was changed
into a swan by his stepmother Aoife.

9. A son of Miodhchaoin. He and his two brothers, Corca and Conn,
were slain by the three sons of Tuireann, Brían, Iuchar and Iucharba.
However, before their death they mortally wounded the sons of
Tuireann. See **Tuireann** 3.

10. A giant. Sometimes given as Aeda. A young man, smooth-featured and of surpassing beauty, who bore a red shield and a huge spear. He slew Bebhionn, daughter of Treon of the Land of Maiden, because she refused to wed him. Bebhionn, a beautiful giantess, sought aid from Fionn Mac Cumhail and his Fianna because she had been bethrothed to Aedh against her will. After Aedh slew her, the Fianna gave chase but when they reached the sea they found Aedh had a great war galley waiting for him and he escaped. Before she died, Bebhionn distributed her jewels to the Fianna. They buried her at a spot called Ridge of the Dead Woman and placed an Ogham-inscribed stone over the grave.

11. Aedh Dubh. He slew the High King Diarmuid Mac Cearbal in the house of Banbán in accordance with a prophecy given by the druid Bec Mac Dé. Bec foretold that Diarmuid would be killed in Banbán's house when he wore a shirt grown from a single flax, when he drank ale brewed from a single grain of corn, and when he ate bacon from a swine that was never farrowed. The manner of his death would be from a spear, from drowning, from burning and from a ridge pole falling on his head. Incredibly, all these things came to pass. See **Diarmuid** 2.

Aeí, Plain of. The place of the bull strife. At the end of the *Táin* saga (q.v.) Donn, the Brown Bull of Cuailgne, and Finnbhennach, the White Horned Bull of Connacht, had their last great battle on this plain. Bricriu Mac Carbad, asked by the men of Ireland to judge the terrible contest, was trampled to death as the Bulls clashed. They fought for three days and nights before the White Horned Bull was slain but the Brown Bull, mortally wounded, turned back to his home before dropping dead at Druim Tarb, the Ridge of the Bull. See **Donn** 6 and **Finnbhennach**.

Aenghus. See **Aonghus**.

Áes. Sometimes Oes. People or folk, etc. *Áes sídhe*, 'the people of the hills', is the name given to the old Irish gods who dwell in hills (*sídhe*) who were later relegated to fairies in popular imagination. Hence the modern Irish word *sióg* for fairy. See under **Sídhe**. *Áes dana* were a learned class who were said to have been ennobled by their art. The class included the *filí* (poets) as well as judges, doctors of medicine, metal-workers and wood-workers.

Age, Feast of. Fleadh Áise. One of the annual festivals of the Tuatha Dé Danaan held at each of their palaces in rotation. It was when Aoife, the second wife of the ocean-god Lir, was on her way to the

Feast of Age at the *sídhe* of Bodb Dearg that she turned her
stepchildren into swans.

Agnoman. Father of Nemed who led his people from Scythia to Ireland
but who had to fight with the Fomorii. See **Nemed** and **Nemedians**.

Aí. Sometimes given as Aoi Mac Ollamain. The poet of the Tuatha Dé
Danaan. When his mother was pregnant the house was rocked by a
great wind and a druid foretold that the child would have wonderful
powers. The king ordered the child to be slain but his father,
Olloman, saved him. The child grew up to ask a boon of the king and
from his poetical pleadings he was accorded the name Aí which,
according to Cormac's Glossary, meant 'poem'.

Aibell. Sometimes Aoibhell. She ruled a *sídhe* in north Munster but
little is recorded of her before she became relegated to 'fairy' status by
popular folklore. She became the guardian spirit of the Dál gCais, the
Dalcassians or Ó Bríen clan. Her dwelling place was at Craig Liath,
the grey rock, two miles north of Killaloe. Her name signifies
'beautiful' (*aoibhinn*). She was the lover of Dubhlainn Ua Artigan and
she possessed a magic harp. Whoever heard its music did not live long
afterwards.

Aichleach. He slew Fionn Mac Cumhaill during a rebellion of the
Fianna. See **Uigreann**.

Aidín. Sometimes Aideen. She is described as a foreigner who became
the wife of Oscar son of Oisín. Hearing of his death at the Battle of
Gabhra, she died of grief and was buried by Oscar's father on Ben
Edar (Howth) where an Ogham stone was set up in her memory.

Aige. A daughter of Broccaid Mac Bric. Because of envy she was turned
into a fawn and slain by the warriors of Meilge, the High King. See
Fafne and **Meilge**.

Ailbe. 1. A daughter of Cormac Mac Art who answered a set of riddles
put to her by Fionn Mac Cumhail, won his love and was invited to live
with him.

2. The hound of Mac Da Thó in one version of the tale. See **Mac Da
Thó**. See also **Ossar**.

Aileach. A major fortress in Ulster. Its ruins still stand in Co. Donegal,
five miles north-west of Derry. The remains are of a circular stone
wall 77 feet in internal diameter and 13 feet thick at its base. It was
built by the Tuatha Dé Danaan and it was here that Mac Cuill, Mac
Cécht and Mac Gréine and their wives, the goddesses Banba, Fótla
and Éire, decided to divide Ireland between them. Aileach is mentioned in the *Great Book of Lecan*, compiled by Giolla Íosa Mac

Firbhisigh (d. 1418). It was the royal residence of the kings of Ulster and later of the kings of Ireland until the fourth century AD. It became the seat of the Ó Néill kings until the early twelfth century when it was destroyed by Murchertagh, king of Munster, in retaliation for the destruction of Kincora in 1088. After that it was abandoned.

Ailill. 1. Ailill Áine son of Laoghaire, king of Leinster. He was poisoned by Cobhthach, king of Bregia, and his son was made to eat his flesh. The trauma struck the boy dumb so that he became known as Móen (dumb). When the boy recovered his speech he was named as Labraid Loinseach. See **Móen**.

2. Ailill Mac Máta, king of Connacht and husband of Medb who features prominently in the saga of the *Táin Bo Cuailgne*. He is depicted as a weak man, easily swayed by the powerful Medb. She taunted him into going to war with Ulster in order to acquire the Brown Bull of Cuailgne, which war he lost. He also features in the story of Mac Da Thó's boar. He was eventually slain by Conall who cast a spear at him while he was bathing in a lake with Medb. Conall killed him in revenge for the death of Fergus Mac Roth.

3. The brother of Eochaid, High King of Ireland. Ailill fell in love with his brother's wife, Étain Echraide, and succumbed to a wasting sickness during which time Étain nursed him. While Eochaidh was on a tour of his kingdom, Ailill vowed his love for Étain. The girl did not want to see a man die for love of her even though she did not reciprocate his love. She arranged an assignation with Ailill but, at the appointed time, Ailill fell into an enchanted sleep and when he awoke his love-sickness was cured. During the sleep a man in Ailill's shape came to her. It was the god Midir. Étain was one of the Tuatha Dé Danaan who had been reborn as a mortal and Midir had been her husband. See **Étain** 2.

4. Ailill Agach or Edge-of-Battle of the sept of Eoghan of Aran. He was the father of the hero Mael Dúin. On a raid to the mainland from the Aran islands, Ailill ravished a nun, Aoife, who bore a son, Mael Dúin. Soon after, Ailill himself was slain by marauders.

5. Ailill of Aran, not to be confused with Ailill Agach (4). He was the father of three beautiful daughters, Aebh, Aoife and Arbha. The god Bodb Dearg was their foster-father and Ailill offered them in marriage to the ocean-god, Lir.

6. Ailill Dubh-dédach, son of Mongán Minscothach and known as 'Black-toothed Ailill'. No weapon could harm him yet he was slain by Art during his quest for the beautiful Delbchaem.

7. Ailill Olom, or Bare-ear, a king of Munster who raped the love-goddess Áine. Áine cut off his ear and afterwards slew him by magic.

8. Ailill, a king of Ulster and father of Étain Echraide. When the love-god Aonghus Óg came to him seeking the hand of Étain on behalf of Midir of Brí Léith, Ailill set him three tasks: clearing twelve plains; draining them by making twelve rivers flow from them to the sea; and, finally, giving his daughter's exact weight in gold and silver. Aonghus Óg accomplished these tasks with the help of his father, the Dagda.

Áille. Áille Shnuadh-Gheal, the Fair. She was wife to Meargach of the Green Spears who was slain by Oscar at the battle of Cnoc-an-Air. In revenge Aille had her druid, Fer Gruadh (The Grey Man), drug and capture Fionn Mac Cumhail, the leader of the Fianna and Oscar's grandfather. The Fianna pursued Fer Gruadh but the druid placed them all under his control until Conan tricked him into releasing them. Oscar killed him and Áille committed suicide.

Aillén. Son of Midhna. A malevolent Otherworld creature which came out of the cave of Cruach each year at the feast of Samhain and burnt down the royal residence at Tara after lulling the defenders asleep with enchanted music. Fionn Mac Cumhail was able to resist the music by pressing his spear to his forehead. Fionn drove off the beast and beheaded it. In one of the several variants, Amairgen is given as the slayer of the beast.

Aillinn. Sometimes given as Ailinn. The daughter of Laoghaire Mac Fergus Fairge (another version gives her as the daughter of Eoghan Mac Daithi). She is the grand-daughter of the king of Leinster. She falls in love with Baile, son of Buain, and heir to the kingdom of Ulster. Ulster and Leinster were deadly enemies and here we have an embryonic 'Romeo and Juliet' tragedy. Aillinn and Baile arranged to meet on the shore near Dun Dealgan (Dundalk). Baile reached the appointed place first. A stranger approached and told him that the warriors of Leinster had discovered Aillinn's assignation and had prevented her coming. Sick with grief, Aillinn had died. Baile then died from a broken heart. The stranger then went to Aillinn and told her of Baile's death whereupon she also died of grief. We are not told who the malevolent stranger is apart from the fact that he must be one of the gods. Baile was buried at Traigh mBaile (Baile's Strand) and a yew tree grew from his grave. From Aillinn's grave grew an apple tree. The poets of Ulster and Leinster cut branches from the trees and carved the tragedy in Ogham on the wands they made from the branches. According to the end of the story, two hundred years later, when Art the Lonely was High King, the Ogham wands were gathered from Ulster and Leinster and taken to the *Tech Screptra* or library at Tara for safe-keeping. As the wands were put into the library they sprang together and could not be separated.

Aimend. A sun goddess who was daughter of the king of Corco Loigde.

Áine. The goddess of love and fertility. She was the daughter of Eogabail, foster-son of the sea-god Manannán Mac Lir, and a druid of the Tuatha Dé Danaan. Áine has been identified with Anu, mother of the gods, and also with the Mórrígán, goddess of battles, but these identifications seem suspect and unlikely. Áine was continually conspiring with mortals in passionate affairs. She was raped by Ailill Olom (see **Ailill** 7) and slew him with her magic. A second legend, which obviously had its roots in the Ailill Olom tale, occurred in the fourteenth century, when it was said that Maurice, first Earl of Desmond (d. 1356) raped Áine who bore a son Gearóid Iarla (third Earl of Desmond, 1359–98) who is known for the courtly love poetry he wrote in Irish. The historical dating is obviously suspect. When Gearóid died it was said that he was but asleep and would rise again on an enchanted steed from the waters of Loch Guirr. Another version is that Gearóid lives beneath the waves of the loch and is seen riding around its banks on a white horse once every seven years. Yet another version has it that Áine turned him into a goose on the banks of the loch. It is an historical fact that Gearóid's son John actually drowned in the River Suir in 1400. The poems of Gearóid Iarla are preserved in Irish manuscripts.

Near Loch Guirr is Áine's dwelling place, Cnoc Áine (Knockainy, Áine's Hill, in Co. Kerry). Even up to the last century Áine was worshipped on St. John's Eve, Midsummer Eve, when local people carried torches of hay and straw tied to poles and lit up Cnoc Áine at night. They would then invoke Áine na gClair (Áine of the Wisps) to guard them against sickness and ensure fertility. They would disperse among their own cultivated fields and pastures waving the torches over their crops and cattle to bring luck and increase. According to D. Fitzgerald in 'Popular Tales of Ireland' (*Revue Celtique*, Vol. IV): 'A number of girls had stayed late on the Hill watching the *cliars* (torches) and joining in the games. Suddenly Áine appeared among them, thanked them for the honour they had done her, but said she now wished them to go home, as they wanted the hill to themselves. She let them understand whom she meant by "they" for calling some of the girls she made them look through a ring, when behold, the hill appeared crowded with people before invisible.' The cult of Áine has been a long time in dying.

Ainlé. Sometimes Ainnle. Son of Usna and one of the two brothers of Naoise who followed him into exile and was eventually slain at the Red Branch Hostel. See **Naoise** and **Deirdre**.

Ainmire. Father of Aedh of Tara. See **Aedh** 7.

Airgialla. See **Oriel**.

Airgtheach. The White House, one of the islands of earthly paradise seen during the Voyage of Bran. See **Bran** 2.

Airitech. A supernatural creature which came out of the Cave of Cruachan, one of the entrances to the Otherworld. Airitech had three daughters who assumed the shape of werewolves and raided the country. The warrior Cas Corach played music to enchant the werewolves and persuaded them that they should assume human forms in order to listen to the music in greater comfort. When they did so his companion Cáilte threw his spear at them so that all three were impaled. Cas Corach then struck off their heads.

Airmid. Sometimes Airmed. Sister of Miach and daughter of Dian Cécht, the god of medicine. She was also a physician like her brother and father and helped Miach sew a cat's eye into the socket of the one-eyed porter of Nuada's palace. When Miach proved a better physician than his father Dian Cécht, the god of medicine slew him in a jealous rage. Airmid gathered the herbs that grew on Miach's grave and laid them out on her cloak in the order of their various healing properties. Dian Cécht, still jealous of Miach, overturned the cloak and hopelessly confused the herbs so that no human would learn the secret of immortality by their use. Airmid also helped Dian Cécht guard a secret Well of Healing.

Airoch Feabhruadh. A son of Mileius and Seang.

Aisling. A vision or dream. A motif that frequently occurs in Irish myth. The most popularly known is 'Aislinge Oenghus' (The Dream of Aonghus Óg) who saw a beautiful maiden in a dream and enlisted the help of his mother, the goddess Boann, to find her. The maiden was identified as Caer and Aonghus took her to his palace on the River Boyne where they dwelt together. A twelfth-century tale is 'Aislinge meic Con Glinne' (The Vision of Mac Con Glinne) which is thought to be an early tale which received its final form in the twelfth-century version. It is an extraordinary and brilliant skit on the clergy and is consistently amusing. During the sixteenth to nineteenth centuries the word was used to describe a form of Irish Poetry.

Aitheach-Tuatha. A pre-Milesian people who staged a revolt against the Milesian conquest of Ireland and were, for a while, successful, but the Milesians regained control.

Aithechda. Son of Magog. He is acclaimed as progenitor of all the races which inhabited Ireland after the Deluge.

Aithedha. Elopements. A class of tales of which 'The Pursuit of Diarmuid and Gráinne' is the best known.

Alba. Sometimes Albu and Albain. Scotland. The modern Scottish Gaelic name for Scotland is still Alba and the root seems connected with 'high hills'. The same Celtic word root is to be found in The Alps, Albania, etc. The original name for the entire island of Britain came from the same root, hence Albion.

Ale, of Goibhniu. Whoever drank it obtained immortality.

Allen, Hill of. Anglicised from the dative form Almain of the name Almu. A great fortress said to be built by Nuada, chief druid of Cahir Mór, King of Ireland, the maternal ancestor of Fionn Mac Cumhail. Fionn made this fortress his chief dwelling, 'its ramparts enclosing many white-walled dwellings and the great hall towering high in its midst.' The story of 'Cath Almaine', the battle of Allen (not to be confused with the historic battle of AD 722) was when the men of Leinster fought with the hero Fergal Mac Máile Dúin. Fergal was slain and his head cut off. His enemies treated his head well, washing it and dressing the hair. It was then set up on a pike while Badb, the battle goddess, hovered around it in the form of a raven. That night, during a feasting around the head, the head of Donn Bó, a youth famed for the sweetness of his song who had also been slain and decapitated in the battle, began to sing a song in praise of Fergal. The story demonstrates the reverence for the human head in Celtic society.

Amairgen. Sometimes given as Amergin and Amorgin.

1. A son of Milesius, a warrior and poet. He also appears as the first of the druids in Ireland. His wife Scena died on the voyage to Ireland and was buried at Inverskena (Kenmare River, Co. Kerry). It is Amairgen who pronounced the first judgement delivered in Ireland and who decided that Eremon should become the first Milesian king of the country. Three poems are accredited to Amairgen. Perhaps the most famous is the extraordinary incantation to Ireland, given in the *Leabhar Gabhála* (Book of Invasions), in which Amairgen subsumes

everything into his own being with a philosophical outlook that parallels the Hindu *Bhagavadgita*.

I am the Wind that blows over the sea;
I am the Wave of the Ocean;
I am the Murmur of the billows;
I am the Ox of the Seven Combats;
I am the Vulture on the rock;
I am a Ray of the Sun;
I am the fairest of Plants;
I am a Wild Boar in valour;
I am a Salmon in the Water;
I am a Lake in the plain;
I am the Craft of the artificer;
I am a Word of Science;
I am the Spear-point that gives battle;
I am the God that creates in the head of man the fire of thought.
Who is it that enlightens the assembly upon the mountain, if not I?
Who tells the ages of the moon, if not I?
Who shows the place where the sun goes to rest, if not I?

2. The father of Conall Cearnach (of the Victories). His foster father was the poet Áthairne. He slew the three-headed Ellén, a supernatural creature which emerged from the cave of Cruachan, the entrance to the Otherworld. He married Findchaem, daughter of Cathbad, the druid of Conchobhar Mac Nessa, king of Ulster. At Bricriu's Feast, Amairgen boasted that he was praised in valour, for his wisdom, his fortune, age and eloquence, and that, as a poet, he was the bane of every chariot-warrior. An eleventh-century manuscript describes how Áthairne, his foster father, came to visit him one autumn and when he tried to take his departure, Amairgen composed a poem suggesting autumn was not the correct time to depart; a similar poem was composed in winter, also in spring, but at the start of the summer Amairgen's poem said, 'A good season is summer for a long journey.'

Andoid. One of the four people who survived the Deluge outside Noah's Ark, the story obviously entering Irish myth with the coming of Christianity.

Angus. See **Aonghus**.

Animal cults. Animals, as gods, malevolent beings and companions, appear profusely in Irish myth just as they play an important part in the myths and religions of most peoples of the world. The divine bull and magical cows are an important motif and the *Táin Bó Cuailgne* is, perhaps, the most famous demonstration of this. Boann is one of the goddesses connected with cattle and her very name seems to signify 'she of the white cattle'. The Mórrígán turned Odras into a pool of water when Odras tried to stop the Mórrígán's bull making off with the cow of Buchat Buasach. The god Lugh is recorded as creating magic cows. However, it is the boar which is the Celtic cult animal *par excellence*. The meat of the boar is a sacred dish served during the feasts of the gods in the Otherworld. Irish myth is littered with destructive pigs and boars. The boar of Formael killed fifty hounds and fifty warriors and the hero Failbhe Finnmaisech. Supernatural pigs (*mucca gentliuchta*) emerged from the Cave of Cruachan, the entrance of the Otherworld. Manannán Mac Lir, the sea-god, chased a giant pig, and his hounds were drowned when the pig sprang into a lake, hence Loch Con (Lake of Dogs), where it swam to an island called Muc Inis (Pig Island). Cats don't often play a prominent role although we find Cairbre Caitcheann (Cat Head) as a divine ancestor of Erainn and in one voyage a little cat is the guard of an Otherworld treasure. This animal is able to change itself into a ball of fire.

Horses play their part and the wife of the god Midir, Étain Echraide, is by her very name connected with this animal. It is recorded that when Cúchulainn was born a mare foaled at the very same time and the two foals were given to him, being named the Grey of Macha and the Black of Sainglend. Horses with fantastic colours appear from the Otherworld. Cúchulainn witnessed a chariot drawn by a single red horse which had only one leg. The chariot yoke went right through the beast and was held by a peg in the centre of its forehead. In the chariot was a woman of red skin, obviously a goddess. Enchanted horses, such as the one Eisirt and later Oisín use to make their journey to the Otherworld, are numerous.

Stags, deer and fawns also have magical qualities. In one stag hunt Súlbhnede, a son of a king of Munster, with thirty warriors, thirty hounds and thirty attendants, died while chasing a supernatural stag. Shape-changing into deer and fawns, such as in the story of Oisín's mother, is also common. Coel was killed by Cairbre while he was in the shape of a deer. Dogs and hounds are not only companions to warriors but also magical beasts. Most famous of the hounds in Irish myth is Culann's hound, slain by Cúchulainn. There is also Mac Da

Thó's hound and the hounds of Fionn Mac Cumhail. Shape-changing into dogs and hounds is another popular motif. Lugh's mother Ethlinn was slain while in the shape of a dog while Fionn Mac Cumhail's sister was changed into a dog in which form she gave birth to Bran and Sceolang, who became his hounds. The bear also plays its role and the name Art (bear) occurs in many Irish proper names. Math is another form of bear as in Mac Mathghamhna (son of the bear). Fish are also important, for example the Salmon of Knowledge. Many horned animals are indicated as being supernatural by the fact that they have three horns – the mystical Celtic trinity. Stags appear with three antlers, rams with three horns and boars with three horns.

Anind. A son of Nemed. Loch Ennell, Co. Westmeath is said to have burst from his grave when it was being dug. He is associated with Dún na Sciath (Fort of Shields) which stone circular fort still stands on west bank.

Anluan. Son of Maga, a Connacht warrior who was slain by Conall Cearnach. Anluan was the brother of Cet. They went to battle against Ulster in the service of Ailill and Medb at the head of three thousand warriors. During the challenging for the hero's portion in the story of Mac Da Thó's boar, Conall, challenging Cet, produced the severed head of Anluan and threw it at him.

Answerer, The. See **Freagarthach**.

Anu. The mother goddess. Sometimes given as Ana and also occurs as Búanann, 'the lasting one', mother of all heroes. It is generally accepted that she is one and the same deity as Dana or Danu. Hence the gods are the Tuatha Dé Danaan, children of Dana. The mountains, The Paps of Anu in Co. Kerry, are named for her.

Aobh. Sometimes Aebh. The eldest daughter of Ailill of Aran (see **Ailill** 5) and foster-child of the Bodb Dearg. Her sisters were Aoife and Arbha. She was chosen to be the wife of the ocean-god Lir and had four children by him. The first two were twins, Fionnuala and Aedh; the second two were also twins, Fiachra and Conn. But she died in childbirth. See **Aoife** 2.

Aoi Mac Ollamain. See **Aí**.

Aoife. 1. Daughter of Árd-Greimne, and sister of Scáthach. A warrior princess of the Land of Shadows. Her sister Scáthach instructed Cúchulainn in the martial arts. Scáthach went to war with Aoife but tried to leave Cúchulainn behind in case Aoife killed him. However, Cúchulainn followed her to the Land of Shadows and was challenged to single combat by Aoife. Cúchulainn asked Scáthach what Aoife cared about most and Scáthach told him that she valued her chariot and horse. During the combat Aoife had shattered Cúchulainn's sword and while she was raising her weapon for the death blow Cúchulainn called out that her horse and chariot had fallen. Aoife glanced round and Cúchulainn ran in and caught her. Defeated by cunning, Aoife submitted to her sister after Cúchulainn offered to spare her on condition she made peace. She fell in love with Cúchulainn and he stayed a while in the Land of Shadows with her. When he left he gave her a gold ring. She told him that she would bear his child. Years later a young warrior came to Ulster named Connlaí. Cúchulainn challenged and slew him not knowing, until the boy was dying, that he was his own son by Aoife.

2. The second daughter of Ailill of Aran. See **Ailill** 5 and **Aobh**. On the death of her eldest sister, Aobh, she married Lir, the ocean-god, and became stepmother to her sister's children. She was jealous of them and, going to attend the Feast of Age at the *sídhe* of Bodb Dearg, she asked her attendants to slay them. They rebuked her and so she used her magic to change them into swans. The children of Lir, in swan-shape, must spend three hundred years on Loch Darravagh (Westmeath); three hundred years on the Strait of Moyle (between Ireland and Scotland); and three hundred years on the Atlantic by the islands of Erris and Inishglory. According to the enchantment, when a southern princess married a northern prince, they would be released from the spell. When Bodb Dearg found out what Aoife, his foster-daughter, had done he changed her into a demon of the air and no more was heard of her. See also **Lir**.

3. She became lover of Ilbrec, the son of Manannán Mac Lir. She was changed into a crane and, while in this form, was killed. Her skin was used to make the Treasure Bag of the Fianna, sometimes called 'The Crane Bag'. See **Treasure Bag of the Fianna**.

Aonbharr. A magical horse which could travel both on land and sea.

Aoncos. An Otherworld island which was supported on a single pillar of silver rising out of the sea. It was seen by Mael Dúin on his fabulous voyage.

Aonghus. 1. Aonghus Óg, also Mac Óg (Young Son). The god of love. He was son of the Dagda and Boann and his palace was Brugh na Boinne by the River Boyne at New Grange. He was of beautiful appearance and four birds, representing his kisses, always hovered around his head. In the story 'The Dream of Aonghus' he saw a beautiful maiden in a dream and fell sick for love of her. He asked his mother for help and she enlisted the support of her brother, the god Bodb Dearg. The girl was identified as Cáer Ibormeith, daughter of Ethal Anubhail of the Dé Danaan of Connacht. Aonghus Óg enlisted the aid of Ailill and Medb, the rulers of Connacht, to persuade Ethal Anubhail to give him his daughter. But Ethal Anubhail said it was not in his power to do so because Cáer lived in the shape of a swan and on the Feast of Samhain would be found with a hundred and fifty other swans swimming on Loch Bel Dragon (Lake of the Dragon's Mouth). If Aonghus could identify her, it would be up to Cáer to decide if she wanted to go with the love-god. Aonghus Óg went to the lake and identified Cáer; they went to his palace by the Boyne and lived together. Aonghus Óg was also foster-father of Diarmuid Ua Duibhne (of the love spot) and tried to save him and his lover Gráinne from the vengeance of Fionn Mac Cumhail by magical devices. When Diarmuid was slain by a magic boar (actually the son of Aonghus Óg's steward, Roc, by Diarmuid's own mother) it was Aonghus Óg who placed the body on a gilded bier and transported it to his palace where he was able to breath a soul into it whenever he wanted a conversation with Diarmuid.

2. Aonghus of the Terrible Spear. A chieftain of the Dési who killed Celleach, son of the High King Cormac Mac Art, with a spear and knocked out the eye of Cormac with its butt. This was in revenge for Celleach raping his niece. This incident starts the tale '*Inndarba inna nDési*' (The Expulsion of the Dési).

3. Aonghus Bolg. An ancestor of the Firbolg, also regarded as an ancestor of the Dési.

4. Son of the Bodb Dearg.

5. Aonghus Mac Aedh Abrat, brother of Fand, who visited Cúchulainn as he lay on his sickbed and sang to him, after which Cúchulainn awoke cured from his sickness.

6. Mac Lámh Gabuid. A warrior who challenged Cet of Connacht during the bragging contest in the tale of Mac Da Thó's boar. He is described as tall and fair-haired. Cet cut off his father's hand and this is why he challenged Cet.

Arannan. A son of Milesius born in Galicia. He climbed to the top of the mast of his ship as the Milesians were invading Ireland and fell into the sea and was drowned.

Arbha. The youngest daughter of Ailill of Aran. See **Ailill** 5.

Arca Dubh. He slew Cumal, father of Fionn Mac Cumhail, chief of the

Fianna. There are two versions of the story. In the first, Cumal could only be slain by his own sword while lying with his wife, and this was accomplished by Arca Dubh who was a servant of Cumal. The other version has it that Arca Dubh was hiding in the grass by the river and threw his spear into Cumal while he was swimming. In yet another version of Cumal's death the killer is named as Goll Mac Morna who became the new leader of the Fianna.

Árd-Greimne. The name signifies 'High Power' (*greimm*). He is named as lord of Lethra, referred to as a place of 'red brightness'. He is the father of two famous female warriors – Scáthach, who taught Cúchulainn the martial arts, and Aoife, who nearly defeated Cúchulainn in single combat.

Árd Macha. The capital of Ulster (Armagh). It was said to have been founded in 370BC by Macha Mong Ruadh, a queen. But the story is interwoven with stories of Macha the goddess of battles. Armagh was situated a short distance from Emain Macha which, throughout the Ulster Cycle, is the seat of the kings of Ulster: see **Emain Macha**. St. Patrick decided to form his religious centre there. It is now the primacy of the Catholic Church in Ireland. The *Book of Armagh*, now in Trinity College, Dublin, is of 442 pages and was completed by Ferdonnach at Armagh in AD807.

Ard Rí. Old spelling Ard Rígh. High King. The seat of the High Kings of Ireland was at Temhair (Tara) in Co. Meath. According to the ancient bardic lists, Slaigne the Firbolg was the first High King and from his accession to AD1 there were one hundred and seven High Kings consisting of nine Firbolg, nine Dé Danaan, and eighty-nine Milesians. From AD1 the first High King was Conaire Mór, and the last High King was Ruaraidh Ó Conchobhar (1161–98) who finally accepted Henry II of the Angevin Empire as suzerain of Ireland at the Treaty of Windsor signed in October 1175. Between Conaire Mór and Ó Conchobhar, eighty-one High Kings are listed. There were no High Kings in Ireland after Ó Conchobhar.

Ardan. A son of Usna and one of Naoise's two brothers (Ainlé and Ardan) who followed him to exile in Alba and was eventually killed with his brothers at the Red Branch Hostel. See **Naoise**.

Argadnel. Silver Cloud. One of the islands of earthly paradise seen during Bran's fabulous voyage.

Argetlámh. See **Nuada** 2.

Art. High King of Ireland. Son of Conn of the Hundred Battles. Art is an example of the confusion between the historical and mythological in Ireland. According to the king lists he ruled at Tara from AD220 to 250. Yet according to the *Annals of the Four Masters* he was killed at the battle of Moy Muchruinne in AD195. He was known as Art Aenfer, the Solitary. In Irish myth, however, Art won the love of Delbchaem (fair shape) and his son is the famous Cormac Mac Art, the great patron of Fionn Mac Cumhail and his Fianna.

According to one tale, Art's father Conn had taken, as one of his concubines, Bécuma Cneisgel, a goddess who had been expelled from the Otherworld. Because of her, the country grew infertile and miserable. One evening she was playing *fidchell* with Art and winning because she had enlisted the aid of invisible servants. Because she won the game she was able to place a *geis* on Art whereby he had to undertake a journey to find and win Delbchaem. By this means Bécuma hoped to get rid of Art for she was jealous of the king's son.

Art set out and faced terrible dangers on his voyage in search of Delbchaem. Hideous toads, a river of ice, a giant and the choice between two cups, one containing poison, barred his way to the beautiful maiden. Finally he had to destroy Delbchaem's evil parents, Morgan, king of the Land of Wonder, and Coinchend, a monstrous warrior woman. Art then brought Delbchaem safely to Ireland and was able to banish Bécuma, who admitted defeat.

Art, on his way to the battle at Moy Muchruinne, where he was to perish at the hands of a rebel, Lugaide Mac Con, passed the night at the house of a smith named Olc Siche. He slept with Achtan, the smith's daughter. Knowing that his death had been foretold, he gave Achtan his sword, golden ring and ceremonial clothing for safe-keeping so that her child would claim his inheritance. She bore his child, who became Cormac Mac Art.

Arthur. In Irish myth Arthur appears as the son of the king of Britain. He stole the hounds of Fionn Mac Cumhail, Bran and Sceolan. The Fianna pursued Arthur to Britain and recovered the hounds. Arthur is said to have sworn fealty to Fionn. There are several later Arthurian stories in Irish manuscript but these stories are obviously translations and re-tellings from Brythonic Celtic sources.

Artrach. A son of Bodb Dearg.

Artur. a son of Nemed who led his people in battle against the Fomorii at Cramh Ros. The Nemedians were all but destroyed.

Astrology. See **Divination**.

Áthairne the Importunate. A druid and poet who is described as an overbearing satirist from Ben Edar (Howth), he is reported to have compiled a code of laws with Forchern, Feirceirthé and Néide under the title of Breithe Neimhidh, which was incorporated into the Brehon Laws. According to Fergus Mac Roth: 'The lakes and rivers receded before him when he satirised them and rose up before him when he praised them.' He was the foster-father of the poet Amairgen (see **Amairgen** 2). He made a progress round Ireland demanding the wives and treasures of his hosts. In Connacht he visited the one-eyed King Luain and demanded his eye. Under the laws of hospitality the hosts could not refuse but when he asked Mesgora Mac Da Thó, king of Leinster, for his wife Búan, Mac Da Thó refused. He then demanded of Conchobhar Mac Nessa that Ulster made war on Leinster for this affront and Conchobhar agreed. This led to the death of Mac Da Thó.

Áth Liag Fionn. The ford into which Fionn Mac Cumhail threw a flat stone attached to a golden chain which had magical properties. It had been a present from a Dé Danaan. A prophesy said the stone would be found on a Sunday morning which would mark exactly seven years before the world came to an end.

Áth Nurchair. Ford of the Sling Cast in Westmeath. This is the river ford where Cet lurked in ambush, using his sling to hurl Conall's 'brain ball' at Conchobhar Mac Nessa of Ulster. Conchobhar fell to the ground with the ball lodged in his forehead. He was still alive and taken back to Emain Macha. Fingen, his physician, said if the ball was extracted Conchobhar would die. He therefore had the ball sewn up with golden thread and forbade Conchobhar to ride horses, give vent to vehement passion or make any other exertion. Seven years later Conchobhar fell into a rage, the ball burst in his head and he died.

Avon Dia. Anglicised from Abhainn Dea, a stretch of river which held back its waves for fear of the mighty duel in the river ford (Ath Ferdia, now Ardee, the Ford of Ferdia) between the champions Cúchulainn and Ferdia.

B

B. *beithe* (birch) in the Ogham alphabet.

Babal. A follower of Partholón who brought the first cattle to Ireland.

Bachorbladhra. A follower of Partholón who became the first to institute the practice of fosterage in Ireland.

Badb. 1. A goddess of battles who is regarded as one of a triune: Badb, Macha (Nemain) and the Mórrígán. Badb's name signifies a crow, which is a constant symbol of the war goddesses. She was married to Net who appears as a more shadowy god of war. In an account of the historical battle of Clontarf, in AD1014, when the High King Brían Bóramha defeated the Vikings, it is said that Badb appeared shrieking over the heads of the warriors during the battle.
2. A daughter of Calatin who took the form of a handmaiden of Niamh, wife of Conall of the Victories, to entice Niamh into a wood where she laid a spell on her so that Niamh would remain lost. She went in the form of Niamh to Cúchulainn in order to persuade him to rise up and rescue Ulster from the forces of Ailill and Medb. She is sometimes confused with Badb 1 although she appears to be a separate entity.

Badba. Obviously linked with the war goddess, Badb 1, the Badba is recorded as a separate supernatural creature which frequents battlefields.

Badh. A *bean sidhe* (banshee) in Munster.

Baile of the Honeyed Speech. See **Aillinn**.

Bainleannan. A female spirit.

Baire. A team game, often played by the heroes, perhaps similar to the modern game of hurly. A hole is dug in the ground for a goal and the purpose is to score goals by getting a ball into the hole.

Balba. One of Cesair's companions on her voyage to Ireland.

Ballyconnell. A spot in Co. Cavan (Bel-atha-Chonaill), the mouth of the ford of Conall where the Red Branch champion was slain.

Balor of the Evil Eye. A god of death and the most formidable of the Fomorii. His father was Buarainech. He had one eye whose gaze was so malevolent that it destroyed whoever gazed upon it. His wife was Cethlenn. It was prophesied that he would be slain by his own grandson and to prevent this happening he had his only daughter Ethlinn locked in a crystal tower on Tory Island so that she might never know a man. Hearing of Ethlinn's beauty, the Dé Danaan, Cian, with the help of a druidess named Birog, managed to reach her. Cian slept with Ethlinn and she gave birth to a boy. Discovering this, Balor had the child cast into the sea to be drowned. Birog, the druidess, saved the boy and he was fostered by Manannán Mac Lir (in other versions by Goibhniu). He grew up to become Lugh Lámhfada, of the Long Arm, the god of arts and crafts. At the Second Battle of Magh Tuireadh, when Balor had slain Nuada and Macha, Lugh took a *tathlum*, a magic stone ball, and waited until Balor's eye was drooping. Then he sent the stone into the Fomorii's eye, knocking it out and destroying twenty-eight Fomorii warriors who were unlucky enough to be within sight of it. Balor was slain and the Fomorii defeated.

Banba. A triune goddess – Banba, Fotla and Éire – representing the spirit of Ireland. She was the wife of Mac Cuill, son of Ogma. With her sisters, Fotla and Éire, she met the Milesians on their arrival in Ireland and each asked that her name be given to the country. The names have since been synonyms for Ireland in Irish literature and poetry; however, it is the name of Éire from which Ireland takes its modern name.

Banbán. The name signifies 'little pig'. He invited the High King Diarmuid to his house for a feast. Aedh Dubh and his warriors attacked the house and burnt it, slaying Diarmuid in accordance with a prophecy. See **Diarmuid** 2.

Banishments or Exiles. A class of tales.

Banshee. See **Bean Sídhe**.

Bard. A class of poets. Bardic schools flourished in historical Ireland as in mythological Ireland. They were finally suppressed in the late seventeenth century.

Barinthus. It was his tales about the Land of Promise which caused Brendan to set out on his fabulous voyage.

Barran. Sometimes Barrfhind, one of Cesair's companions on her voyage to Ireland.

Baruch. A Red Branch warrior who met Fergus, Naoise and Deirdre on their return from Alba. He persuaded Fergus to leave the lovers, whom he was guarding, to go on to Emain Macha alone in order that he might feast with Baruch at his fortress Dun Baruch, which looked out over the River Moyle, across which Naoise, Deirdre and Naoise's brothers sailed on to their doom. See **Naoise** and **Deirdre**.

Beag. A Dé Danaan who had a magic well, guarded by her three daughters. When Fionn Mac Cumhail came to the well to ask for a drink the daughters tried to prevent him from getting the water. One of them threw water over him to scare him away and some of it went into his mouth. From the water he gained wisdom.

Bealcu. A champion of Connacht during the *Táin* war. He found the Ulster champion Conall of the Victories lying wounded having just slain Cet in combat. Bealcu refused to kill Conall. 'I will not slay a man at the point of death, but I will bring you home to heal you and when your strength is come again you will fight me in single combat.' Bealcu kept his promise to nurse Conall but his three sons were worried that Conall might recover sufficiently to slay their father. They plotted to assassinate Conall before he was well. However, Conall found out and tricked them into killing their father; then he killed them and took their heads back to Ulster.

Bealtaine. See **Beltaine**.

Beann. A son of Conchobhar Mac Nessa of Ulster, who took his clans south. They argued and divided, some settling in Wexford and some in Cork. Both section of the clan gave their names to the areas – Beantraighe (the followers of Beann), which is the barony of Bantry in Wexford and the town and bay of Bantry in Cork.

Bean Sídhe. Popularly known to English speakers as a banshee. Literally, 'woman of the hills' or, in modern usage, 'woman of the fairies'. After the gods went underground and were, in popular folk memory, transformed into fairies, a banshee became a female fairy attached to a particular family which warned of approaching death by giving an eerie wail.

Beara. The daughter of a king of Spain who married Eoghan Mór of Munster (Magh Nuadat). It had been prophesied that the man who would wed her would come to her on a certain night if she went to the River Eibhear where she would find a salmon wearing shining clothes. The prophecy fulfilled, she wed Eoghan. On their landing in Ireland, they arrived on the north side of Bantry Bay which Eoghan renamed in honour of his wife. The peninsula still carries the name Beara or Beare.

Beara, Hag of. See **Cailleach Beara**.

Bebhionn. A beautiful giantess, daughter of Treon of the Land of Maidens. She was promised to Aedh against her will and sought help from Fionn Mac Cumhail and the Fianna. But Aedh followed her and slew her. Fionn and his warriors buried her on the Ridge of the Dead Woman. See **Aedh** 10.

Bebo. The wife of Iubdan, king of the Faylinn or little people. She had an affair with Fergus Mac Léide. See **Iubdan** and **Fergus** 8.

Bécuma. (Cneisgel – of the Fair Skin) She dwelt in the Land of Promise and had an affair with Gaiar, a son of Manannán Mac Lir, the sea-god. Because of this she was banished to the human world where she persuaded Conn of the Hundred Battles, the High King, to take her as his wife or concubine. She grew jealous of his son Art and tried to get him banished. See **Art**.

Bec Fola. A wife of Diarmuid, a king, who left him in bed one morning to spend a day and a night in the Otherworld. On returning she found that it was still the same morning and her husband was only just stirring from his sleep.

Bec Mac Dé. A druid who prophesied the death of the High King Diarmuid (see **Diarmuid** 2) in the house of Banbán. In spite of the unlikely conditions of the prophecy, it was fulfilled.

Bé Find. Sister of the goddess Boann. She became the wife of Idath and mother of Fraoch, the most handsome warrior in Ireland. See **Fraoch**.

Bel. See **Bilé**.

Beltaine. The feast of the fires of Bel, one of the four major festivals of the Celts falling on May Eve and 1 May and marking the beginning of the summer. Also known as Cetshamhain. It was customary to observe the festival by lighting bonfires, hence Bel-tinne, the fires of Bel. It was a time when the Celts offered praise to Bel, the life-giver, represented by the sun, for having brought victory over the powers of darkness and for bringing the people within sight of another harvest. On that day the fires of every household were extinguished. At a given time, the druids would rekindle the fires from torches lit from 'the sacred fires of Bel', the rays of the sun, and the new flames would symbolise a fresh start for everyone. Numbers of cattle from each herd would be driven in ancient circles through fires as a symbol of purification. Some scholars have argued that, because of this, the ceremony was the start of the Celtic New Year but it is widely agreed that Samhain marks this point. The festival was widely known and practised throughout the Celtic world and not just in Ireland. Survivals of May Day bonfire ceremonies are to be found in many places from France to Scotland. In Cornwall the ceremony is still observed with incantations offered in the old Cornish language. The modern Irish word for the May month is still Bealtaine. In Scotland, while Màigh has replaced the native word, May Day is still Latha Bealltainn. Until the nineteenth century, the Scottish Law Term starting in May was designated the Beltane Term. In Manx, May is known as Boaldyn and May Day as Laa Boaldyn. Significant events always happened at Beltaine not only in Irish tradition but also in Welsh myth. It was at Beltaine that Partholón came to Ireland, the Dé Danaan arrived and the Milesians invaded. The pre-Christian ceremony was claimed for Christianity and merged with the feast day of St. John the Baptist. See **Bilé**.

Beo. A destructive sow killed by Fionn Mac Cumhail who gave its head to Cruithne, daughter of Locham the smith.

Beothach. Son of Iarbanel.

Bilé. A god of death who is cognate with Bel and Belinos in Brythonic tradition and whose feast day was on May Eve and 1 May: see **Beltaine**. In some texts Bilé is known as 'Father of Gods and Men' and husband to Dana. In other texts he appears as father of Milesius who significantly comes from 'Spain', a synonym for the Land of the Dead. This deity had a profound influence throughout the ancient Celtic world, apparently as god of both life and death. There are many places throughout Europe named after him. In London, for example, Belinos' Gate has come down to modern times as Billingsgate. His name is also to be found in personal names such as that of one of the most notable kings of Britain before the Roman invasion – Cunobelinus. The Celtic form is Cunobel – the Hound of Bel. In 5BC the Romans regarded Cunobelinus as High King of Britain. William Shakespeare has given him greater fame as *Cymbeline*.

Biobal. A Partholón who brought the first gold to Ireland.

Birog. A druidess who helped Cian to gain access to the crystal tower of Balor where the Fomorii ruler had imprisoned his daughter Ethlinn so that she would know no men, for it had been prophesied that his grandson would kill him. Later Birog saved the life of the child of Cian and Ethlinn when Balor had him cast into the sea. The child grew up as Lugh Lámhfada, god of arts and crafts.

Bith. 1. Son of Noah and father of Cesair who took Barran and sixteen women to start a kingdom in the north of Ireland where he subsequently died.

2. Father of Adna, chief poet of Ireland.

Black of Sainglend. Sometimes given as Saingliu. One of Cúchulainn's two famous horses born on the same night as the hero.

Bladh. A Milesian hero who had one of the twelve chief mountains of Ireland named after him – Sliabh Bladh (Slievebloom).

Blaí Bruige. Son of Fiachne who asked if he could foster the boy Sétanta who became the hero Cúchulainn. He was slain by Celtchair after it was discovered he was having an affair with Bríg Brethach, Celtchair's wife.

Blathnát. Sometimes given as Blanid. Daughter of Mend, king of Inis Fer Falga. The Munster king Cú Roí carried her off to become his wife. However, she had fallen in love with Cúchulainn, who was an enemy of Cú Roí. Cú Roí's fortress at Sleemish was so constructed that no one could find its entrance. Blathnát gave Cúchulainn a signal by emptying milk into a stream which ran through the fortress. Cúchulainn's attack was successful. Cú Roí was slain and Blathnát carried off. Among those taken, however was Cú Roí's bard Fer Cherdne (sometimes Ferchertnae) who waited his chance to avenge his king. As Cúchulainn progressed along the Beara peninsula, they paused and Blathnát stood by some cliffs. Fer Cherdne leapt forward, seized her by the waist and jumped over the edge, killing them both.

Blocc and Bluigne. Two 'king stones' which opened before Conaire Mór when he demanded recognition as High King at Tara. The assembled chieftains then accepted him.

Boann. Sometimes given as Boand. The name signifies 'she of the white cattle'. She is a water-goddess and wife of Nechtan, a water-god: see **Nechtan.** Sídhe Nechtan (the Hill of Carbery, Co. Kildare) held a sacred well, the well of Segais or Connla's Well, which was the source of the inspiration of knowledge: see **Nuts of Knowledge.** Only four persons were privileged to go there – Nechtan and his three cupbearers. Boann ridiculed this *geis*; she went to the well and walked contemptuously around it in a left-hand circle, whereupon the waters of the well rose up and pursued her eastwards and drowned her. Its course formed the river named after her – the Boyne. However, another version states that she escaped but the waters never returned to the well, thus forming the river.

In yet another version Boann is listed as the wife of Elcmar of the

Bruig. The Dagda wanted to sleep with her and sent Elcmar on a long
errand making nine months seem like one day. Through this union
Aonghus Óg, the love god, was born. He was called Óg or Mac Óg
because Boann said: 'Young is the son who was begotten at break of
day and born betwixt it and evening.' See **Aonghus Óg**. Some
Christian monks have confused things by trying to make Boann into
the wife of the Dagda in accordance with Christian morality. It was
Boann who organised the search for the girl who Aonghus Óg
dreamed of, Cáer the daughter of Ethal Anuabhail.

Bochra. The father of Fintan, the husband of Cesair. The name means
'ocean' and it may be significant that Fintan escaped the Deluge by
turning himself into a salmon which could live in the ocean.

Bodb Dearg. Bodb the Red, a son of the Dagda who succeeded him as
ruler of the gods. Yet in some versions he is called the *brother* of
Boann. He had his palace or *sídhe* at Loch Dearg on the Shannon,
contracted from Loch Dergdherc, the lake of the red eye. His domain
was Connacht and he helped Boann identify the girl in Aonghus Óg's
dream as Cáer, the daughter of Ethal Anubhail of Connacht. He had a
daughter Sadb who was turned into a fawn by a druid and in this guise
met Fionn Mac Cumhail. She changed back into human form and
conceived Fionn's son Oisín. The druid pursued her and changed her
back into a fawn. Bodb Dearg had another daughter, Daireann,
whose love Fionn refused; in revenge she drove him mad with an
enchanted drink but the madness passed. Bodb Dearg also had a
goldsmith named Len who gave his name to the lakes of Killarny,
Loch Lena, the Lakes of Len of the Many Hammers.

Bóramha. Also given as Borúmha and Anglicised as Boru. A tribute
placed on the people of Leinster by the High Kings. According to the
Book of Leinster the High King Tuathal Teachtmhair, the Legitimate, had two daughters – Fithir and Dairine. Eochaidh, the king of
Leinster, wanted to marry the younger daughter but could not while
the elder was unmarried. To achieve his purpose he married Fithir,
the elder daughter, and took her to his palace. After a while he
returned to Tara saying that Fithir had died. After a period he wed
Dairine, the younger daughter, and took her back to his palace. Here
Dairine found her sister alive and both sisters died of shame and grief
at the deception. When the news reached Tara, Tuathal vowed
vengeance and led an army against Eochaidh of Leinster. He killed
Ecohaidh and forced Leinster to agree to a tribute and from that time
onwards the High Kings of Ireland exacted a tribute known as 'cattle

counting' or the Bóramha. It seems the tribute was seldom paid unless exacted by the use of force. One of the most famous historical High Kings of Ireland was Brían Bóramha (Brian Boru) – 941–1014 – who won the nickname by successfully imposing the tribute on Leinster.

Bran. 1. A son of Lir and brother of Manannán. The name signifies a raven. In Brythonic Celtic myth he appears as a god of the Other-world and, as a son of Lir, this may have been his role in the Goidelic tradition. But apart from a brief reference in the *Book of Leinster* little is known about him. The other two surviving Brans are human in origin. There were several Brans in the Celtic world, such as the Celtic leader who conquered Rome in 390BC, following the battle at Allia, and the Celtic leader whose armies swept through Greece and sacked the Temple of the Oracle of Apollo at Delphi in 279BC. However, it has been argued that rather than being a personal name, Bran or Brennus (as history records them) might have been a title. *Brenin* remains the modern Welsh word for a king.

2. Son of Febal. He is the hero of the most famous 'Voyage' tale – 'Immram Brain' or the Voyage of Bran, which has been dated to the eighth century AD. The story, however, is essentially pre-Christian in character. It starts one day when Bran was walking near his fortress. He heard sweet music which caused him to fall asleep. When he awoke he found a branch of silver with white blossom beside him. He went back to his fortress and even though the gates were bolted that night a beautiful woman appeared clad in strange clothes and sang a long lay to Bran describing the splendour and delights of her world beyond the sea. As she departed the silver branch sprang from Bran's hand to her own. The next day Bran, his three foster brothers and twenty-seven warriors (the mystical $9 \times 3 = 27$ figure) set out on a voyage to find the land of which the woman had sung. After two days and nights they met Manannán Mac Lir riding on the ocean waves. He was on his way to the land of the Dál nAraide to beget his son Mongán by its queen. A Christian embellishment is that Manannán told of the coming of Christ to save the world. The fabulous voyage continued with Bran coming to the Island of Joy where he was forced to leave one of the men who wanted to stay there. Eventually he came to Tir na mBan, the Land of Women, where he saw the beautiful woman on the shore. She threw a ball of thread to Bran and drew his ship to the shore. Bran and his crew stayed for what they thought was but a single year before the crew began to get restless and demanded

to return home. The woman warned them that centuries had passed
in the human world but Bran was persuaded to leave. The woman
warned them that if they set foot on Ireland they would suddenly age
all the centuries they had been away. They neared land and one of the
crew leapt ashore, heedless of the warnings. He immediately turned
to dust. Bran wrote his story on Ogham wands and threw them ashore
before turning his ship back into the unknown. 'And from that hour
his wanderings are not known.' This is one of the earliest voyage tales
and it is distinguished by the beauty of its incidental poetry, the
descriptions of the snowy cliffs of the Land of Silver hazed in mist, of
glistening sea horses and flowering plains.

3. The hound of Fionn Mac Cumhail which was also his nephew.
Fionn's sister, Tuireann, had been turned into a bitch dog in which
state she gave birth to Bran and Sceolan who become her brother's
faithful hounds. In finding Sadb, who becomes Oisín's mother, in the
shape of a fawn, Fionn had to crush Bran to death between his legs to
prevent the dog from savaging the fawn.

Brandubh. 1. A board game played by the heroes and gods. The
name signifies 'black raven'. It seems similar to *fidchell*. There
have been several archaeological finds of board games in Celtic
graves. A wooden board with sockets for movable pegs was found in
Ballinderry, Co. Westmeath.

2. A king of Leinster. The *Annals of Ulster* say he died in AD604.
His father was Eochaidh of Leinster and his mother was Feildem
(Feldelma). She gave birth to twin boys but exchanged one of them
with the twin daughters of King Aidan of Alba. Her remaining son,
Brandubh, grew up to become king. He was a good friend of Mongán
of the Dál nAraidi but coveted Mongán's wife, Dubh Lacha. He
tricked Mongán into giving him Dubh Lacha although Mongán, the
son of Manannán Mac Lir, used his magic powers to get her back.
Brandubh treacherously slew the son of the High King Aedh and
Aedh made war on him. Brandubh sent a spy to kill Aedh (see **Aedh**
7) but was later slain by Saran. A Christian embellishment has
Brandubh raised from the dead by a miracle.

Branfad. Another board game, which appears to resemble chess or
draughts.

Brea. 1. Son of Belgan, one of five Dé Danaan left in Ulster to stir up
discord among the Milesians when the Dé Danaan were driven
underground.

2. Battle of; a ford on the Boyne where Fionn Mac Cumhail is

supposed to have been killed trying to put down a rebellion of his own Fianna.

Breasal. The High King of the World. He is said to have built Barc Bresail in Leinster, a formidable fortress which was eventually destroyed by the High King Tuathal Teachtmhaire during his war on Eochaidh of Leinster. Breasal lived in the west and his country was known as Hy-Brasil and sometimes Ó-Brasil. In later folklore Hy-Brasil became a legendary Atlantic island which was only visible every seven years. Anyone who looked on it when it was visible would die. It was suggested that it was a sunken land of which the Aran Islands were a remnant. Ruairí Ó Flaithearta, writing his *A Choregraphical Description of West of H-Iarr Connaught* (London, 1684), told of a man named O'Ley who claimed to have been kidnapped and taken to the island. The name of Hy-Brasil appeared on maps as a real place. A. Dalorto (*circa* AD1325), the Genoese cartographer, placed it in the latitudes south of Ireland. So fixed in people's minds was Hy-Brasil as a reality that when explorers came to South America they thought they had found the legendary country and thus gave the name Brazil to the land they discovered.

Breg. A goddess who appears as the wife of the Dagda. She seems to be a triune goddess for she is also known as Meng and Meabal and confused with Boann.

Bregon. A son of Milesius. He is said to be father of Bilé and Ith, although Bilé also appears as father of Milesius. Bregon built a tower in 'Spain', the synonym for the Land of the Dead, from which Ith, one fine winter's night, saw the land of Ireland and set out to visit it.

Brehon Laws. The ancient laws of Ireland and the oldest surviving law system in Europe, named from *breitheamh*, a judge. The laws are very sophisticated and complex, the result of many centuries of practice. It is recorded that the first codification of the laws occurred in the fifth century at the instigation of St Patrick. Until that time the laws had been handed down in oral tradition. It has been said that the Irish law tracts are probably the most important documents of their kind in the whole tradition of western Europe by reason of their extent, archaism and of the tradition that they preserve. Their roots are in ancient Indo-European custom and not in Roman Law. Of the surviving tracts the *Senchus Mór* deals with civil law while the *Book of Acaill* deals with criminal law. Both of these are to be found in the *Book of the Dun Cow* which is one of the most complete copies of the tracts that survives. The language of Irish law is ancient, Bérla Féini as it is called. In spite of English attempts to destroy this law system it persisted, with many English colonists turning to it for judgements. Even through the seventeenth century the laws were in use in parts of Ireland. However, they were finally suppressed during the Penal Law period.

Brendan. The historical Christian saint appears as an entry here because of his fabulous voyage '*Navigatio Sancti Brendani*' (the Voyage of St. Brendan) which became one of the most popular stories of the Middle Ages and played an important part in inspiring the voyages which later resulted in the discovery of America. The tale seems to have been based on the earlier 'Voyage of Mael Dúin' by a late ninth- or early tenth-century Irish Latinist. The tale was translated into many European languages. Brendan the Voyager (or Navigator) – to differentiate him from his contemporary, St. Brendan of Birr – was born in Co. Kerry *circa* AD486 and died in 578. He became a disciple of St. Ita of Kileedy and founded the monastery of Cluain-ferta (Clonfert), Co. Galway. According to the story of his voyage he was inspired by one Barinthus who told tales of the Land of Promise. Brendan first set out in a curragh but this was driven back so he then set out in a wooden vessel. Like Mael Dúin he came to an island populated by spirits in bird form, found a crystal column in the sea, sailed a translucent sea and came to an island of giant smiths. Differing slightly from Mael Dúin's voyage, he landed on an island which turned out to be a giant whale, Jasconius, and also found himself in the Sargasso Sea.

Breoga. A follower of Partholón who introduced single combat (monomachy) into Ireland as a means of settling conflicts without recourse to full-scale war.

Bretnas. The name of Celtic Britain before the coming of the English.

Bres. 1. A Dé Danaan warrior who was sent to negotiate with the Firbolg ambassador, Sreng, when the Dé Danaan landed in Ireland. Bres proposed that the two peoples divide Ireland into two halves but the Firbolg refused and the first battle of Magh Tuireadh took place in which Bres was killed.

2. A son of the Fomorii Balor mentioned in the tale of the 'Children of Tuireann'. Lugh was approaching the land of the Fomorii from the west and Bres arose saying: 'I wonder that the sun is rising in the west today.' The Fomorii druids informed him that it was not the sun but the countenance of Lugh.

3. Son of Elatha, king of the Fomorii, and of Eri, a Dé Danaan

woman. He married Brigit, goddess of fertility. When Nuada lost his hand at the first battle of Magh Tuireadh, Bres became king because the blemish prevented Nuada from keeping office. Bres was a very beautiful person but an oppressor who proved unpopular. After Miach the physician had replaced Nuada's silver arm with a real one, and Nuada became able to rule again, Bres was deposed. He fled with his mother to the land of the Fomorii to seek the aid of his father, Elatha. This led to the second battle of Magh Tuireadh. He was captured during the battle and in return for his life he promised the Dé Danaan that he would advise them about agriculture, about planting and sowing, and thus seems to have become, for a while, an agricultural divinity.

Bresal. See **Etarlann.**

Brí. The daughter of Midir the Proud.

Brían. The eldest of the three sons of Tuireann by the goddess Brigid. With his brothers Iuchar and Iucharba he slew Cian, Lugh's father. As compensation Lugh demanded that the three brothers must fulfil eight tasks. They had to get three apples from the Garden of Hesperides; a pig-skin from Tuis, king of Greece; a poisoned spear from Pisear of Persia; two horses and a chariot from Dobhar, king of Siogair (Sicily); two pigs from Easal, king of the Golden Pillars; the hound-whelp of the king of Ioruiadh; the cooking spit of the women of Fianchuibhe, which lies at the bottom of the sea; and then give three shouts on the Hill of Miodchaoin. The adventures of the brothers in fulfilling these tasks have been compared to the voyage of Jason and the Argonauts. Brían in all these adventures plays the leading and dominant role.

Bricriu. Nemthenga, of the Poisoned Tongue. A son of Carbad, he was an Ulster champion renowned for his bitter tongue and a desire to create trouble. It was Bricriu who caused strife between Cúchulainn and the other Red Branch warriors as to who was the greatest champion. In the famous tale '*Fled Bricriu*' (Bricriu's Feast) it is mentioned that eight swordsmen had to guard Bricriu. He is also a creator of trouble in the 'Tale of Mac Da Thó's Boar'. Bricriu is the trouble-maker of the Ulster Cycle. At the end of the *Táin* war he was asked by the men of Ulster to judge the contest between the Brown Bull of Cuailgne and the White Horned Bull of Connacht on the Plain of Aeí. Bricriu was trampled to death by the fighting bulls.

Bríg Betach. The wife of Celtchair who had an adulterous affair with the Red Branch champion Blaí Bruige.

Brigid. Sometimes Brigit. A triune goddess.
  1. The goddess of healing.
  2. The goddess of smiths.
  3. The goddess of fertility and poetry. It is in this last form that we know more about her. She appears as a daughter of the Dagda. For a while she was married to Bres, the half-Fomorii ruler of the Dé Danaan. By Tuireann she had three sons – Brían, Iuchar and Iucharba. In many tales she appears as an equivalent to Dana, mother of all the gods. She has her counterpart in Brythonic and Gaulish culture for she appears as Brigindo among the Gauls and Brigantia in Britain. The name seems to represent 'High One'. She is obviously the totem of the Brigantes of Britain. Her festival was one of the four great feasts of the Celtic world and was held on 1 February. The feast seems to be connected with the coming into milk of the ewes and was a pastoral festival.
  4. The Christian saint, known in Ireland as 'Mary of the Gaels'. She is mentioned here as her traditions are often confused with those of the goddess. St. Brigid was born in Faughart in AD450 and died in Kildare in 523. As an Irish saint she takes second place only to St. Patrick. There were numerous written accounts of her life soon after her death and her cult became widespread. However, many ceremonies and traditions associated with her predecessor, the goddess, were ascribed to her, not least her feastday: 1 February is now the feast of St. Brigid. R. A. S. MacAlister put forward the theory that the saint was actually a priestess of Brigid who converted to Christianity. In most accounts of her life, her father is named as Dubhtach, a druid.

Brí Leith. The *sídhe* or palace of Midir the Proud at Slieve Golry near Ardagh, Co. Longford. Midir had a great playing field nearby where Aonghus Óg played during his fosterage with three times fifty boys and three times fifty girls. It was here that Aonghus Óg fell out with Triath, son of Febal, another foster child of Midir. Triath told Aonghus Óg the truth of his parentage. Brí Leith was stormed by the High King Eochaidh Airemh in order to secure the release of Étain whom Midir had abducted. See **Midir**, **Eochaidh Airemh** and **Étain 2**.

Britan. A Nemedian who, having fled from Ireland after the victory of Morca and the Fomorii over his people, settled in the island of Britain and gave his name to it.

Briun. Son of Bethar. He was 'no mean warrior, who on the ocean's eastern border reigned'. It was Briun who fashioned the *tathlum*, sling shot, for Lugh to use to take out Balor's eye during the second battle of Magh Tuireadh.

Bruigh na Boinne. Palace of the Boyne, identified with New Grange. It was first the fortress of Nechtan and later the home of Aonghus Óg, the love-god.

Bruree. Bruigh-rígh, palace of the king. The chief seat of Ailill Olom in Munster.

Brythonic Celts. Consisting of the modern nationalities of the Welsh, Cornish and Bretons. The Gauls were also classed as Brythonic. See **Celt.**

Buain. A king of Ulster and father of Baile of the Honeyed Speech.

Buan. 1. Daughter of Samera who fell in love with Cúchulainn and, in trying to spring after his chariot, fell and struck her head on a rock and died.

2. Wife of Mesgora Mac Da Thó. The Ulster poet and druid Áthairne the Importunate stayed with Mac Da Thó, the king of Leinster, and demanded that he give Buan to him. Under the laws of hospitality a host is not supposed to refuse the request of a guest but Mac Da Thó refused. Áthairne returned to Ulster and persuaded Conchobhar Mac Nessa to make war on Mac Da Thó for this insult. Conall of the Victories was the warrior who eventually slew Mac Da Thó but Buan, rather than go with him, died of grief; her grave is named Uaig Búana.

Búanann. 'The mother of heroes', an Amazon-type lady who taught the martial arts and ran a school for warriors. The name signifies 'lasting one'. See **Anu.**

Buí. Sometimes given as Bói. An alternative name for the Cailleach Beara (Hag of Beara). It signifies 'yellow'. She is described as a wife of Lugh. See **Cailleach Beara.**

Buic. Son of Banblai, a warrior of Medb of Connacht who led a raid in search of the Brown Bull of Cuailgne. He was successful in capturing the beast but Cúchulainn slew him although he was unable to rescue the bull at that point. 'This was the greatest affront put on Cúchulainn during the course of the raid.' See **Natchrantal.**

Buile Shuibhne. The Frenzy of Sweeny. A warrior named Suibhne of the Dál Riada was maddened by his injuries at the battle of Moira. He took off on a mad flight through the wild places of Ireland in search of peace of mind. The tale is a powerful image of a frenzied mind. Suibhne returned to an almost animal familiarity with nature and the nature poetry contained in the story is excellent. It was apparently a common thing for poets to compose nature poetry in the name of Suibhne for several centuries, and the eighth-century poem '*M'airiuclan ni Tuaim Inbhir*', an account of a retreat, is supposed to one of his utterances.

Buinne the Ruthless. A son of Fergus Mac Roth. When Naoise and his brothers were besieged at the hostel of the Red Branch, Buinne and his brother Iollan defended them. Iollan was slain and Buinne killed many of Conchobhar Mac Nessa's men before the Ulster king offered him a mountain as a reward if he would cease fighting. Buinne accepted but did not enjoy his treachery for the mountain turned barren.

Bull. As in other cultures, the bull as a symbol of strength and virility features prominently in Irish mythology. The saga of the *Táin* war is perhaps the most famous story in which the bull cult is prominent. The ancient Irish used to hold a Bull Feast and according to the Book of the Dun Cow a special ceremony was performed by druids before a new High King was chosen. A white bull was sacrificed and a druid would eat of its flesh and drink its blood. The druid then slept and the man he dreamed about would be the rightful king. If the sleeper uttered a falsehood about his vision it was said that he would perish from the wrath of the gods.

C

C. *Coll* (hazel) in the Ogham alphabet.

Cael. A warrior of the Fianna who won the hand of Credhe, daughter of a king of Kerry, after reciting a poem in praise of her possessions. Cael makes an interesting point about cosmetics in the ancient Irish world. He says: 'A bowl she has whence berry juice flows with which she colours her eyebrows black.' When Cael died Credhe lamented him, praising his valour, and among the things she says is that 'his shield never uttered a moan in time of battle' meaning that he never came near to being vanquished in a fight.

Cáer Ibormeith. Daughter of Ethal Anubhail of the *sídhe* Uaman in Connacht. Aonghus Óg, the love-god, dreamed of her and, having his dream interpreted, set out to find and woo her. See **Aonghus** 1.

Cahir Mór. A High King (according to the king lists, he ruled in AD174) who was overthrown and slain by Conn of the Hundred Battles who succeeded him.

Cailleach Beara. The Old Woman, or Hag of Beara. Originally she appears as a triune goddess with her sisters Cailleach Bolus and Cailleach Corca Duibhne. She is also said to have been named Buí (Yellow) and been the wife of the god of arts and crafts, Lugh. The *Book of Lecan* mentions that she had seven youthful periods, marrying seven husbands and having fifty foster-children who founded many tribes and nations. Her domain was the Beara peninsula (see **Beara**) on the Cork-Kerry border.

Caílte. Sometimes Caoilte. The thin man. Son of Ronán and a cousin of Fionn Mac Cumhail, he is one of the chief warriors of the Fianna and is one of their foremost poets. He is said to have killed the god Lir in battle in the fight in which the Fianna helped the god Midir against Bodb, the new ruler of the Tuatha Dé Danaan. A Christian embellishment has him returning from the Otherworld to recount to St. Patrick the adventures of the Fianna.

Cairbre. 1. Foster brother of Conaire Mór.

2. Son of the king of Leinster who, with his brother Muredad, features in 'The Destruction of Da Derga's Hostel'.

3. Son of the god of eloquence and literature, Ogma, and his wife Étain. He is a bard of the Tuatha Dé Danaan who visited the half-Fomorii king Bres, received poor hospitality and therefore satirised him which forced him from his office. In the second battle of Magh Tuireadh he promised to curse and satirise the Fomorii to help the Dé Danaan win.

4. Son of Cormac Mac Art. He succeeded Cormac as High King and, with Fionn Mac Cumhail already dead, proceeded to exterminate the Fianna. His daughter Sgeimh Solais (Light of Beauty) was to marry and, according to custom, on the wedding night the Fianna had the right to receive her weight in gold to distribute among them as the royal bodyguard. Cairbre refused to pay and recreated the old animosity between Clan Morna and Clan Bascna. This led to the battle of Gabhra, said to have taken place in AD284, in which Oscar, then the leader of the Fianna, slew Cairbre but himself was mortally wounded and all the Fianna were destroyed.

5. Cairbre Caitcheann or Cathead. So called because he had the ears of a cat. A usurper who was set up as ruler when the Aitheach-Tuatha staged their revolt against the Milesians. During his reign 'there was only one grain on each stalk of corn and one acorn on each oak, the rivers were empty of fish, the cattle milkless'.

6. Son of Iliu. His son Fer Chertnae was a champion of the Red Branch.

7. Cairbre Músc. One of the three young sons of the High King, the others being Obléne and Oball, who features in 'The Destruction of Da Derga's Hostel'.

Cairell. 1. A son of Fionn Mac Cumhaill who was killed by Goll Mac Morna. Conán called him *crechtingech* or 'ragged-nailed' as a sign of abuse. This referred to his finger-nails: well-kept finger-nails were considered a mark of beauty and aristocracy by the ancient Irish.

2. A fisherman who caught Tuan (see **Tuan Mac Cairell**) in his reincarnation as a salmon. His wife ate the salmon and Tuan was reborn in human form as Tuan Mac Cairell.

Cairenn Chasdubh. Mother of Niall of the Nine Hostages and the second wife of Eochaidh Muigmedon. She was the daughter of Scál Móen, the Dumb, king of the Saxons. She was hated by Eochaidh's first wife, Mongfhinn (polygamy was practised in early Irish society), and forced to do menial work even though late into her pregnancy. She gave birth to Niall while she was working.

Caladcholg. The sword of Fergus Mac Roth, meaning 'hard dinter'. The famous sword of King Arthur of Britain, Excalibur, is a Latin corruption of this name.

Calatin. A druid, probably of Fomorii origin, who was sent by Medb to cast spells on Cúchulainn to incapacitate him during the *Táin* war. The Clan Calatin, twenty-seven sons and a grandson who had studied sorcery in Alba for seventeen years, attacked Cúchulainn. It was said that they never missed a throw with their poisoned spears and everyone they hit died in a week. All the members of the Clan Calatin were mutilated: the left hand and right foot were missing from each of them. Cúchulainn was worsted by them and was actually being drowned in a stream when a Connacht warrior, Fiachra, felt compassion for him and went to his rescue, cutting off the remaining hands of the Clan Calatin. Cúchulainn then slew them all. One version says that three daughters were born to Calatin's wife after his death; all were blind in the left eye and tried to draw Cúchulainn out to fight during his sickness by making the appearance of an army invading Ulster. They could shape-change. See **Badb** 2.

Camel. A door-keeper at Tara in the days of Nuada.

Cano. Son of Gartnán, king of Alba. He was in exile in Ireland where he was honoured by the High King Aedh Slane (AD656). He went to visit Guaire, king of Connacht, and while he was there he met Marcán, an old chieftain, who had a young wife named Cred. Cred fell in love with him and drugged everyone attending a feast so that she could be alone with him. Cano refused to make love to her while he remained under the laws of hospitality. However, he did love her and he gave her a stone which he said contained his life. After he returned to Alba to become king he made an assignation with Cred. Attempts to keep the assignation were frustrated by Cred's stepson Colcu. Cred, waiting at Loch Crede, became so anguished that she dashed her head against a rock and dropped the stone, which was thereby fragmented. Cano died three days later.

Cano Gall. The Foreigner. He was enlisted as pilot of a ship bearing an embassy from Conchobhar Mac Nessa during the tale of *Cath Ruis na Ríg* (Battle of Rosnaree).

Caoilte. See **Cáilte**.

Caoranach. A monster which dwelt in Lough Dearg.

Capa. One of three fishermen who first discovered Ireland, being driven there from Spain. They perished in the Deluge.

Caplait. A druid who taught the two daughters of Laoghaire, the High King.

Carmán. A goddess who came to Ireland from Athens with her three ferocious sons – Calma (Valiant), Dubh (Black) and Olc (Evil). They laid Ireland to waste but were eventually overcome by the Tuatha Dé Danaan. Carmán died of grief and it is recorded that death 'came upon her in an ungentle shape'. She was subsequently remembered in Leinster by a Festival of Carmán held at Lugnasad, 1 August.

Cas Corach. A minstrel and son of a minstrel of the Dé Danaan who 'plays so sweet a strain that all fall asleep'. See **Airitech.**

Cassmail. A Dé Danaan slain at the second battle of Magh Tuireadh.

Cat. 1. A mystical creature in Irish myth. As in most European languages the common name 'cat' applies in Irish (*catt*) but there are eight other words for a cat. The word *puss* has been borrowed into English as a pet-name for a cat. Cats permeate the myths, for example Irusan of Knowth who would often make off with people. Three monstrous cats dwelt in the Cave of Cruachan, the entrance to the Otherworld. One of the most poetic names given to an Irish cat is Luchtigern (Mouse Lord).

2. Son of Cruithne, founder of the Tuatha Cruithne (Picts) who gave his name to the ancient province of Cat, still known as Caithness.

Cath. Battle. A popular class of tales among which are '*Cath Almaine*' (Battle of Allen), '*Cath Maige Léna*' (Battle of the Plain of Léna), '*Cath Maige Mucruime*' (Battle of Mucruime's Plain), '*Cath Maige Rath*' (Battle of the Plain of Rath), '*Cath Maige Tuireadh*' (Battle of Moytura), '*Cath Fionn Trágha*' (Battle of White Strand or Ventry) and '*Cath Ruis na Ríg*' (Battle of Rosnaree).

Cathbad. A druid from the Tratraige of Mag Inis. He was the personal druid of Conchobhar Mac Nessa and some versions say he was Conchobhar's father. He married Maga, widow of Ross the Red, and his children were Dechtire, the mother of Cúchulainn, Elbha, the mother of Naoise, and Findchaem, mother of Conall of the Victories. He prophesied that Deirdre would have great beauty and would bring about Ulster's destruction. He also prophesied that Cúchulainn would be a glorious warrior but his life would be short. He was persuaded to lure Naoise and his brothers out of the Red Branch Hostel but when Conchobhar had them slain in contravention of the laws of hospitality and his own personal promise of safety, Cathbad cursed him and Emain Macha, his capital.

Cathubodua. A name for the crow or raven of battle. A title for the goddesses of war.

Cauldron, Magic. In pre-Christian myths a popular Celtic motif was the quest for a magic cauldron. The Dagda had a magic cauldron from Murias and no one parted from it hungry. Cúchulainn and Cú Roí stole a magic cauldron from a mysterious fortress. Out of this cauldron streamed gold and silver. The god Midir the Proud owned another magic cauldron. The cauldron, as a mythological symbol, provided abundance and restored people to life. Such a cauldron features in the adventures of Nera. There are parallels in the Welsh sagas: Annwfn, an Otherworld deity, had a cauldron, as did Didwarnach, Ogyrvan the Giant, Peredur and Bran. The tale 'The Spoils of Annwyn' is said to be the prototype on which later Christian writers modelled the Holy Grail quest in the Arthurian myths. Celtic cauldrons varied greatly in size and material, often being made of bronze, copper or silver and always richly decorated. A magnificent surviving cauldron is the Gundestrup Cauldron, dated to the first century BC and now in the National Museum, Copenhagen.

Caves. Like all early peoples the Irish held that caves were of supernatural and religious significance. They provided entrances into the Otherworld, like the Cave of Cruachan, and were places wherein dwelt the gods. In Christian times, when it was no longer fashionable to speak of the gods, it was the fairies who dwelt in the caves.

Cé. 1. The druid of Nuada who was mortally wounded at the second battle of Magh Tuireadh. Lough Cé burst out of his grave.

2. Son of Cruithne, founder of the Tuatha Cruithne (the Picts), who gave his name to an ancient province of Alba, now the area of Marr and Buchan.

Cébha. Of the Fair Skin. A daughter of Fionn Mac Cumhail who married Goll Mac Morna.

Céile Dé. The Culdees or 'servants of God'. Although they do not appear in Irish myths, being an historical order, they deserve an entry because it is mostly through their writings that the myths have come down to us. They were a monastic order founded by St. Mael Ruain of Tallacht (d. AD792). It was a loose-knit order with no central authority. They appeared in Ireland and in Scotland, existing in Scotland well after the absorption of the Celtic Church into that of

Rome – the last known reference to their existence in Scotland was in the fourteenth century.

Céis Churainn. A mysterious cave where three sorceresses imprisoned some of the Fianna who were then rescued by Goll Mac Morna in the tale 'The Dwellers of Céis Churainn'.

Cellach. Son of Cormac Mac Art who raped a relative of a Dési chieftain, Aonghus of the Terrible Spear. He was slain by Aonghus in the Great Hall of Tara in front of Cormac. Cormac, in trying to defend his son, had his eye taken out by the butt of the spear. It was this incident which led to the expulsion of the Dési. See **Aonghus 2** and **Dési**.

Celt. The Irish are a Celtic people. It is a linguistic term and not a racial one, marking out a member of the Celtic-speaking peoples. In modern times the Celts are divided between the Goidelic (Q) Celts – the Irish, Manx and Scottish Gaelic speakers – and the Brythonic Celts, being the Welsh, Cornish and Breton speakers. The Gauls (Gaulish dying out around the fourth or fifth century AD) were a Brythonic Celtic-speaking group and the term Gaulish may be applied to the language spoken by the Celts in all parts of the European mainland.

The Celts were the first transalpine people to emerge into recorded history. The term *keltoi* was first used by the Greek Hectaeus (*circa* 517BC) and is equivalent to Hyperborians and Gauls. The name seems to have derived from a Celtic word meaning 'hidden people', perhaps because of the Celtic reluctance to commit their vast store of knowledge to records written in their own language, passing things on only by oral tradition. This reluctance was due to a taboo imposed by the druids rather than a lack of literary knowledge. Celts did use Greek and Latin letters and sometimes wrote in those languages although modern archaeology has pushed back the date of surviving Celtic inscriptions to around the fifth century BC. For example, in 1983, the discovery of a lead tablet inscribed in Celtic at La Vayssière, France (known as the Larzac inscription) has provided us with our longest text in Gaulish. The etymology of the word Celt may well be from the same root that gives us *ceilt*, an act of concealment, and *kilt*, the short male skirt of traditional Celtic dress.

The Celts began an expansion around 900BC at which time they possessed great skill in metal work, especially in the use of iron, itself a Celtic word borrowed into the Germanic languages (Old Irish = *iarn*). This metal was only just becoming known to the craftsman of the 'Classical' world. With their iron weaponry and tools, the Celts were able to cut roads through the impenetrable forests of Europe. An ancient Irish word for road, still in use, is *slighe* from *sligim*, I hew. The road-builders of the ancient world, as modern archaeology shows, were Celts, whose roads were of wood. The Romans simply built over the top of these roads with stones. There is a preponderance of Celtic loan-words in Latin connected with roads and transportation, such as vehicles like *carpentum* (which gives us car and carpenter), *carruca*, *carrus*, *essedum*, *rheda*, *petorritum* etc.

The Celts pushed southwards and at their greatest expansion in the third century BC had settled in an arc throughout Europe with its eastern part being Galatia (around Ankara, in Turkey), from which country we have the earliest records of the workings of a Celtic state, through to the British Isles which some scholars now believe were settled by them between 2000 and 1000BC with the last major settlement in the second century BC.

During the sixth century BC they had extensively settled in northern Italy and were in constant war with the expanding Roman Empire. However in 390BC they defeated the Roman armies and sacked Rome itself. Polybius tells us that it was not until 345BC that the Romans were strong enough to reassert their independence. The 'Italian Celts' (Cisalpine Gauls) remained independent until 196BC when they were finally incorporated into the expanding Roman Empire. Many Latin writers were therefore of Celtic origin, including the famous poet Virgil and others such as Gallus, Cornelius Nepos and Trogus Pompeius.

In 280BC the Celts swept through the Greek States, smashing the Greek armies, and in 279BC they sacked the temple of Apollo's Oracle at Delphi. They even made an attempt to take over Egypt during the reign of Ptolemy II Philadelphus around 277BC. Although Julius Caesar led two expeditions to Britain in 55BC and 54BC, Britain remained independent of Rome until AD43. Ireland was never conquered by Rome.

The Celts were an exciting and an inventive civilisation with a highly developed religion which unified all their tribes from Ireland to Galatia. They had a sophisticated law system, as witnessed by the Brehon Laws and the Laws of Hywel Dda. They were among the first to develop the concept of the immortality of the soul. Aristotle, Sotion and Clement acknowledged that much of early Greek philosophy was influenced by the druids and Pythagoras' thesis on immortality, which bears a resemblance to druidic teachings, owed much to the fact that he had a slave who was a Celt.

It is believed that the two linguistic groups (Brythonic and Goidelic) diverged over 2500 years ago, the Brythonic group simplifying itself in its case endings and in the loss of the neuter gender and dual number. The two groups also differ in the matter of initial mutation and aspiration. There is the famous substitution of 'P' for 'Q' in the Brythonic languages (hence the designation P and Q Celtic). Thus the word for 'head' in Irish, *cenn*, becomes *pen* in Welsh; the word 'worm' in Irish, *cruiv*, becomes *pryv* in Welsh and so forth.

Celtic civilisation was smashed first by the Romans and later by the expanding English and French empires. But the Celts have managed to survive into the modern world with 2,500,000 speaking a Celtic language today out of the 16,000,000 who now populate the Celtic countries. One must add a further 1,000,000 Celtic-speakers to this figure among those who live outside a Celtic country. Only Ireland (in part) and the Isle of Man have any degree of self-government and only the Irish and Welsh languages have any legal status. Irish is the first official language of the Irish Republic (the 1981 Population Census for the Irish Republic gives 31.6 per cent of its population as able to speak Irish – that is 1,018,312 people). The language is also one of the official languages, though not one of the seven working languages, of the European Economic Community (EEC). No figures of Irish speakers have been given for Northern Ireland since Partition but it is generally estimated that there are about 60,000 speakers there.

Celtchair. Son of Uthecar Hornskin. A Red Branch warrior. His wife Bríg Bethach had an adulterous affair with Blaí Bruige. Celtchair took the opportunity to slay Blaí Bruige one day in the royal palace at Emain Macha. At the time Conchobhar Mac Nessa and Cúchulainn were playing *fidchell* and a drop of blood from Celtchair's spear fell on to the board. For violating the laws of hospitality Celtchair was ordered by Conchobhar to rid Ireland of three scourges. The first was in the person of Conganchas Mac Daire, the brother of Cú Roí, who was laying waste the country and whom no weapon could kill. Celtchair asked his daughter Niamh to marry him and learn the secret of his invulnerability. She did so and discovered that Conganches could only be killed by having spear tips thrust through the soles of his feet and the calves of his legs. Celtchair was thus able to kill him. The second scourge was in the form of an infernal dog which Celtchair killed by cunning. The third and last scourge was also in the

form of a dog and, as Celtchair despatched it, a drop of blood trickled
from his spear on to his flesh and, symbolically remembering the
drop of blood of the *fidchell* board, Celtchair was killed by its venom.

Cendchaem. Smooth-faced. The name of a *fidchell* board on which
Conchobhar Mac Nessa played with Fergus Mac Roth.

Cerband. Wife of Rudraidhe, son of Partholón. The name of her
husband does vary in other texts with Partholón's other two sons.

Cermait of the Honeyed Mouth. A son of the Dagda who was killed by
Lugh when he found out that his wife was having an affair with him.
Lugh, in turn, was killed by Cermait's son Mac Cuill. The name
Cermait is apparently given as a synonym for Ogma.

Cesair. 1. Daughter of Bith and granddaughter of Noah. Bith was
denied a place in the Ark and so Cesair advised him to build an idol
with Fintan and Ladra. The idol advised them to build a ship as Noah
had done, taking refuge in it. However the idol could not tell them
exactly when the Deluge would occur. They acted on the advice of
the idol, built the ship then sailed off. After seven years they came to
the shores of Ireland. Cesair became the wife of Fintan but he
eventually abandoned her. She died with most of her followers just
before the Deluge which Fintan escaped by changing into a salmon.
2. The wife of Ugaine Mór, High King of Ireland, and mother of
Laoghaire Lorc and Cobhthach.

Cet. Son of Maga. A Connacht warrior who enjoyed slaying the men of
Ulster. He was responsible for the death of Conchobhar Mac Nessa,
the king. He struck Conchobhar in the forehead with a 'brain
ball' from his sling, and after seven years the 'brain ball' caused
Conchobhar's death. Conall Cearnach challenged Cet's right to the
hero's portion at the feast of Mac Da Thó's boar. Cet accepted that
Conall was the better warrior but said his brother Anluan was even
greater. Whereupon Conall tossed Anluan's head at Cet's feet. In the
following mêlée Conall slew Cet but was sorely wounded himself.

Cethe. Son of Dian Cécht, the god of medicine.

Cethern. A lightly armed foot soldier, Anglicized as 'kern'.

Cethlenn. The name signifies 'crooked tooth'. The wife of Balor of the
Evil Eye who also fought at the second battle of Magh Tuireadh and
wounded the Dagda.

Cethor. A Dé Danaan and husband of Erí.

Cethren. 1. A son of Fintan and a poet who instructed Fionn Mac
Cumhail.
2. A warrior slain by Medb of Connacht in the war of the *Táin*.

Cetshamhain. An alternative name for the feast of Beltaine.

Chariots. Righairled, the fourteenth king of Ireland after Eber, son of
Milesius, is said to have introduced the first war chariots to Ireland.
In the myths, the chariot features mostly in the Red Branch Cycle. In
the Fenian Cycle there is scarcely any reference to chariots, although
in historical times there is a reference to war chariots in use at the
Battle of Crinna in AD226. St. Patrick is said to have ridden in a
chariot, and the Greeks and Romans frequently mention Celtic war
chariots. Julius Caesar was greatly worried by the British chariots
during his campaigns in Britain although, in Gaul, he observed that
war chariots had been given up two centuries before. The chariot
usually contained a charioteer and a warrior – as demonstrated in the
tales of Cúchulainn and the charioteer Laeg. While the charioteer
drove, the warrior could run along the yoke between the horses and
cast his spear over the heads of the galloping beasts before returning
to the car.

Ciabhan of the Curling Locks. The mortal lover of Cliodhna
who brought her from the Land of Promise to Ireland. Manannán
Mac Lir chased them to Cork and sent a great wave to return her
to the Otherworld leaving Ciabhan desolate. See **Cliodhna** and
Tonn.

Cian. A son of Dian Cécht, god of medicine. In the disguise of a woman,
he went to Balor's tower to retrieve his stolen cow, Glas Gaibhnenn.
In this enterprise he was helped by the druidess Birog. He met
Manannán Mac Lir on the way. He heard of Balor's daughter
Ethlinn, imprisoned in the tower of crystal on Tory Island so that she
would know no man, because it had been prophesied that Balor
would be slain by his own grandson. Cian seduced Ethlinn and then
returned to his own country with his cow. Ethlinn later gave birth to a
son Lugh Lámhfada. Cian was eventually slain by the three sons of
Tuireann and in reparation for his death they had to set out on their
famous quest. See **Ethlinn**, **Lugh**, **Brían** and **Tuireann** 3.

Cichol Grinchenghos. The footless. A Fomorii who preceded
Partholón to Ireland and lived by fishing and hunting birds. He was
eventually slain at the battle of Magh Ibha. His mother was Lot, a
monstrous woman with bloated lips in her breast and four eyes in her
back. His father was named Goll.

Cingris. Pharaoh of Egypt whose daughter Scota married Niul and was
mother of Goidel, the progenitor of the Gaels.

Clan(n). A tribe or descendants of an individual.

Cletiné. A spear owned by Cúchulainn which was coveted by Medb of Connacht. See **Uman-Sruth**.

Cliamh Soluis. The sword of light. Nuada's sword which no enemy could resist once it was unsheathed.

Cliodhna. A goddess of beauty who dwelt in Tír Tairnigiri (the Land of Promise). She fell in love with a mortal named Ciabhan of the Curling Locks. They fled from the Land of Promise and landed in Glandore, Co. Cork. While Cliodhna rested on the shore, Ciabhan went off to hunt. Cliodhna was lulled to sleep by music played by Manannán Mac Lir who then sent a great wave to sweep her back to his domain of Tír Tairnigiri leaving her lover desolate. Later folklore tradition made the goddess degenerate into a fairy queen worshipped at Carraig Cliodhna, Cork. The 'Wave of Cliodhna', however, was regarded as one of 'The Three Great Waves of Ireland'. See **Tonn**.

Clonach. A brother of Teideach. See **Teideach**.

Clothra. A daughter of Eochaidh Féidhleach. She drowned her own sister Ethné while she was pregnant. She had affairs with each of her three brothers and bore a son who became High King. He was called Lugaid Riab nDerg, of the Red Stripes, because he had two red stripes which divided his body into three sections, each section resembling one of Clothra's brothers, thereby proclaiming him to be the son of all three. When he grew up he begot a son on Clothra himself. The boy was called Crimthann Nía Náir, the modest warrior, who also became High King. The verse runs:

> Lugaid Riab nDerg to fair Crimthann
> Was father and was brother,
> And Clothra of the comely form
> Was grandmother to her son.

Cnu. Fionn Mac Cumhail's dwarf and jester.

Cobhthach Coel. The Slender. A son of Ugaine Mór, the High King. He became king of Bregia but was jealous of his brother Laoghaire Lorc, king of Leinster. He was so jealous, in fact, that he fell ill and his flesh withered thus earning him his nickname of Coel. He planned to kill his brother but, knowing that his brother was always well guarded, he devised a plot to get him alone. He sent word that he had died. Laoghaire came to pay his respects and, as in custom, entered the funeral chamber without his bodyguard. As Laoghaire bent over his brother's body, Cobhthach drew a knife and stabbed him in the stomach. Cobhthach then contrived to poison Laoghaire's son Ailill Áine and made Ailill's son eat his father's heart. The trauma of this incident struck the child dumb so that he was called Móen (dumb). Cobhthach now assumed the kingship of Leinster, ruling from Dinn Rígh, the fortress of the kings. Móen was taken into exile and when he recovered his speech and grew to manhood (becoming known as Labraidh Loingsech) he returned with an army of Gauls to exact vengeance. He attacked Cobhthach in his fortress at Dinn Rígh and eventually Cobhthach with thirty of his warriors were burnt to death in a great hall. See **Móen.**

Cochar Crufe. A warrior who acted as guardian at Dún Scáthach. He challenged Cúchulainn after the hero had accidentally broken the finger of Uathach, Scáthach's daughter. Cúchulainn slew him and became Uathach's lover. See **Uathach.**

Coinchend. Wife of Morgan. She was a monstrous warrior woman who was slain by Art when he rescued Delbchaem, their daughter, from the tower in which they had imprisoned her in the Land of Wonder. See **Art.**

Coinn Iothair. 'The Hound of Rage'. A dog belonging to Cromm Dubh.

Coire-Bhrecain. Corryveckan. Brecan's cauldron or whirlpool. Brecan, a grandson of Niall of the Nine Hostages, was sailing a fleet of fifty ships to Alba when he encountered a terrible whirlpool near Rathlinn Island. He and his fleet were swallowed up. See **Mórrígán.**

Colcu. Cred's stepson. See **Cano** and **Cred.**

Colm Cuaillemech. A smith of the Dé Danaan.

Colpa. A son of Milesius who died before the arrival of the Milesians in Ireland and was buried on the island of Gotia.

Conaing. Sometimes given as Conand and Concinn. A son of Ferbar. He was a leader of the Fomorii who lived on Tory Island and built a tower there, perhaps the same structure as Balor's Tower. He levied tribute on the Nemedians who rose against him and attacked Tory Island. He was killed but his brother Morc avenged him.

Conaire Mór. High King of Ireland. The son of Mess Buachalla and Nemglan, a mysterious bird-god. On the night before Mess Buachalla was due to marry the High King Eterscél, she was visited by Nemglan. It was he and not Eterscél who was the father of Conaire Mór. Mess Buachalla raised him in secret, not disclosing who his father was. His foster father was Désa and his foster brothers were Fer Lee, Fer Gar and Fer Rogán. In due course Eterscél died and

Conaire Mór followed a flock of birds towards Tara. They suddenly turned into warriors and their leader identified himself as Nemglan, his father. He told Conaire Mór to proceed to Tara where he would be acclaimed as High King. Conaire Mór had a sword which could sing. But he was weighed down by more *geise* (taboos) than any other king or champion. These *geise* he was eventually forced into breaking on his way to Da Derga's hostel. The Mórrígán, goddess of battles, appeared to warn him of his doom. At Da Derga's hostel, Conaire Mór and his followers were surrounded and attacked. Conall of the Victories, Sencha and Dubhtacht stood with him until the last. However, Conaire Mór was overcome with thirst and Conall volunteered to go for water. When he returned the final attack had been made and Conaire Mór's head had been struck off. He gave the severed head a drink whereupon it spoke and thanked him for his deed.

Conall. 1. See Conail.

2. Conall Anglonnach, a son of Iriel Glumar, one of the three chief warriors of Ulster – the others being Conall Cearnach and Laoghaire of Ráth Immel.

3. Conall Cearnach, of the Victories. Son of Amairgen and Findchaem. A warrior of the Red Branch, foster brother to Cúchulainn as well as being a blood cousin. It was he who avenged the death of Cúchulainn by slaying his killers. He killed Mesgora Mac Da Thó, the king of Leinster, and took his brain, mingling it with lime, to make a 'brain ball' – a magical slingshot. It was this which Cet of Connacht stole and used in an attempt to kill Conchobhar Mac Nessa. The 'brain ball' lodged in Conchobhar's head and caused his death seven years afterwards. Conall Cearnach is one of the great Ulster heroes and many adventures are attributed to him.

Conan. 1. of Cuala, a daughter of Medb of Leinster, wife of nine kings of Ireland in succession.

2. Mac Lia, son of the chieftain of Luachar. He spent seven years harrying and attacking the Fianna in revenge for Fionn's killing of his father. Eventually he made his peace with them and became one of their number. He is not to be confused with Conan Maol.

3. Mac Morna, sometimes known as Maol (bald). The son of Morna and brother of Goll. A warrior of the Fianna. He appears as something of a buffoon, a glutton and a coward, as foul-mouthed as Thersites and as great a braggart as Pistol. Nevertheless, he was a

leading member of the Fianna and several times saved the day for the warriors.

Conaran. A Fomorii who dwelt at Dún Conaran and sent his three sorceress daughters to take captive members of the Fianna. They were all slain by Goll.

Conchobhar Mac Nessa. King of Ulster during the Red Branch Cycle. The son of Fachtna Fathach, king of Ulster, and Nessa. When Fachtna Fathach died Nessa married Fergus Mac Roth who had become king. She married him only on the condition that her son Conchobhar could become king for a year. Under his mother's instructions Conchobhar ruled so well that the people did not want Fergus Mac Roth to return. Conchobhar then refused to give up the kingdom. Fergus Mac Roth, for a while, served under him. He is said to have been married at one time to Medb of Connacht but later married Mughain. He fell in love with Deirdre but rather than wed him Deirdre eloped with the Red Branch champion, Naoise. Using Fergus Mac Roth, Conchobhar enticed Deirdre and Naoise back from their exile in Alba on a false promise of safety. While in the Red Branch Hostel in Emain Macha, Conchobhar had Naoise and his brothers slain and Deirdre brought to his palace. Deirdre killed herself. Fergus Mac Roth, appalled by Conchobhar's treachery, offered his services to Ailill and Medb of Connacht during their war against Ulster. Even Conchobhar's druid, Cathbad, said to be his real father in some versions, is said to have cursed him and Emain Macha for his treachery over Naoise. After conducting a war against Mac Da Thó, at the instigation of Athairné the Importunate, Conchobhar was ambushed by the Connacht warrior Cet. He had stolen a magic 'brain ball', a slingshot, made by Conall of the Victories from the brains of Mac Da Thó. While the shot, which struck Conchobhar in the centre of the forehead, did not kill the king, it lodged in his head. His physicians could not remove it and Conchobhar was told never to get into a rage nor ride horses. After seven years Conchobhar did get into a rage and the 'brain ball' killed him. It was during Conchobhar Mac Nessa's reign that Cúchulainn's adventures took place, and it is the main period of the Red Branch Cycle.

Concinn. Sometimes Conand and Conaing. See **Conaing**.

Congal. Foster brother of Mael Fhorthartaig. He offered to intercede to help Mael Fhortartaig's stepmother in her plan to seduce Mael Fhortartaig.

Conganchas Mac Daire, Brother of Cú Roí. He ravaged Ireland with impunity because no weapon could harm him. He married Niamh, daughter of the Red Branch champion Celtchair. She discovered that he could only be slain by spear points penetrating the soles of his feet and the calf of his legs. She told her father, who slew him.

Conlaí. 1. Son of Cúchulainn and Aoife of the Land of Shadows. When he had grown to manhood Conlai went to Ulster. He defeated Conall Cearnach in single combat. Cúchulainn went to challenge this young warrior, despite a prophetic warning from his wife Emer. Cúchulainn mortally wounded his son. As he lay dying, Conlaí revealed his identity to his father, who was struck with grief. In some texts the name is given as Conall.

2. Son of Conn of the Hundred Battles. He went on an adventure to the Otherworld. Seeing a vision of a beautiful woman in a glass boat he sprang into it and 'from that day forward they were never seen again'. He was brother of Art who also voyaged to the Land of Wonders.

Conlaí's Well. See **Nuts of Knowledge**.

Conmac. A king of Britain who was grandfather of Ingcél, Caech and Eccell who led the attack on Conaire Mór in the tale of 'The Destruction of Da Derga's Hostel'.

Conmaicne Réin. A mountain in Connacht where the Tuatha Dé Danaan first made their appearance in Ireland.

Conn. 1. One of the sons of Lir, the ocean-god, who was transformed into a swan with his brother and sisters by their evil stepmother.

2. A son of Miodchaoin who was killed with his father and two brothers by the sons of Tuireann, though not before the sons of Tuireann were themselves mortally wounded.

3. Conn of the Hundred Battles. High King of Ireland. One day, before his accession to the throne, he and his followers were enveloped in a mist. A man appeared in it and invited them to a *ráth* where Conn met the symbol of Sovranty, a girl seated on a crystal chair and wearing a golden crown. Lugh, the god of arts and crafts, also appeared and prophesied concerning Conn's descendants who, he said, would reign in Ireland. According to the king lists Conn was High King from AD177–212.

Connachta. The Province of Connacht, an ancient kingdom and also known as the kingdom of Cruachain. Its original boundaries stretched from the Shannon to Donegal Bay and incorporated Co. Cavan. It was often in rivalry with Ulster and the most notable war

was that of the *Táin Bó Cuailgne*. Its most famous ruler was Queen
Medb, who is said to have ruled there for eighty-eight years.

Corc. A son of Miodchaoin who, with his brothers Conn and Aedh,
mortally wounded the three sons of Tuireann before they were killed.

Cormac. 1. A king of Ulster who married Étain Oig. See **Etain** 3. The
real father of Mess Buachalla.

2. Cormac Cond Longes. Son of Conchobhar Mac Nessa. He sided
with Fergus Mac Roth in protest at his father's treachery in slaying
the sons of Usna (Naoise etc.). He went to live in exile in Connacht.
When Conchobhar was dying he asked Cormac to come home and be
king in his stead. A prophetess warned Cormac that death awaited
him if he returned to Ulster but he went anyway. During the journey
he stopped at a hostel and during the night warriors attacked him.
Craiftine, the harpist of Labraid Loinseach of Leinster, lulled him
to sleep with music so the warriors could slay him. The attack was
instigated by Craiftine as revenge for the fact that Cormac had had an
affair with his wife.

3. Cormac Mac Art. High King who is said to have ruled in the
historical period AD254–277. He was the patron of the Fianna, the
royal bodyguard, and reigned during the period of the adventures of
Fionn Mac Cumhail, their greatest leader. He succeeded as High
King after defeating Fergus Dubdedach, Fergus Black Tooth. He
became friendly with the gods and Manannán Mac Lir invited him to
the Otherworld and gave him a magic branch of silver which bore
golden apples. When it was shaken such sweet music sounded that
the wounded and sick forgot their pain. Cormac kept this treasure all
his life but, at the point of death, he returned it to the gods. His
daughter Gráinne was engaged to Fionn Mac Cumhail but eloped
with one of Fionn's warriors, Diarmuid, which led to 'The Pursuit of
Diarmuid and Gráinne'. One of his sons, Cellach, was slain by a Dési
chieftain, Aonghus of the Terrible Spear, because Cellach had raped
his niece. In trying to save his son, Cormac had his eye put out by the
butt of Aonghus' spear. This disfigurement caused him to lose the
High Kingship. In vengeance, Cormac ensured that the Dési were
expelled from their lands. His son Cairbre succeeded him and
destroyed the Fianna.

Corpre. See **Cairbre**.

Cothulín Druith. A magical cap which, put on, enabled a person to
survive under the sea.

Craiftine. A harpist of Móen. His music lulled to sleep the parents of

Moriath so that Móen could make love to her. His playing also lulled to sleep the defenders of Dinn Rígh so that Móen's warriors could overcome them. See **Móen**. It was his harp, however, that revealed the secret of Móen's equine ears. Craiftine's wife became the lover of Cormac Conloingeas, son of Conchobhar Mac Nessa. In revenge Craiftine lulled him to sleep with his harp so that his comrades could slay him.

Crane Bag, The. See **Treasure bag of the Fianna.**

Crann-tabuáll. A staff sling. A favourite weapon of the heroes. A normal sling is called a *tailin* or *teilim* and a *taball*. In the *Táin* epic the staff sling is frequently used in battle. A sling shot is called *lic-tailme* and some sling shots become mystical weapons. The most famous was the 'brain ball' made by Conall Cearnach from the brain of Mac Da Thó. The Dé Danaan had a special sling shot composed of the blood of toads, bears and vipers (although no such snakes existed in Ireland) mixed with sea sand and hardened.

Crebhán. A High King who was accompanied by Náir, a goddess from the Otherworld. He led an expedition there and returned with wonderful treasures.

Cred. The wife of Marcán who tried to become the lover of Cano. See **Cano**.

Credhe. A daughter of the king of Kerry. She wed Cael after he composed a song about her possessions. She bore him a son named Luchra. When Cael died, she died of grief and they were both buried in the same grave. See **Cael**.

Credné Cred. The goldsmith of the Tuatha Dé Danaan who helped make the weapons for the second battle of Magh Tuireadh. Brother of Goibhniu and Luchtar.

Créide Fírálaind. A goddess who presented Art, son of Conn, with a splendid mantle and tried to persuade him to stay with her when he arrived in the Otherworld in search for Delbchaem.

Creidne. A female champion of the Fianna. She joined the Fianna having fled from her home after an incestuous relationship with her father which resulted in three sons.

Crimmal. An uncle of Fionn Mac Cumhail. He was a follower of Fionn's father Cumal when he was leader of the Fianna. He escaped from the slaughter of the Battle of Cnoc where Cumal was slain, then lived in penury with some followers in the forests of Connacht until Fionn sought him out and he rose with Fionn's fortunes.

Crimthann. 1. Son of the High King Lugaid Riab nDerg (of the

Red Stripes) who was High King in AD65. His mother was Lugaid
Riab nDerg's own mother, Clothra. Crimthann became known as
Crimthann Nía Náir, the modest warrior, and he became High King
in AD74. See **Clothra.**

2. Crimthann Cass. A king of Connacht, and father of Laoghaire,
who recovered the wife of Fiachna who had been abducted by Goll of
Magh Mell.

3. Crimthann Mac Fidhaigh. He perished at the hands of supernatural women on the feast of Samhain.

Cromm Cruach. Sometimes Crom Cróich. An early golden idol who
was reported to have twelve gods who served him. He was worshipped by the king Tigernmas (Lord of Death) on Magh Slécht (Plain of
Adoration) and human sacrifices were offered.

Cromm Darail. A druid and foster son of Cathbad who, with his
brother Cromm Deróil, features in the tale of 'The Intoxication of
Ulster'.

Cromm Deróil. A druid and foster son of Cathbad. See **Cromm
Darail.**

Cromm Dubh. An idol worshipped by the people of Connacht and
Munster.

Cronánách. He first appeared as an enormous misshapen churl who
played sweet music to Fionn Mac Cumhail on the pipes. Then he
turned into a handsome youth and revealed Fionn's destiny. He came
from the *sídhe* of Fermuin.

Crow. Also Raven. A symbol of the goddesses of battle. In this form
they appear hovering over the battlefields. The symbol was common
to all the Celtic peoples. It is fascinating to read the story of the Gallic
Wars by the Roman Livy (T. Livius Patavinus, d. 16BC). He speaks
of a Roman named Valerius Corvus (Crow) who was rescued while in
single combat with a Celtic chieftain by a crow who pecks the Celt's
face and hides the Roman with its wings. It is such a typical Celtic
motif that one has to examine Livy more closely. It is not the only
Celtic motif he uses. Camille Jullian (*Histoire de la Gaule*, 3rd ed.,
Paris, 1920) claims that Livy's history is made up from Celtic epics.
This is not so hard to believe when we realise that Livy was raised in
Cisalpine Gaul at a time when the Celtic language and traditions still
held sway there. The story of Valerius Corvus is much like the
famous episode in the *Táin Bó Cuailgne* in which the Mórrígán,
goddess of battles, attacks Cúchulainn in the form of a crow because
he has scorned her love.

Cruacha. Étain's maid who went with her when she married the god Midir the Proud. It is thought that Cruachan, in Connacht, was named for her although it is generally accepted that it derives from the word for a piled-up hill.

Cruachan, Ráth. Ailill and Medb's capital in Connacht. Sometimes called Rathcroghan. The site still remains three miles north-west of Tulsk, Co. Roscommon. It is a circular site of about an acre in extent but is surrounded by numerous other fortresses so that it has been described by Dr John O'Donovan (*Annals of the Four Masters*) as 'a town of fortresses'. Ráth Cruachan was still in use as the Connacht royal capital when, in AD645, the Connacht king Ragallach was assassinated there. Connacht was also called 'The Land of Cruachan'.

Cruachan, Cave of. Famous as an entrance to the Otherworld, sometimes called the 'Gate of Hell' by Christian scribes.

Crúadín. The magic sword of Cúchulainn, sometimes confused with Caladcholg (hard dinter) of Fergus Mac Roth and sometimes written as Caladbolg. The name derives from the same root – *crúaid* (hard) – but it is given in the diminutive form.

Cruithne. 1. The Progenitor of the Tuatha Cruithne or the Picts. Pict is the Latin name – *pictii*, painted people – for the Tuatha Cruithne. Cruithne had seven eponymous children who divided Alba between them forming the ancient provinces of the country: Cet (Marr and Buchan), Fiobh (Fife), Cirech (Angus and Mearns), Cat (Caithness), Fotla (Atholl), Moireabh (Moray), Fortriu (Strathearn).
2. Daughter of Locham the smith. Fionn Mac Cumhail killed a magic sow called Beo and gave it to her as a wedding present.

Crunnchu. Son of Agnomain. He was the father of the famous twins of Macha. One day a beautiful woman came to his doorstep. He took her in and she lived with him and became pregnant by him. Crunnchu boasted that she could win any foot race. His boasting forced her to race a chariot and, although she won, she gave birth to twins and died. Before doing so, she cursed the men of Ulster. See **Macha** 3.

Cú. A son of Dian Cécht, the god of medicine.

Cuailgne. A district of Ulster (modern Carlingford Peninsula) in which Daire kept his famous Brown Bull which became the object of Ailill and Medb's envy in the famous *Táin* epic. The place is frequently Anglicised as Quelegny or Cooley.

Cuan. A chief of the Munster Fianna who took part in the 'Pursuit of Diarmuid and Gráinne'.

Cúchulainn. The Hound of Culann, sometimes called the Hound of

Ulster. Perhaps the most famous hero of Irish mythology, he has been called the Irish Achilles. His mother was Dechtire, daughter of Cathbad, and on the eve of her wedding to Sualtaim Mac Roth she was spirited away to the Otherworld with fifty of her handmaidens in a mysterious bird flock. When she returned she had a baby boy named Sétanta. The father was the god Lugh Lámhfada. Sualtaim became his mortal father.

One day Culann the smith was holding a feast for the king Conchobhar Mac Nessa and his retinue. Sétanta arrived late at Culann's fortress after the gates were closed for the night and Culann's hound had been unleashed to guard against enemies. The hound attacked Sétanta who seized and killed it. Culann was angry when he learnt that his favourite hound had been killed but Sétanta promised him that until he acquired and trained another hound he would become Culann's hound and guard the fortress at night. It is by the name of Culann's hound – Cú Chulainn – that he became famous.

Cúchulainn was cousin to Conall Cearnach, whose mother Finchaem became his foster mother, and also cousin to Naoise and his brothers, the sons of Usna and his mother's sister Elbha. He took up arms on the day which Cathbad, druid of Conchobhar Mac Nessa, declared auspicious. Cathbad said that the man who took up arms on that day would become famous, albeit short-lived.

On his first battle foray he slew the sons of Nechtan Scéne and returned still in a battle frenzy, his chariot decorated with the heads of his enemies. Conchobhar's wife, Mughain, led the women of Emain Macha forth naked so that the hero, suffused with embarrassment, began to calm down. Whereupon he was seized and immersed into three tubs of ice-cold water; the first of these burst, the second boiled and the third just grew warm.

He fell in love with Emer, daughter of Fogall the Wily. Fogall, to delay Cúchulainn's suit, as he did not want his daughter wed to the champion, told him that no warrior could consider himself fit unless he trained with Domhnall the Warlike of Alba. Cúchulainn, with Conall Cearnach and Laoghaire, went to train there. Domhnall taught them all he could but said they could not be regarded as really trained until they attended the school of martial arts run by Scáthach, the female champion. Cúchulainn, having rejected the love of Domhnall's daughter, set off to find Scáthach but Domhnall's daughter caused Conall Cearnach and Laoghaire to turn back to

Ireland. Cúchulainn studied under Scáthach and had an affair with her daughter. He helped Scáthach overcome her sister Aoife of the Land of Shadows and had an affair with Aoife who bore his son Conlaí, whom he eventually killed not recognising him.

He returned to Ireland and went to the fortress of Forgall the Wily to claim the hand of Emer. Forgall refused; Cúchulainn slew many of Forgall's warriors and entered the fortress, whereupon Forgall leapt to his death from the ramparts to escape Cúchulainn's wrath. Cúchulainn and Emer were married. However, women were always falling in love with him, including Cú Roí's wife Blathnát, whom he took from Cú Roí's fortress in Munster after slaying him. Fand the Pearl of Beauty, a goddess and wife of Manannán Mac Lir, also fell in love with him and he spent a while with her in the Otherworld. However, Fand finally yielded him to Emer.

Cúchulainn is chiefly famous for his single-handed defence of Ulster during the war of the *Táin* when Ailill and Medb of Connacht invaded. He was acknowledged champion of all Ireland. He is also a tragic hero. During the *Táin* he was forced to slay his best friend Ferdia during a terrible combat at the ford. He rejected the love of the goddess of battles, the Mórrígán, and roused her wrath. His doom was sealed. In the final fight he strapped himself to a pillar stone because he was so weak. His enemies finally slew him but only dared approach his dead body when a crow (the Mórrígán) perched on his shoulder and an otter began to drink his blood. Through most of his adventures, Cúchulainn's charioteer and faithful companion is Laeg, who was also killed during the final conflict. Laeg drove Cúchulainn's two famous horses – the Grey of Macha and the Black of Sainglend. Cúchulainn had some mystical weapons such as his sword, Caladín, and his spear, the Gae-Bolg.

Cuimne. A hag who assisted Mongán in rescuing his wife, Dubh Lacha, from the clutches of Brandubh. Mongán changed her into a beautiful princess so that Brandubh agreed to swap Dubh Lacha for her. After Mongán and Dubh Lacha had gone, Cuimne changed back into a hag.

Cuirithir. A poet who was in love with Liadin. See **Liadin**.

Culann. The smith who forged Conchobhar's weapons and who was thought to be Manannán Mac Lir in human form. He was referred to as an Otherworld smith dwelling in the *sídhe* of Slievegallion. One evening he was giving a feast for Conchobhar and his retinue at his fortress in Cuailgne. The gates were locked at sunset and his hound was unleashed to guard the fortress. Young Sétanta arrived late and was attacked by the hound, which he killed. Culann was angry that his favourite hound was dead but Sétanta offered to become his hound until a new one was trained. Henceforth he was known as Cúchulainn – the hound of Culann. Culann's daughter was said to be responsible for the enchantments of Fionn Mac Cumhail.

Culdubh. A *sidhe* dweller who was slain by Fionn Mac Cumhail because he stole some food.

Cumal. Son of Trenmor, chief of the Clan Bascna and leader of the Fianna. He fell in love with Murna of the White Neck but her father, Tadhg, a druid, opposed the marriage because it had been prophesied that the union would bring about the end of his line. However, Murna eloped with Cumal. The druid then persuaded Goll of the Clan Morna, who was a contender for the leadership of the Fianna, to fight against Cumal. Goll attacked Cumal and Clan Bascna at Cnoc, scattering Cumal's men. Cumal was slain, either by Goll or one of his men. Murna escaped and bore Cumal's son, Demna, who later grew up as Fionn Mac Cumhail, the greatest leader of the Fianna. It is interesting to note that Cumal signifies 'sky' and seems cognate with the Brythonic Celtic name Camulos who was also known among the Continental Celts, particularly the Remi of Gaul, as a god of war. This god was commemorated in the one-time capital city of Britain, Camulodunum, the fortress of Camulos, or Colchester. The same name was given to Almondbury in Yorkshire, while Camulosessa, the seat of Camulos, appears in southern Scotland. It also seems cognate with King Arthur's famous court at Camelot.

Cup, Magic. see **Cauldron**.

Curad-mir. The Hero's Portion. A motif that features in such tales as 'Mac Da Thó's Boar' and 'Bricriu's Feast'. It was a choice cut of meat, usually a piece of thigh, reserved for the greatest champion attending a feast and therefore its apportionment was often the start of a quarrel between the warriors.

Cú Roí. Son of Daire and a king of Munster. His judgement was binding when he chose Cúchulainn as champion of Ireland over his rivals Conall Cearnach and Laoghaire. In one version he disguised himself as a giant and presented himself to the heroes, challenging each to cut off his head and then to let him retaliate. Sure that no retaliation could occur, Laoghaire and Conall Cearnach struck their blows but Cú Roí picked up his head and replaced it. Neither would let him give the return blow, and they fled. Cúchulainn, however, was quite prepared to allow Cú Roí to retaliate and was therefore declared champion. A similar story is told in 'Bricriu's Feast' with other characters.

In most stories, however, there is nothing supernatural about Cú Roí. At first, he was a friend of Cúchulainn and together they raided Inis Fer Falga and made off with the king's daughter, Blathnát, and other spoil. Blathnát fell in love with Cúchulainn but Cú Roí quarrelled with him and bested Cúchullain by burying him up to the armpits before making off with Blathnát and the rest of the loot. He took Blathnát to his fortress in Munster and married her. However, she sent a message to Cúchulainn that she would signal him as to the best way to attack Cú Roí's fortress at Sleemish. This she did by emptying milk into a stream which ran through the fort. When Cúchulainn and his men saw the white stream they followed it and attacked. Cúchulainn slew Cú Roí and carried Blathnát off but Cú Roí's bard, to avenge his king, seized Blathnát and leapt over a cliff to their common death.

Curragh. Sometimes *curach.* Cognate with the Welsh coracle (*cwrwgl*). The most popular of Irish boats and often used in the sagas and tales. The Irish had considerable knowledge of ship-building and classical writers record their extensive trade with European ports. In the Brehon Laws there are three main classes of ships recorded: the *ler longa* (sea ship), the *barca* (a coastal vessel not suitable for long voyages) and lastly the *curragh.* It had a wicker-work frame and was covered in hide. The *curragh* is still in use in Ireland today although the hide has been replaced by a tarred canvas covering.

Cuscraid Mend Machae. A son of Conchobhar Mac Nessa who made a claim for the hero's portion in the tale of 'Mac Da Thó's Boar'.

D. *Dair* (oak) in the Ogham alphabet.

Dabilla. Boann's lapdog.

Da Choca. He owned a hostel in Meath considered one of the five great hostels of Ireland. The others were those of Forgall Manach and Mac Da Reo in Bréifne, Mac Da Thó's hostel in Leinster and Da Derga's hostel in Cúala.

Da Derga's Hostel. A hostel by the River Dodder owned by a Leinster chieftain. Conaire Mór the High King journeyed there in spite of the fact that he had received warnings of impending doom on the way. It was the spot where fate contrived to break all his *geise* (taboos) by which his doom was sealed. The hostel was besieged by Ingcél, a Briton, and his followers including a number of Irish dissidents, such as Conaire Mor's own foster brothers and the sons of Medb of Connacht. Conaire Mór and his men wrought a great destruction on the attackers before perishing. 'The Destruction of Da Derga's Hostel' is one of the most popular tales of a king ignoring the foretelling of his fate.

Dael Duiled. An *ollamh* and poet of Leinster who entered a contest with Marbán the swineherd for the honour of the title of chief poet and philosopher of Ireland. He lost.

Dagda, The. Father of the gods. His name signifies 'the good god'. He is sometimes referred to as Eochaidh Ollathair (All-Father), also as Aedh (Fire) and Ruad Rofessa (Lord of Great Knowledge). He is also the patron god of druidism. He is drawn as a man clothed in rustic garb carrying a gigantic magic club which he dragged on wheels. With one end of the club he could slay his enemies and with the other he could heal them. He had a black horse, Acéin (ocean), and his cauldron, brought from the city of Murias, was one of the major treasures of the Dé Danaan. No man went hungry away from it. The Dagda also had a magical harp which was stolen by the Fomorii. With

Ogma and Lugh he set off in pursuit and found it in the Hall of the Fomorii. At the sound of the Dagda's voice the harp leapt from the wall, killing numerous Fomorii, and began to sing a pæan in praise of the Dagda.

At the second battle of Magh Tuireadh the Dagda appeared in the form of Ruad Rofessa, degenerated into a grotesque old man 'so fat and unwieldy that men laughed when he attempted to move about'. He carried a cauldron which held eighty gallons of milk and as much meat, whole goats, sheep and swine, all of which went to make his meal. His ladle was big enough to hold a man and a woman. As the other gods never seem to lose the splendour of their appearance, one wonders why the Dagda, the father of the gods, does so.

After the defeat of the Tuatha Dé Danaan, it was the Dagda who allotted spiritual Ireland to the gods, giving a *sídhe* to each. Aonghus Óg was not allotted a *sídhe* because the Dagda wanted his palace Bruigh na Boinne for himself. However, Aonghus Óg extracted the promise that he could spend a day and a night at the palace before he left it. Thereafter he refused to leave because he had tricked the Dagda by subtle wording into promising he could spend day and night there, meaning eternity. So the Dagda had to abandon his chosen palace.

As the Dé Danaan departed to their underground *sídhe* (eventually to change from gods into fairies in popular folklore) the Dagda resigned as leader of the gods. A council was held at which his son the Bodb Dearg was chosen as ruler. All accepted this decision except Manannán Mac Lir, who simply left the proceedings, and Midir the Proud, who started a war against Bodb Dearg. In this war between the gods, the Fianna, although mortals, were enlisted on Midir's side. Aonghus Óg, the Dagda's most famous son by the goddess Boann, does not seem to have played a part in this conflict. The Dagda no longer took any significant part in the affairs of Ireland although he does make a later appearance in the guise of the chief cook of Conaire Mór.

Daire. 1. Son of Dedad and father of Cú Roí and Conganchas.

2. Son of Fachtna and owner of Donn, the Brown Bull of Cuailgne. He refused Medb's request that he sell the bull to her. The refusal started the war of the *Táin*.

3. A son of Fionn Mac Cumhail who was swallowed by a monster but used his sword to cut his way out of its stomach.

4. A druid of Cormac Mac Art who identified Diarmuid for Gráinne

during the feast which Cormac held for Fionn Mac Cumhail and the Fianna.

5. A king who had five sons. A druid prophesied that one of them would be High King and so he gave them all the name Daire. The druid said that the chosen one would be he who caught a golden fawn. Lugaide Láigde Daire was the one who did so.

Daireann. A daughter of the Bodb Dearg. She fell in love with Fionn Mac Cumhail and asked him to have her as his only wife for one complete year and thereafter give her half of his time. When Fionn refused she gave him a cup of poison which drove him mad so that his Fianna deserted him. It was Cáilte who persuaded them to return at nightfall when the madness had passed and Fionn was well again. Daireann's sister, Sadb, was mother of Fionn's son Oisín.

Dairine. The younger of the two daughters of the High King Tuathal Teachtmhair. When Eochaidh, king of Leinster, came to Tara and told Tuathal that his wife, Fithir, Tuathal's elder daughter, was dead, Tuathal allowed him to marry Dairine. But when Eochaidh took Dairine to his fortress in Leinster, she found her elder sister still alive. Both girls died of shame. When Tuathal heard about this he went to war with Eochaidh and Leinster and exacted a tribute. This was the origin of the Bóramha. See **Bóramha.**

Daithlín. One of Mael Fhothartaig's hounds.

Dál. A division, a sept, a tribe or land inhabited by a tribe, for example Dál Fiatach, a kingdom on the eastern seabord of Co. Down; Dál nAraidi, around Lough Neagh; Dál Riada, in Co. Antrim in Ireland and in Argyll in Scotland.

Dalan. A druid who informed Eochaidh Airemh that Étain his wife had been carried off by the god Midir the Proud to his *sídhe* at Brí Leith.

Dall. The father of Fedilmid, Conchobhar Mac Nessa's story-teller.

Dallan. Son of Manech, a king of Ulster.

Daman. A Firbolg chieftain who was the father of Ferdia, Cúchulainn's friend.

Dana. Sometimes given as Danu and cognate with Anu. A mother goddess from whom the Tuatha Dé Danaan take their name. There is a school that believes that Dana is not the same deity as Anu, though most agree that she is. If her counterpart in Brythonic Celtic tradition is anything to go by, then her husband, never mentioned in the Irish tradition, is Bilé, god of death. The Dagda is her son. In some texts it is she, not Brigid, who is said to be the mother of Tuireann's children, Brían, Iuchar and Iucharba.

Dán Direch. An ancient Irish poetical system equivalent to the Welsh *Cynghanedd*, a metrical system of multiple alliteration and rhyme within every line of the Irish strict metres.

Daolgas. Son of Cairill. When he lay dying, his daughter stopped over him and kissed him. As she did so a spark of fire flew from his mouth to her mouth and she became pregnant. The child was also called Daolgas.

Dara. See **Daire.**

Dark Druid, The. See **Fer Doirech.**

Darvra. Now Lough Derravargh, Co. Wesmeath. The lake in which the children of Lir were bathing when their stepmother, Aoife, turned them into swans. They spent three hundred years on this lake and were visited annually by the Dé Danaans and the Milesians so that the gathering became a yearly festival. After three hundred years the children of Lir left for the Sea of Moyle.

Dathi. A nephew of Niall of the Nine Hostages and a king of Connacht. On Niall's death he became High King and went on a raid to Thrace. He came to a tower occupied by Formenius, king of Thrace, and demolished it but Formenius called upon the gods and a bolt of lightning killed Dathi.

Dead, Land of the. See **Otherworld.**

Deaf, Valley of the. Gleann na Bodhar. To which Cúchulainn was taken in order to recover from the enchantments of the daughters of Calatin.

Dealgnaid. The wife of Partholón who had an affair with her servant Todga when her husband was away. On returning and discovering this, Partholón acknowledged the fault was his for neglecting her.

Debility. Of the men of Ulster. See **Macha 3.**

Dechtiré. Sometimes Dectera. Daughter of the druid Cathbad and of Maga, daughter of the love-god Aonghus Óg, she was half-sister of Conchobhar Mac Nessa and mother of the hero Cúchulainn. Her sisters were Findchaem and Elbha. She was to wed with Sualtaim Mac Roth, an Ulster chieftain, when, at her wedding feast, a fly flew into her cup and she drank it. Afterwards she fell into a deep sleep and a handsome man, the god Lugh Lámhfada, appeared to her and commanded her to take fifty handmaidens and follow him. He changed them into birds and they flew away to the Otherworld. Three years later a bird flock appeared before Emain Macha and the warriors of Ulster went out to see them. The birds coaxed the warriors to follow them and led them to the Boyne. Here, at nightfall, they changed into Dechtiré and her handmaidens and the god Lugh. Dechtiré had a new-born baby whose name was Sétanta, the son of Lugh. Dechtiré returned to Sualtaim who accepted the child as his son. Sétanta grew up to be Cúchulainn.

Decies. See **Dési.**

Dedad. Alternative form of Degad. He formed the military élite of Munster, and was father of the warrior Lí.

Dé Danaan. See **Tuatha Dé Danaan.**

Degad, The. Also Dedad. The Munster equivalent to the Red Branch of Ulster. Their most famous leader was Cú Roí whose fortress was at Cathair Chonroi (the stone fortress of Cú Roí), now Caherconree, near Tralee.

Deirdre. Sometimes Derdriu. Deirdre of the Sorrows, daughter of Felim Mac Dall, a chieftain of Ulster. She was born when Felim was entertaining Conchobhar Mac Nessa, the king, in his fortress. Cathbad the druid cast her horoscope and said she would be fairest of all the women in Ireland and would wed a king but, because of her, only death and ruin would come upon the land. Conchobhar's warriors wanted the baby put to death at once but Conchobhar saved the child by saying that he would raise her and when she was old enough she would become his wife. In this manner no foreign monarch would wed her and so cause any war or dissension in Ulster. Lebharcham the poetess was charged with nursing her.

When the time came for her marriage to Conchobhar, Deirdre did not want to wed an old man. Looking over the ramparts of Emain Macha she saw a handsome young warrior, 'his hair like the raven's wing, his cheek the hue of blood and skin as white as snow'. She asked Lebharcham to identify him. He was Naoise, son of Usna, a hero of the Red Branch. Deirdre engineered a meeting. She fell in love with Naoise and he with her. Accompanied by his two brothers, Ainlé and Ardan, Naoise eloped with Deirdre and fled to Alba. Here the sons of Usna took service with the king of the Cruithne and, for a while, Naoise and Deirdre lived happily in Glen Etibhe.

The years went by and Conchobhar Mac Nessa became increasingly bitter. Outwardly, however, he pretended that he had forgiven Naoise and Deirdre, and sent Fergus Mac Roth to invite them to return to Ulster in peace. Deirdre foresaw their doom but Fergus Mac Roth was known to be a man of his word. His assurance of safety in Conchobhar's name was enough to reassure Naoise. They returned and were met by Baruch who sought to detain Fergus Mac Roth by inviting him to a feast. He pointed out that it was a *geis* (taboo) for Fergus to refuse to attend. So Fergus sent Deirdre, Naoise and his brothers on to Emain Macha under the protection of his two sons, Iollan and Buinne.

Conchobhar, having ascertained that Deirdre was as beautiful as ever, ordered his warriors to attack the hostel of the Red Branch where they were staying. Iollan was killed and Buinne was bribed. Ardan and Ainle were slain and finally Naoise was killed by Eoghan Mac Duracht, using Naoise's own sword. Deirdre was forced to wed Conchobhar. For a year she was his unwilling wife, never smiling. Conchobhar, angered by her attitude, asked her who she hated most in the world. Deirdre replied: 'You and Eoghan Mac Durthacht!' Enraged, Conchobhar told her that she would be Eoghan's wife for a year. When Deirdre, her hands bound to prevent escape, was placed in Eoghan's chariot, she contrived to sling herself head-foremost from it and dashed her head against a rock which killed her. From her grave grew a pine and from Naoise's grave a second pine grew. When full-grown the two trees met and intertwined above the graves; nothing could part them. Deirdre's story is one of the great love stories from the myths and is classed by the ancient bards as one of the 'Three Sorrows of Story-telling'.

Déisi. See **Dési**.

Dela. His five sons led the Firbolg invasion of Ireland.

Delbáeth. 1. Son of Ethlinn and Aonghus Óg, described as 'a noble youth of the Tuatha Dé Danaan'. He is said to be father of Éire, Banba and Fótla by the goddess Éirinn.

2. Son of Cas Mac Tuil, seventh in line from Ailill Olomh. He was banished with his five sons. He went to the cairn of Fiachu and kindled a druidic flame from which burst five streams of fire. Hence *Delbaed*, shape-fire. See **Delvin**.

Delbchaem. Fair Shape. Daughter of Morgan, king of the Land of Wonder, and his wife, Coinchend, a terrible warrior woman. She was imprisoned by her parents in a tower set on a high pillar. Art, son of Conn, who had been sent on his quest in search of Delbchaem by his stepmother, the goddess Bécuma, slew her parents, rescued her and brought her back to Ireland.

Del Chliss. A spear of Cúchulainn with which he slew the sons of Nechtan Scéne. Originally, it meant a split piece of wood and was given as the name for a charioteer's goad.

Delga. A Fomorii chieftain, father of Morca. He built a fortress called Dún Dealgan (Dundalk) which became the fortress of Cúchulainn.

Deluge. The story of the Great Flood occurs in the legends of many lands and not only in the Hebrew tales of the Bible. One school of thought is that Christian missionaries were responsible for the wide dispersal of the story while others claim that the legends have a basis in history, that a flood was common to all the peoples of the world. It is questionable whether the Irish Deluge was due to Christian influence; however, the Irish story does have some unique qualities in that there were four survivors of the Deluge outside the Ark, one of whom, Fintan, turned himself into a salmon to escape.

Delvin. Dealbhna or Delbáeth's descendants, from where Delvin in Co. Westmeath takes its name. See **Delbáeth** 2.

Demna. The original name of Fionn Mac Cumhail. Sometimes given as Deime and Demne.

Deoca. A daughter of a Munster chieftain who was betrothed to Laoghaire, a Connacht chieftain. She asked him to give her, as a bridal gift, the four singing swans who were the transformed children of Lir.

Derbfine. Descendants of a common great-grandfather whose rights as a sept of four generations are made clear in the Brehon Laws.

Derbhorgill. Sometimes given as Derbforgaille. Daughter of a king of Lochlann. She had been left for the Fomorii in lieu of tribute on a deserted beach. Cúchulainn happened by and slew the Fomorii and she fell in love with him. She turned herself into a swan, with a handmaiden, and followed Cúchulainn back to Ireland. Cúchulainn was hunting with a companion, Laoghaire, and he cast a stone with his slingshot bringing down one of the swans that flew over. It was Derbhorgill. He sucked out the slingshot and healed her but, being now united to him by blood, Derbhorgill was forbidden to wed him. Cúchulainn gave her to Laoghaire to wed.

Derbrenn. The first love of Aonghus Óg. Her six foster children were turned into pigs by their mother.

Derc-Ferna. The cave of Dunmore, Co. Kilkenny. In this cave dwelt Luchtigern (Mouse Lord), a great cat which was eventually slain by a female champion (*ban-gaisgidheach*) of Leinster.

Dér Gréine. Tear of the Sun. The daughter of Fiachna Mac Retach, who married Laoghaire Mac Crimthann of Connacht.

Derg-druimnech. Red-backed. The shield of Domhnall Breac, king of the Dál Riada of Alba. The Ulster hero Conall is said to have cast a

spear at him during the battle of Moira (said to have happened in
AD637) and while three warriors placed their shields before their
king, Conall's spear, *lúin*, went through their shields, through them,
through Domhnall's shield and wounded him. However, it is
recorded that Domhnall was still victorious in this battle.

Désa. Also Donn Désa. A champion who became foster father
to Conaire Mór. He had three sons, Fer Le, Fer Gar and Fer
Rogain, who joined Ingcél against their foster brother and took
part in the attack on Da Derga's hostel where Conaire Mór was
killed.

Dési. Sometimes Déisi and Decies. A clan of Bregia in the province of
Mide (Meath). The name appears to signify 'vassals'. They feature in
a story *'Inndarba inna nDési'* (The Expulsion of the Dési) which,
according to Professor Kuno Meyer, is stylistically dated back to the
third century AD. Cellach, a son of Cormac Mac Art, the High King,
riding through the Dési territory, raped a niece of a chieftain,
Aonghus of the Terrible Spear. Aonghus (Gae-Adúath) went to Tara
to demand justice. Cellach denied his act. In a rage Aonghus seized
the spear of a guard and killed Cellach. Cormac Mac Art, trying to
save his son, had his eye taken out by the butt of the spear. This
disfigurement, under Celtic law, disbarred Cormac from the kingship and his son Cairbre became High King. Nevertheless, the Dési
were subject to a terrible vengeance from Tara. They were expelled
from their lands. Some settled in Munster; others were pursued from
Ireland and, after a voyage of many adventures, settled in south
Wales. The Dési settlement is an historical one. There is an Ogham
inscription which survives in the Carmarthen Museum, dated to the
sixth century. It is to Voteocorigas, a Dési ruler, who is believed to be
the Voterporius whom the sixth-century Gildas attacked as a tyrant.
The story survives in *Annála Ríoghachta Éireann*, a seventeenth-
century copy of an earlier book known in English as the *Annals of the
Four Masters*.

Destructions. A class of tales such as 'The Destruction of Da Dearga's
Hostel', 'The Destruction of Dinn Rígh', etc.

Dian. A young chieftain of the Fianna who was captured by the gods of
the *sídhe*. Cáilte met him and asked him how life was with the gods.
Dian told him that he would rather be a slave among the Fianna than
a prince among the gods.

Dian Cécht. The god of medicine. After Nuada lost his hand in the first
battle of Magh Tireadh, Dian Cécht supplied him with a silver hand,

thus earning Nuada the name Airgetlámh. However, this blemish precluded Nuada from kingship and Bres, the half-Fomorii, became king. Dian Cécht's son, Miach, proved himself a better physician by providing Nuada with a new hand of flesh and blood, allowing him to regain the kingship. However, Dian Cécht grew jealous of his son and slew him. With his daughter Airmid he guarded a spring of health which restored the dead and wounded members of the Dé Danaans. Among the Brehon Law tracts is one called 'The Judgements of Dian Cécht', relating to the practice of medicine, which Professor Binchy dates as early as the sixth century AD (*Eriu* Vol. XX). See **Airmid** and **Miach**.

Diarmuid. 1. A king whose wife Bec Fola left one morning to visit the Otherworld. She stayed a day and a night but on her return found that it was still the same morning and Diarmuid was only just stirring.

2. Son of Fergus Cearbaill. An historical High King, sometimes confused with the husband of Bec Fola, who reigned about AD545–568, according to the king lists. There are several stories about him. One of his officers was killed by a chieftain named Aodh Guaire, related in fosterage to St. Ronán (Ruadan). When the king sent men to arrest Aodh, St. Ronán hid him and so Diarmuid had Ronán arrested and tried in his stead. He was condemned by the ecclesiastics for this act and Ronán himself uttered the famous curse: 'Desolate be Tara for ever!' Soon after Tara was abandoned never to achieve its former splendour, so the story went.

His wife was Mughain who had an affair with Flann, son of Dima. Diarmuid had Flann's fortress burnt over his head. Sorely wounded, Flann sought to avoid the flames by climbing into a vat of water where he drowned. In one version St. Ronán prophesied that a roof beam would fall on Diarmuid's head and kill him. In another St. Ciarán foretold that Diarmuid would suffer the same death as Flann. However it was Diarmuid's druid Bec Mac Dé who made the most interesting prophecy. He said that Diarmuid would be killed by Flann's kinsman, Aedh Dubh, in the house of Banbán. His death, however, would only be encompassed on the night he wore a shirt grown from a single flax seed, when he drank ale brewed from one grain of corn, and when he ate pork from a sow which was never farrowed. The manner of his death would be by slaughter, by burning, by drowning and by the ridge pole of a roof falling on to his head. The prophecy seemed so unlikely that Diarmuid scorned it

even when Banbán invited him to a feast. Mughain his wife warned
him of his doom and refused to accompany him.

At Banbán's house Banbán suggested that since the king's wife was
not with him his own daughter would 'this night be your wife'. The
girl brought Diarmuid a nightshirt, food was brought and ale. The
girl told him that the nightshirt was made from a single flax seed; the
pork was from a sow that had not farrowed and the ale brewed from a
single grain of corn. Realising the impending doom, Diarmuid
sprang to the door. Aedh Dubh was there and stabbed the High King
with his spear. Wounded, Diarmuid fled back into the house. Aedh
Dubh's men set fire to it. Seeking to escape the flames, Diarmuid
scrambled into a vat of ale. A burning ridge pole fell on to his head.
The prophecy was fulfilled.

3. Ua Duibhne. Diarmuid of the Love Spot. His father was Donn
who took him to be fostered by the love-god Aonghus Óg. While at
Bruigh Na Boinne, Donn discovered that his wife had been having an
affair with Roc, Aonghus Óg's steward. She gave birth to another
child and Donn crushed this child to death. Roc took a wand and
smote his dead son with it, whereupon the dead child turned into a
great magical boar. Roc told the boar to bring Diarmuid Ua Duibhne
to his death and the boar ran off to the forests around Ben Bulben,
Co. Sligo, to await its destiny.

Diarmuid grew up to be a beautiful youth and became a member of
the Fianna. Out hunting with Goll, Conan and Oscar, he arrived late
one night at a hut in a wood where an old man, a young girl, a wether
sheep and a cat were living. When they sat down to eat the cat jumped
on the table and not one of the four Fianna champions could throw it
off. The old man told them that the wether sheep was the World and
the Cat was death. The four champions then went to bed and the
young girl, whose beauty made a light like a radiant candle, went to
sleep in the same room with them. Each of the champions sought to
make love to her but she chose Diarmuid, saying: 'I am Youth and I
will put a mark on you that no woman can ever see you without loving
you.' She touched his forehead and gave him his famous love spot.

Diarmuid was one of the active members of the Fianna and played
a role in the chase of Abarta. He also had adventures in the
Otherworld.

Fionn Mac Cumhail became bethrothed to Gráinne, the daughter
of the High King Cormac Mac Art. Fionn was now elderly, war-worn
but still a great warrior. The Fianna accompanied him in his wedding

feast at Tara. Gráinne, however, was not anxious to wed an old man however great a warrior he was. She asked first Oisín if he would elope with her. When he refused she asked Diarmuid and contrived to put a *geis* on him so that he had no choice. He sought advice from Oisín, Oscar and Celta. They pointed out that he must not break his *geis*. In spite of his reluctance, Diarmuid eloped with Gráinne from the palace of Tara.

Burning with rage, Fionn summoned his Fianna, and set out in pursuit. At first Diarmuid treated Gráinne as a sister and sent messages to Fionn to this effect. But Gráinne eventually seduced him and he fell in love with her. The pursuit is graphically described and many times Diarmuid rescues Gráinne and himself from the vengeance of Fionn. After sixteen years of outlawry, at the intercession of both Cormac Mac Art and the love-god Aonghus Óg, Fionn begrudgingly made peace. Diarmuid and Gráinne settled in their palace at Rath Gráinne at Tara. Gráinne bore four sons and a daughter to Diarmuid.

However, Gráinne was not satisfied that peace had been made until both Fionn and her father Cormac Mac Art had become their guests at Ráth Gráinne. Fionn and Cormac agreed and were feasted there for a year. Towards the end of this feasting, Diarmuid was awoken by the sound of a hound baying. It was an omen. He decided to go out hunting with Fionn and the Fianna. While they were traversing Ben Bulben, Co. Sligo, they discovered that they were no longer the hunters but the quarry. They were pursued by an enchanted boar, Diarmuid's own stepbrother. Fionn, still nursing a grudge, knowing that Diarmuid never retreated from danger, enticed him into fighting the boar. Diarmuid's hounds fled in terror as the boar approached. Diarmuid slung a stone at it but while he hit it in the middle of the forehead it made no impact. Diarmuid struck the boar with his sword but the weapon broke in two. The boar sprang on him and gored him but Diarmuid finally succeeded in driving the broken hilt of his sword into the animal's brain.

While Diarmuid was in his death agony, Fionn stood over him and said: 'It likes me well to see you in that plight, O Diarmuid, and I would that all the women in Ireland saw you now, for your excellent beauty is turned into ugliness and your comely form into deformity.' Diarmuid pleaded with Fionn to give him water, for a draught of water from Fionn's hand would have healed his wounds. Fionn refused. Diarmuid reminded him of how he had once rescued Fionn.

Fionn replied that there was no well nearby. Diarmuid pointed to a well nine paces away. Fionn reluctantly got water, but let it fall through his hands.

The Fianna came up and Oscar, Fionn's own grandson, declared that if Fionn did not get water promptly he would kill him. Fionn finally brought the water but it was too late: Diarmuid was dead. The Fianna laid their cloaks over him and returned to Ráth Gráinne. Gráinne, seeing them returning without Diarmuid but with Diarmuid's hound, realised what this meant and swooned on the ramparts. The Fianna left. Sorrowing, Gráinne and her household went to fetch the body. They found the love-god Aonghus Óg there, with others of the Dé Danaan. They raised three bitter cries and placed Diarmuid on a bier. Aonghus Óg told Gráinne he would carry Diarmuid to Bruigh na Boinne. While he could not restore Diarmuid to life, 'I will send a soul into him so that he may talk with me each day'. See **Gráinne**.

Digde. An alternative name for the Cailleach Beara.

Dige. An alternative name for the Cailleach Beara.

Dinn Rígh. The fortress of kings in Leinster. It was formerly known as Duma-Slaigne, the burial mound of Slaigne, the Fomorii king. It was also known as Tuaim Tenba. It is now identified with Ballyknockan, on the west bank of the Barrow in Co. Carlow, where an old earthwork still stands. The ramparts are 237 feet in diameter. In the tale 'The Destruction of Dinn Rígh' it was here that the evil ruler Cobhthach Coel of Bregia was slaughtered with thirty of his warriors when Moén locked then into an iron hall and set fire to it.

Dinnsenchas. 'The lore of prominent places'. It is a comprehensive topography of Ireland and a guide to geographical mythology. It is contained in the twelfth-century Book of Leinster and is one of the richest sources of myth. It is here we find the early versions of the story of the Sons of Usna and many Fianna tales.

Dithorba. A king who ruled Ireland alternately with Cimbaeth and Aedh Ruadh who are variously given as his brothers or cousins. When Aedh Ruadh died his daughter Macha Mong Ruadh was elected to rule. Dithorba and Cimbaeth led an opposition to her but she made peace with Cimbaeth, eventually marrying him, and slew Dithorba. She captured his five sons and made them construct the ramparts of Emain Macha. See **Macha** 4.

Diurán. A poet and one of Mael Dúin's followers during his fabulous voyage. When Mael Dúin's ship reached the Pillar of Silver in the sea, with its top out of sight and a silver net spread around it, Diurán leant out of the boat and hacked away a piece of silver net. When he returned home the Christian embellishment is that he placed the silver on the High Altar at Armagh, the seat of the primacy of Ireland.

Divination. The art of foretelling the future is an essential part of the myths. In most cases the fate of the hero or heroine is foretold at birth. Such is the case of Deirdre whose horoscope is cast by Cathbad. More often than not, it is to escape their fate that the protagonists set out on their adventures which inevitably lead them to the fate they seek to avoid. In some cases, such as the death of Diarmuid the High King at the House of Banbán, the prophecy is so bizarre that its fulfilment seems unlikely. Mortals ignore the warnings at their peril. Such is the fate of Conaire Mór. Divination was widely practised in Celtic society. It was practised in many forms – astrology, dreams, signs and omens from nature and unusual occurrences. One favourite way was the casting of yew wands inscribed with mystic words in Ogham. Divination was the prerogative of the druids, both male and female, who were also the interpreters of people's dreams or visions. Women who prophesied were usually related to druids if they were not part of the druidic order. The Old Irish word for an astrologer was *néladoir* (cloud diviner) and no house or palace could be erected without an astrologer being consulted as to the most propitious time.

Dobhar. King of Siogair, identified as Sicily. He owned two wonderful horses which could run equally well on land and sea. One of the tasks of the Children of Tuireann was to acquire these beasts and the king's chariot. The task was accomplished when Brían killed Dobhar with the poisoned spear of Pisear.

Dobhinia. An ancestress, perhaps goddess, of the people of Corco Duibhne in Kerry.

Doilín. One of Mael Fhothartaig's hounds.

Domhnall. 1. The Warlike. A champion of Alba to whom Cúchulainn was sent to finish his military training. He was accompanied by Laoghaire and Conall Cearnach. In another version Conchobhar Mac Nessa is the unlikely substitute for Conall. After Domhnall had taught them all he could he advised them to go to the school of Scáthach, the famous female champion. Domhnall had a daughter, Dornoll, who fell in love with Cúchulainn.

2. Breac. The name of an historical king of the Dál Riada of Alba. He invaded Ireland and fought in the battle of Magh Ráth, the Plain of

Forts (Moira), in AD637. Confusingly, his opponent was another Domhnall, Domhnall Mac Aedh, who presided over the historic Assembly of Druim Ceata. He is mentioned here because he possessed a shield of magic propensities which Conall pierced during the battle.

Domnu. Goddess of the Fomorii. The name seems to signify an abyss of the sea and, significantly, the name Fomorii appears to translate as 'undersea dwellers'. Indech, the Fomorii leader, is specifically described as the son of Domnu but she appears to be a mother goddess and mother of all the Fomorii. Through the various sagas and tales an eternal struggle is seen between the Children of Domnu, representing darkness and evil, and the Children of Dana, representing light and goodness.

Donn. 1. Irish god of the dead whose abode is at Tech Duinn (House of Donn) which is placed on an island off the south-west of Ireland. See **Tech Duinn**. The house is the assembly place of the dead before they begin their journey to the Otherworld. In modern folklore Donn is associated with shipwrecks and sea storms and sometimes equated with the Dagda and Bilé. In some versions he is said to be the son of Midir the Proud. More often than not he is confused with the eldest son of Milesius. See **Donn 2**.

2. The eldest of Milesius' eight sons whose mother was Seang. He commanded the Milesians in their invasion of Ireland but when he was greeted by the goddess Éire, who asked that the island might take her name, he paid her scant respect. She foretold his doom. The Milesians put the sea again and Manannán Mac Lir caused a great storm to blow up. In one version Donn goes aloft to spy out the land and falls into the sea. Another version says he asked his brothers to bury him on an island off the mainland; this they did, and here his tradition and that of Donn 1 became intermixed.

3. Foster brother of Mael Fhothartaig who slew Eochaidh and his wife and son in retaliation for the killing of Mael Fhothartaig.

4. The father of Diarmuid Ua Duibhne who gave his son to Aonghus Óg to be fostered. His wife was unfaithful with Aonghus Óg's steward Roc and bore him a son. Donn killed this child by crushing it to death and flung its body to his hounds. Roc, however, smote the dead child with a magic wand and turned it into an enchanted boar which was instructed to encompass the death of Diarmuid Ua Duibhne. It then went to Ben Bulben to await its destiny.

5. Donn Désa. See **Désa**.

6. Donn Cuailgne. The Brown Bull of Cuailgne over which the Táin war was fought. He was originally the swineherd of the Bodb Dearg (see **Nár**) whose rival was the swineherd of Ochall. They fought constantly with each other and continued through numerous re-incarnations, as ravens, as water beasts, as demons, as champions, as great water worms until, finally, they were reborn as bulls: the Brown Bull of Cuailgne and the White Bull of Connacht. The Brown Bull was coveted by Medb of Connacht and this provoked the war against Ulster in which Medb attempted to secure the Brown Bull. At the end of the war Donn and his rival, Finnbhenach or the White Bull of Connacht, met and fought. Donn finally killed his ancient rival but he was mortally wounded.

7. Donn Bó. A youth famed for his singing. See **Allen, Hill of.**

Dornoll. Bigfist. The loathsome misshapen daughter of Domhnall the Warlike. She fell in love with Cúchulainn and when he refused her she sought vengeance. She caused his companions Laoghaire and Conall to desert him while he journeyed on to the Land of Shadows.

Dragons. Irish mythology abounds with monstrous serpents or dragons most of whom live at the bottom of lakes. Sometimes they guard palaces or fortresses. However, there have never been any venomous reptiles in Ireland. There is a species of small lizard, called *are-luachra* or lizard of the rushes. Two centuries before St. Patrick was supposed to have driven out all the serpents, writers were stating that no such creatures existed in Ireland.

Druid. Druids were both male and female. They have been mistakenly called 'a religious caste'. It is true that druids presided at religious functions and promulgated the Celtic religion and its rites. However, they were also important political figures, advisers, judges and teachers. The philologist Rudolf Thurneysen believed that the word came from the roots *dru-vid* meaning 'thorough knowledge'. Druids were known throughout the Celtic world and not just in Ireland. According to the classical writers a strenuous training was needed to become a druid: some commentators said it took up to twenty years to learn all the druidical laws and canons. C. Julius Caesar described druids in this way:

> They are concerned with religious matters, perform sacrifices offered by the state and by private individuals, and interpret omens. Many of the youth resort to them for education and they are held in high honour by the Gauls. They have the decision in

nearly all the disputes that arise between the state and individuals; if any crime has been committed, if any person has been killed, if there is any dispute about an inheritance or a boundary, it is the druids who give judgements; it is they who settle the rewards and punishments. Any private person or any tribe refusing to abide by their decision is excluded from sacrifice. This is the heaviest punishment that can be inflicted; for those so excluded are reckoned to belong to the godless and wicked. All persons leave their company, avoid their presence and speech lest they should be involved in some of the ill-consequences of their situation. They can get no redress from injury and they are ineligible to any post of honour.

The druids were not only ministers of religion but were accounted philosophers, natural scientists and teachers, and were able to give legal, political and military judgements. They were trained in 'international law' as well as tribal law and were the arbiters in disputes between territorial groups. The druids had power to prevent warfare between tribes, for the moral and legal authority of the druids was greater than that of the chieftains or the kings or even the High King himself. Conchobhar Mac Nessa could not speak at an assembly before his druids spoke.

The druids appear similar to the eastern Zen masters. Whereas most of the knowledge of Brythonic Celtic and Continental Celtic druids has come down to us from Greek and Latin sources, there is a corpus of native Irish writing describing the role of Irish druids. However, all of this has been written by Christian monks and so contains a Christian outlook and veneer. Their role in Irish myths appears mainly as wizards, masters of the supernatural arts, instead of merely learned men.

Native sources do acknowledge the druids' role as teachers. Even Colmcille (St. Columba) commenced his education under a druid. Druids had to be consulted on all matters of importance: when Conchobhar Mac Nessa contemplated attacking Ailill and Medb he first sought the advice of his druid Cathbad as to the manner and timing of his punitive raid. But while the druids were respected they were not sacrosanct. During his adventures with Clann Calatin Cúchulainn killed a druid working against him.

The *Dinnsenchas* describes the offices of the druids and notes the *ban-drui* or female druid. Before the second battle of Magh Tuireadh, it is stated, two female druids promised to enchant the Fomorii army and cast a spell so that 'the trees and stones and sods of the earth . . . shall become a host against them and rout them'. The role of female druids is also noted in later Christian ecclesiastical writings.

The Latin writers, in particular, were not exactly sympathetic to the Celtic people or the druids, and they spoke of human sacrifices as part of the Celtic religion. There is no native tradition of this, especially connected with the Irish druids. If there had been some hint of such a tradition then the Christian scribes, in their efforts to denigrate the older religion and its practices, would have undoubtedly seized upon it as they did with Cromm Cruach.

Druids in Ireland had a tonsure, as did the later Christian monks. It is recorded that they cut their hair in a mystic figure called *airbacc Giunnae* (perhaps, fence cut of the hair) – a tonsure which ran from ear to ear instead of being a circular form on the crown of the head. The Celtic Christian monks copied this fashion and it became one of the points of contention with Rome. The Roman form of tonsure finally displaced the Celtic form.

Whereas it is recorded that the Brythonic and Continental Celtic druids proscribed the writing down of their lore in any form, the Irish druids are frequently observed as writing things down in Ogham on wands of wood. See **Gods** and **Otherworld**.

Drumcain. The ancient name of Temhair (Tara), which meant 'beautiful hill', where the Dé Danaans and the Milesians first met.

Duanaire Finn. A collection of ballads about Fionn Mac Cumhail. Volume 1 of *Duanaire Finn* was edited by Professor Eoin Mac Neill for the Irish Texts Society in 1908. Professor Gerard Murphy then took over and edited Volumes 2 (1933) and 3 (1954).

Dubgilla. Sometimes Dubh Giolla. Black servant. The shield of Aedh, king of Oriel.

Dubh. Black. Wife of Enna and a druidess. She discovered that Enna had another wife and drowned her rival by magic. She was slain with a slingshot by Enna and fell into a pool which became known as Dubh's pool, *Dubhlinn*. This, it is said, is how Ireland's capital city achieved the name of Dublin. In some of the annals the name is written as *Duibh-linn* and this is translated in the Latin texts as *Nigratherma* – black pool. It was originally the name of a pool on the River Liffey where the city was built. In early times an artificial ford of hurdles was constructed across the river where the main road from Tara to Wicklow crossed. The city that sprang up around this was called the Town of the Hurdle Ford – Baile Átha Cliath. It is by this name that the capital of Ireland is known to all Irish speakers today.

Dubh Lacha. The beautiful wife of Mongán. She was born on the same night that he was. She was coveted by Brandubh who tricked Mongán into giving her to him. However, Mongán, a son of Manannán Mac Lir, used his supernatural powers to secure her release. The tale is told in *Toraigheacht Duibhe Lacha* (The Rescue of Dubh Lacha).

Dubhlaing. The lover of Aoibhell who prophesied he would die in battle unless he allowed her to wrap his body in a cloak of invisibility.

Dubhthach Doéltenga. Son of Lugaid Mac Casrubae. A warrior of the Red Branch who is described as 'a man who has never earned the thanks of anyone. When warriors of Ulster go out he goes out alone.' The nickname Doéltenga means 'backbiter'. He was given on loan the spear of Celtchair, Lúin, which was found discarded after the second battle of Moytura. Dubhthach assisted Fergus Mac Roth in his attempts to avenge the killing of the sons of Usna by helping him against Conchobhar Mac Nessa. It was Dubhthach who slew Conchobhar's son Fiachnae and also Maine. However, Fergus once says of him:

Away with Dubhthach Doéltenga
drag him behind the host.
Never has he done any good
he has slain young women.

Those people he cannot kill
he incites against each other.

Dubhthach is present at 'The Destruction of Da Derga's Hostel' and is also seen stirring up trouble at Bricriu's Feast.

Duineach. An alternative name for the Cailleach Beara. It means 'strong' or 'having a large following'.

Dulachan. Sometimes given as Dullahan. Known to later folklore as a malicious spirit, he was a headless horseman who rode a headless horse. With his whip he took out the eyes of any who saw him.

Dul-Dana. Blind, stubborn-born. Manannán Mac Lir's name for the baby Lugh Lámhfada whom he fosters. See **Lugh**.

Duma. A mound or burial ground. Duma na nGall was 'The Mound of Hostages' at Tara.

Dún. A fortress or fortified palace. Each king and champion had his dún, such as Cúchulainn's famous Dún Dealgan in Muirethemne. The prefix occurs in numerous place names in Ireland, in Britain and on the European mainland. Sometimes it occurs as a suffix as in the well-known case of London, from the Latin Londinium which came from the Celtic Lugdun or Lug's fortress. Lyon in France derived from the same name being, in Roman times, Lugdunum. More usually, the word occurs as a prefix as in Dunboyne (Dún Baeithin), Boyne's fortress; Duncannon, Conan's fortress; Duncormick, Cormac's fortress; Dundalk (originally from Dún Dealgan), Delga's fortress, the chief residence of Cúchulainn, and so forth.

Dún Bolg, Battle of. One of numerous battles in which the men of Leinster fought against the imposition of the Bóramha by the High King. In this particular tale the warriors of Leinster were smuggled into the High King's encampment in baskets loaded on to three hundred teams of twelve oxen. The High King's men were told that the baskets contained food. Once in the enemy camp the warriors of Leinster leapt out and routed the High King's army.

Dunlaing. A king of Leinster who unlawfully slew twelve women for which act he was himself slain by Cormac Mac Art.

Dún na nGéid. Sometimes Dún na nGédh. According to the story 'The Feast of Dún na nGédh', Domhnall Mac Aedh, the High King of Ireland, decided that it should become the seat of the High Kings after the abandonment of Tara. According to the king lists he ruled in Ireland from AD627 to 641. Just before the feast, two horrible black spectres – male and female – appeared to the assembly and, having devoured enormous quantities of food, vanished. They left a baleful influence for it was a subsequent quarrel which led to the battle of Magh Ráth (Moira) in 637.

Dún na Sciath. Fortress of shields. A circular fortress on the western shore of Loch Ennell in Co. Westmeath. It was associated with Anind the son of Nemed and, indeed, it was said that Loch Ennell flooded from his grave. It became a royal residence of the High Kings after the abandonment of Tara.

Dún Scaith. Fort of shadows. A synonym for the Otherworld, sometimes identified with the Isle of Man (see **Mannin**). Cúchulainn and his friends landed there and found, in its centre, a pit out of which came a swarm of loathsome serpents. They fended them off but were attacked by a further swarm of toads with sharp beaks which turned into dragons. Cúchulainn and his companions prevailed and carried off three magic crows and a marvellous cauldron with gold and silver and an inexhaustible supply of meat. They harnessed the crows to pull their ship home to Ireland. However, the gods who protected Dún Scaith conjured a storm and the ship was wrecked. Undaunted, Cúchulainn and his companions managed to swim back but they lost their treasure.

Durfulla. Sometimes Durbhola. A daughter of the king of the merfolk who married a human. When she died she was buried on an island but this was overrun by the sea.

Durthacht. King of Fernmag whose son Eoghan contested the right to the hero's portion in the tale of 'Mac Da Thó's Boar'. In most accounts of the 'Exile of the Sons of Usna' it is Eoghan Mac Durthacht who kills Naoise. See **Eoghan** 3.

E

E. *Eded* (aspen) in the Ogham alphabet.

Eachtra. Adventure. A class of tales in mythology usually connected with a mortal's journey to the Otherworld and often closely allied with the *Immrama* or voyage tales, e.g. *Eachtra Fergus Mac Léide*, a saga of a king of Ulster; *Eachtra Chormaic i dTír Tairnigire* (Cormac's Adventures in the Land of Promise); *Eachtra Chonlae Choím Maic Cuind Chétchathaig* (Adventures of Conla the Fair, son of Conn of the Hundred Battles). The *eachtra* became very popular in Irish literature during the fifteenth to seventeenth centuries and numerous medieval stories survive from this period.

Eadon. The nurse of the poets of the Tuatha Dé Danaan.

Easal. King of the Golden Pillars who had seven magic pigs. Even though they were killed and eaten at feasting every night they were found alive the next day and anyone eating their flesh was never afflicted with disease. Easal befriended the sons of Tuireann and gave them his pigs, which were part of their quest. Easal's daughter was married to the king of Ioruaidhe.

Eber. 1. Eber Finn. A son of Milesius. He slew Mac Cuill, husband of Banba. He refused to acknowledge Amairgen's judgement that his elder brother Eremon should be ruler of Ireland after the Milesian conquest. Eber and Eremon then divided Ireland between them, Eber taking the southern half from the Boyne to the Wave of Cliodhna. He subsequently attacked Eremon and was slain by him. It was a tradition for some chieftains to trace their ancestry to Eber Finn.

2. Eber Scot. Son of Esru, son of Goidel, son of Scota, daughter of the Pharaoh Nectanebes, and therefore founder of the 'Scots' or Irish people.

3. Eber White-Knee. An ancestor of Milesius who ruled his people

when they lived in the land of Gaethluighe, eight generations before they moved to Spain where Bregon ruled them.

Ebhric. Sometimes given as Eric. A young farmer who dwelt on the shores of Erris Bay and saw the children of Lir in their swan-shapes. He heard them singing, found out who they were and wrote down their story.

Ébliu. 1. A sister of Lugh Lámhfada who became wife to Fintan Mac Dóchra. She is associated with Munster and gave her name to one of the glens of Slieve Eelim (Sliabh Eibhlinne) east of the city of Limerick.

2. Stepmother to Ecca and Rib, sons of a king of Munster who fled with her to set up a new kingdom on a plain. But the plain was flooded to form Lough Neagh and they perished.

Ecca. Brother of Rib. See **Ebliu** 2.

Éccell. A brother of Ingcél Cáech and Dartaid, grandsons of a king of Britain who led the attack on Conaire Mór at Da Derga's hostel. See **Conaire Mór** and **Ingcél Cáech**.

Ecet. A hero of the Red Branch and father of Amairgen. See **Amairgen** 2.

Echbél. A hero of the Red Branch, son of Deded, who slew Inloth Mar son of Fergus Mac Léide at Temuir Luachra.

Echuir. A warrior and one of the three doorkeepers at the High King's palace at Tara. He is the son of Ersa and Comla. The other doorkeepers are his brothers, Tochur and Tegmong.

Ecne. The name signifies knowledge or poetry. Said to be the son in common of the three sons of the goddess Dana. A curious example of the 'Trinity' motif. See **Triads**.

Eibhir. Wife of the hero Oisín who is described as a yellow-haired stranger who came from a sunny country.

Éire. Sometimes Eriu. A Dé Danaan goddess who gave her name to Ireland. She was wife of Mac Gréine, son of Ogma, and grandson of the Dagda. Her sisters were Banba and Fótla. When the Milesians landed in Ireland, Éire, with her two sisters, greeted them, each wanting the Milesians to name the country after them. 'Welcome warriors,' cried Éire. 'To you who have come from afar this island shall henceforth belong and from the setting to the rising sun there is no better land. And your race will be the most perfect the world has ever seen.' Donn, the Milesian leader, did not treat her with respect and a war ensued between the gods and the Milesians in which Donn perished. Amairgen, however, the Milesian druid, promised the goddess that Éire would be the country's principal name. While the names of her sisters, Banba and Fótla, are used in poetic reference to Ireland, Éire still remains the Irish name for the country. In its genitive form this becomes **Éireann (hence Erin, Erinn etc.).**

Éirinn. Given as mother of Éire, Banba and Fótla by Delbáeth. See **Delbáeth** 1.

Eiscir Riada. The traditional boundary line which divides Ireland into two halves running along a broken ridge of low mounds from Dublin to Galway Bay. *Eiscir* – sand hill; *riada* – to travel by horse or chariot. From mythological times there are references to the two halves of Ireland, starting with the partition of Eber Finn and Eremon. In the days of Conn of the Hundred Battles it was divided into Leth Conn (Conn's half) and Leth Moga (Mug's half).

Eisirt. The poet of Iubdan, king of the Faylinn, a diminutive people. He made fun of Iubdan's boastfulness. Eisirt told him that the people of Ulster were giants and to prove it he went to the court of Fergus Mac Léide and returned with Aedh (see **Aedh** 5) who was a dwarf but seemed a giant to the Faylinn. Eisirt then laid a *geis* on Iubdan to go to Emain Macha himself and be the first to eat the porridge there the next morning. He foretold that Iubdan would fail and be a prisoner for a year and a day before being released. He would only be released, however, by parting with his dearest possessions. See **Iubdan.** By extra-sensory perception, Eisirt was able to tell that Fergus Mac Léide was having an affair with the wife of his steward and that his queen was having an affair with her foster son.

Eithne. See **Ethné.**

Eithniu. See **Ethné.**

Elatha. Sometimes Elathan. A Fomorii king whose land lay under the sea. He was an exception to the rule that all Fomorii were hideous or deformed. He was 'a man of fairest form, with golden hair down to his shoulders'. He was the son of Delbáeth of the Fomorii. He arrived in a silver ship on the shore and met Eri, wife of Cethor, a Dé Danaan queen, walking there. He slept with her and foretold that she would give birth to a son. He gave her a ring and told her to give it to the boy when he was big enough. Then he sailed off. Eri gave birth to Bres who became king of the Dé Danaan. When the Dé Danaan threw him out, Eri and Bres went to Elatha and sought his help. This caused the second battle of Magh Tuireadh. See **Eri, Bres** 3 and **Magh Tuireadh** 2.

Elcmar. Sometimes referred to as the husband of Boann instead of

Nechtan. He was sent by the Dagda on a long journey and so enchanted that nine months passed as one day. This was in order that the Dagda could sleep with Boann and she could bear a child without her husband knowing. Her son was called Aonghus Óg, the love god, for Boann observed: 'Young is the son who was begotten at break of day and born betwixt it and evening.' Elcmar returned knowing nothing. See **Boann**, **Dagda** and **Aonghus** 1.

Ellén. A three-headed monster which came out of the cave of Cruachan. See **Amairgen** 2.

Eltar, Plain of. It was the only plain in Ireland when Partholón landed, a place on which no twig ever grew.

Emain Abhlach. Emain of the apple trees, an island paradise said to be off the coast of Alba ruled by Manannán Mac Lir. The fabulous voyage of Bran started when a strange woman appeared to Bran and gave him a silver branch with white blossom from the apple tree of Emain Abhlach. She sang a song describing the splendour and delight of the island and the next day Bran set out in search of it.

Emain Macha. The seat of the kings of Ulster which features prominently in the Red Branch Cycle. Next to Temuir (Tara) it is, perhaps, the best known of the royal residences. It is identified with Navan, a phonetic rendering of *'n Emain*, two miles west of Armagh, where there is still a great mound surrounded by immense circular ramparts, half obliterated but covering eleven English acres. It was said to have been the capital of the Ulster kings for six hundred years, and attained its greater glory during the time of Conchobhar Mac Nessa and the heroes of the Red Branch. In AD355 it was destroyed by the 'Three Collas', Colla Uais, Colla Menn and Colla Dachrigh, cousins of the High King Muiredach. From that time on it was abandoned and left to ruin. It was founded by Macha Mong Ruadh (see **Macha** 4) who, having defeated Dithorba and captured his five sons, marked out the circuit of the city and its ramparts with her brooch and forced her captives to construct the ramparts. Thus the place was named 'the brooch of Macha'. There is another version, see **Macha** 3, which claims another Macha founded the city and called it the 'Twins of Macha'. A fascinating echo of the myths is given in the townland of Creeveroe, near Navan, which is an Anglicised form of Craobh Ruadh, the Red Branch.

In the sagas it is said that there were three great halls at Emain Macha. First, the Craobh Ruadh, the Red Branch, in which the king and his heroes feasted and slept. This hall contained nine rooms of red yew partitioned by walls of bronze and all grouped around the king's apartment which had a ceiling of silver and bronze pillars embossed with gold. Second, the Craobh Derg, also meaning Red Branch, which was the treasure house of the city and also contained the heads of slain enemies. Lastly, there was the Teite Brecc, the speckled house, where all the weapons and armour of the Red Branch heroes were stored, for it was a rule that no weapons should be borne in the feasting halls in case their owners argued when they were the worse for drink. In addition to the main halls there was a hospital for the sick and wounded which was known as the Bron-Bherg, or warrior's sorrow.

Emer. Wife of Cúchulainn. She was the daughter of Forgall Manach, Forgall the Wily, lord of Lusca, a spot a few miles north of Dublin. Emer is said to have 'the six gifts of womanhood – the gift of beauty, the gift of chastity, the gift of sweet speech, the gift of needlework, the gift of voice and the gift of wisdom'. Cúchulainn, coming to her father's fortress, saw her and immediately fell in love. He demanded marriage but Emer replied that she could not marry before her elder sister, Fial, although she returned his love. Forgall, her father, was against the match, and pointed out that Cúchulainn still had his reputation to earn and suggested he go away to train with Domhnall the Warlike in Alba. Cúchulainn was told by Domhnall that his training would best be completed under the female warrior Scáthach. During Cúchulainn's absence Forgall tried to marry Emer to a southern king, Lugaid Mac Ros. But Lugaid heard that Cúchulainn desired to marry Emer and he was fearful of the consequences knowing Cúchulainn's prowess as a warrior. He refused the marriage.

Cúchulainn finally returned and presented himself at Forgall's fortress to claim Emer. Forgall refused him admittance and defended his fortress. Cúchulainn leapt over the battlements and killed twenty-four of Forgall's warriors before Forgall himself leapt to his death from the ramparts. Cúchulainn carried Emer off, plus her foster sister and two loads of gold and silver. Forgall's sister, Scenmed, raised an army against Cúchulainn but he defeated it, and took Emer back to his fortress of Dún Dealgan.

All was not 'smooth' in their subsequent relationship for Cúchulainn was loved by many women. But the only affair which endangered his relationship with Emer was that with Fand, the Pearl of Beauty, the wife of the sea-god Manannán Mac Lir. Cúchulainn fell in love with Fand and spent a month with her in the Land of Promise.

Emer decided to kill Fand. She discovered the spot where Cúchulainn and Fand had an assignation and went there. She and Fand argued over Cúchulainn but when she saw how Fand loved him she proved her own love by suggesting that she give Cúchulainn up for the greater good. In response, Fand realised how much Emer loved Cúchulainn and decided it would be best for all if she returned to her husband Manannán Mac Lir. She was helped in this decision by Manannán who shook his cloak between Fand and Cúchulainn to ensure they would never meet again. Cúchulainn fell sick until the druids of Ulster gave him a draught of forgetfulness. Emer, too, took a similar potion. The affair was forgotten.

Just before Cúchulainn's death at the Pillar Stone, he had a vision of Emain Macha in flames and Emer's body being tossed over the ramparts. He hurried to Dún Dealgan and found her alive and well. But it was a forewarning of his own impending doom. Emer tried to persuade him to stay with her but he went on to the road which would lead him to the Pillar Stone and his own death.

Enna Airgthetch. A High King who made the first silver shields in Ireland and gave them to his chieftains. They were produced at Srgetos (silverwood) at Rathbeag on the Nore, Co. Kilkenny. As well as *airget* there are two other words in Irish for silver, *cimb* and *cerb*. It was mined in Ireland from early times and features prominently in the sagas.

Eochaidh. The name signifies 'horse'.

1. Given as the foster father of Lugh Lámhfada instead of Manannán Mac Lir.

2. A king of Dunseverick who gave his daughter in marriage to Ronán, a king of Leinster. The daughter tried to have an affair with Ronán's stepson, Mael Fhothartaig, and when he rejected her she encompassed his death. Eochaidh, his wife and son were slain by Ronán's champion, Donn, in revenge.

3. A king of the Dési, sometimes Eochaidh Allmuir. See **Aonghus** 2 and **Dési**. He fought seven battles with Cormac Mac Art after the High King attempted to expel the clan from Ireland in revenge for Aonghus' slaying of his son, Cellach. Eochaidh finally took his people to settle in the kingdom of Dyfed in southern Wales. Independent Welsh records show the historical presence of the Dési as late as AD730 when Teudor Mac Regin, a descendant of Eochaidh, ruled them.

4. A king of Leinster who married Fithir, the elder daughter of

Tuathal Teachtmhaire (given as High King AD130–160). Eochaidh actually wanted to wed Dairine, the younger daughter, but could not until Fithir was married. So Eochaidh married Fithir and took her back to his palace. After a while he returned to Tara and said Fithir was dead. Tuathal then allowed him to marry Dairine. When Eochaidh took Dairine back to his palace at Ráth Immil she found her elder sister still alive. Both girls then died of shame and Tuathal went to war with Eochaidh forcing him to pay a tribute which became known as the Bóramha. Eochaidh was killed in this war. The High Kings continued to exact the Bóramha tribute for many years but it was seldom given by Leinster without recourse to warfare. To exact it at least once in a reign was a point of honour and test of the High King's authority. See **Bóramha**.

5. Eochaidh Airemh (Airemh – ploughman). High King of Ireland who married Étain Echraidhe while in her human guise. He was unmarried and looking for a wife when his envoys reported that Étain, the daughter of Etar, was the most beautiful woman in all Ireland. He went to see her, fell in love and married her. Étain was, in fact, a Dé Danaan who was wife to Midir the Proud. Through the jealousy of Midir's first wife, Étain had been reborn as a human. See **Étain** 2. Eochaidh had a brother Ailill (see **Ailill** 3) who fell in love with Étain. However, Midir appeared to Étain and rewoke her memory. She agreed to return with Midir provided Eochaidh agreed. Midir appeared to Eochaidh on the Hill of Temuir (Tara) and then came to his palace and offered to play a game of *fidchell* with him. He allowed Eochaidh to win most of the games and in payment performed several tasks for him, such as clearing forests, building causeways and reclaiming land. But when Midir won the final game he asked, as his reward, Étain. Eochaidh was honour-bound to let Midir return in one month to claim her. Eochaidh then barricaded his fortress against Midir but Midir duly appeared in the feasting hall of the palace, summoned Étain, and both turned into swans and flew off.

Distraught, Eochaidh summoned his druid Dalan and for a year they searched Ireland until Dalan finally tracked down Midir's *sídhe* at Brí Leith. It took Eochaidh nine years to dig open the *sídhe*. Midir finally offered to return Étain and sent fifty maidens to Eochaidh all looking like Étain. Eochaidh, however, recognised the real Étain and she returned to live with him and bear his daughter, Étain Óig (Young Étain).

During one version of this story there is a reference to Eochaidh imposing on the tribes of Tethbae (a district comprising parts of Co. Westmeath and Longford) the task of building a causeway across the Bog of Lamrach. The account describes how the foundations of this road were laid with the trunks of trees. The tale goes on to say that the people resented the task and so they waited until the Feast of Samhain and set fire to Eochaidh's palace with him inside. Eochaidh is said to have perished inside and the road was never completed.

In July 1985, during operations by Bord na Mona (the Irish Turf Board), part of an old road was discovered in a County Longford bog. The Department of Archaeology, University College of Dublin, took over the excavation and discovered 1000 yards of a sophisticated roadway laid on a foundation of oak beams placed side by side on thin rails of oak, ash and alder. The roadway was dated to 150BC. The existence of roads, frequently mentioned in mythology as taking heavy chariots and other methods of transport, is thus confirmed. The Co. Longford road may well be the same as that mentioned in the Eochaidh saga.

6. Eochaidh Bélbuidhe, of the Yellow Lips. A champion of the Red Branch.

7. Eochaidh Bres. Alternative name for Bres. See **Bres** 2.

8. Eochaidh Dála. A king of Connacht who married Medb, daughter of Eochaidh Féidhleach, High King of Ireland. He was appointed High King with the consent of Medb if he married her. See **Medb** 1.

9. Eochaidh Féidhleach, son of Find son of Findlag. High King of Ireland about 140BC, according to the king lists. He was brother of Eochaidh Airemh (see **Eochaidh** 5) and also of Ailill Anubhail. His most famous daughter was Medb of Connacht who is sometimes confused with Medb of Leinster who also appears as his daughter. Another daughter is given as Mughain Attenchaithreach, daughter of his wife Ethné, who married Conchobhar Mac Nessa of Ulster. Conchobhar is also said to have married Medb of Connacht at one time. In one account Eochaidh Féidhleach woos Étain at the time of the Destruction of Da Derga Hostel but dies shortly after their meeting.

10. Eochaidh Iuil. One of three warriors with whom Cúchulainn was asked to fight during the story 'The Wasting Sickness of Cúchulainn'. Cúchulainn was told that if he fought Eochaidh Íuil, Senach Siarbarthe and Eoghan Indh Inbher, Fand would come back to him. At first Cúchulainn refused. Later he attacked the warriors.

Coming across Eochaidh washing in a spring, Cúchulainn cast a spear at him which pierced his shoulder and went on to kill thirty-three of his men. He later said:

> I heard Eochaidh Íuil groan
> a sound that comes from the heart;
> if that truly was one man, and not an army,
> my cast was well aimed.

11. Eochaidh Mac Erc. The Proud. A king of the Firbolg at the time of the Dé Danaan invasion. He was married to Tailtu (sometimes Tailta), daughter of the King of the Land of the Dead. He named his royal palace Tailltinn (now Teltown, Co. Meath) after his wife. He refused to share the kingdom with the Dé Danaans, saying, 'If we give them half they will take the whole.' He fought a great battle at Magh Tuireadh (See **Magh Tuireadh** 1) and finally fled to the strand at Ballysadare (Baile-easa-dara, town of the cataract of the oak) in Co. Sligo where he was slain.

12. Eochaidh Mac Muchtra. A king of Munster in the time of Conchobhar Mac Nessa who formed an alliance with Ailill and Medb of Connacht. He claimed a pedigree reaching back to Ith son of Bregon. But, we are told, he had one eye, which would disqualify him from kingship. In many of the Ulster tales people from Munster appear with deformities, mainly as having one eye. This seems to demonstrate a curious prejudice towards Munster on the part of the Ulster saga writers.

13. Eochaidh Muigl Mheadhoin. Sometimes Muigmedon. Father of Niall of the Nine Hostages who was said to have died in AD366. He traced his lineage back to Eremon.

14. Eochaidh Oll-Athair. An alternative name for the Dagda. See **Dagda**.

15. Eochaidh Sálbuidhe. Yellow Heel. The father of Nessa, mother of Conchobhar.

Eogabail. Foster son of Manannán Mac Lir. A druid who is father of the love-goddess Áine. See **Áine**.

Eoghan. 1. A king of Connacht who was mortally wounded when fighting with the warriors of Ulster. He was buried on the Connacht border facing Ulster as it was said that his spirit would protect his kingdom against their attacks. The Ulster warriors, however, dug up his body and reburied it face downwards near Loughill. The name derives from *leamhchoill*, elm wood, and not from the word *loch*, a lake.

2. Son of Ailill, a king of Munster, who was killed in the same battle as Art. His story parallels Art's tale. On the night before the battle of Moy Machruinne he slept with the daughter of a druid at her father's request. The druid had prophesied that a child of the union, if born on a certain day, would rule all Ireland. Eoghan went on to his death and the girl conceived. But the child was about to be born before the specified time and so the girl sat astride a boulder in the middle of a ford to prevent the child's birth. At the auspicious time, the girl allowed its birth but died in the process. The child, because its head had been pressed against the stone and flattened, was known as Fiachra Broad-Crown and fulfilled the prophecy.

3. Son of Durthacht. A champion of the Red Branch who slew Naoise and his brothers at the request of Conchobhar. In some tales the name of Naoise's killer is given as a Norse prince named Maine. See **Maine** 1. After Naoise's wife Deirdre had lived with Conchobhar for a year, never smiling, Conchobhar asked her who she disliked most in the world. She replied: 'You and Eoghan son of Durthacht.' In a rage Conchobhar gave her to Eoghan to keep as his wife for a year. As she was being placed on Eoghan's chariot, her hands tied behind her to prevent her escape, she threw herself from it, purposefully smashed her head against a rock and died.

4. Eoghan Mór. The true name of Mug (or Mag) Nuadat, a king of Munster who married Beara, daughter of a king of Spain. See **Beara**. He went to war with the High King Conn and forced Conn to split Ireland into two. He then ruled Mug's Half, the southern half of Ireland. Not content he wanted more, seeking a share of the rich merchandise that passed through Dublin. He made a further war on Conn which resulted in the battle of Moy Léana (Moylena) in which he was slain by Conn who thus regained the High Kingship of all Ireland. Eoghan Mór's son was Ailill Olamh who married Sadb, Conn's daughter, and became High King.

Eolas. A son of Partholón's three druids. Another instance of the 'joint parentage' between three fathers or three mothers which occurs in the myths, representing the mystical Celtic trinity. The name signifies 'knowledge'.

Er. A son of Partholón.

Erannán. A son of Milesius who climbed to the mast of his vessel to spy out the land during the invasion of Ireland and fell to his death. In another text this death is accorded to Milesius' eldest son, Donn.

Erc. 1. Son of Fedilimid, a Red Branch champion.

2. Mac Cairbre. One of Cúchulainn's greatest enemies. A king of Leinster. His father was slain by Cúchulainn in battle. It was Erc who cast his spear and slew one of Cúchulainn's horses, the Grey of Macha, just before the Ulster champion met his own death at the hands of Erc's companions. Erc was slain by Conall of the Victories in revenge for Cúchulainn's death.

Ercol. A Connacht warrior and foster father of Medb of Connacht. His wife was Garmuin. When Cúchulainn, Conall and Laoghaire went to the court of Ailill and Medb for their judgement as to which of them was the greatest warrior and deserving of the hero's portion, Ailill and Medb sent them to Ercol. Ercol sent them to Samera but Samera sent them back to Ercol to challenge him to single combat to prove their worth. Laoghaire fought him first but was sent fleeing back to Emain Macha after Ercol's gelding killed his horse. Laoghaire claimed Ercol had slain Conall and Cúchulainn in order to justify his flight. Conall was similarly despatched by Ercol and in his flight his son Rathand was drowned. When Cúchulainn's turn came his Grey of Macha (Liath Machae) killed Ercol's gelding; Cúchulainn defeated the champion and bound him behind his chariot, taking him back as hostage to Emain Macha.

Eremon. Sometimes Anglicised as Heremon. The first Milesian king of Ireland. He was the eldest of the remaining sons of Milesius and Amairgen the druid decreed that he should rule Ireland. His brother Eber refused to accept this judgement and, to keep peace, Eremon agreed to the division of the country. But eventually Eber wanted more and attacked Eremon. See **Eber** 1. Eremon slew him and founded the institution of the High Kingship at Temuir (Tara) which takes its name from the goddess Tea, becoming the traditional seat of central government in Ireland.

Eri. Wife of Cethor, a Dé Danaan. She was gazing out to sea one day when a handsome young man arrived on a silver ship. He was Elatha, a Fomorii king. He made love to her and prophesied the birth of a son, giving her a ring which she was to put on her son's finger when he was man enough to wear it. The boy was born and named Bres. He became king of the Dé Danaan after Nuada lost his arm and was thus precluded from kingship. However, the Dé Danaan rose up against Bres' tyranny and Eri took him on a journey to the Fomorii kingdom to seek his father's aid. See **Elatha** and **Bres** 3.

Eric. A penalty or compensation fine imposed particularly for the crime of homicide or bodily injury in ancient Irish law. It consisted of an honour-price (*log-enech*) which was carefully specified according to the rank and position of the dead or injured person.

Erin. See **Eirinn**.

Eriu. See **Éire**.

Erni. The female keeper of the treasures of Medb of Connacht. She is also chief of her handmaidens at Rath Cruachan.

Ersa. Husband of Comla and father of the three doorkeepers of the High King at Temuir (Tara) – Echuir, Tochur and Tegmong.

Esa. Sometimes Ess. She appears in a conflicting tradition as the mother of Mess Buachalla in the place of Étain Óig. Through incest with her father Eochaidh Airemh, the High King, she conceived the child which Eochaidh then ordered destroyed. See **Étain** 3 and **Mess Buachalla**.

Étain. 1. Wife of Ogma. The daughter of Dian Cécht, god of medicine, she was an artificer in her own right. Her sons were Tuireann and Cairbre.

2. Étain Echraidhe. The daughter of Ailill of Echraidhe in Ulster. The god Midir the Proud fell in love with her and asked his foster son, the love-god, Aonghus Óg, to go to Ailill and make the arrangements for the wedding. Ailill, however, demanded that Aonghus Óg perform three tasks for him before he would allow the marriage: he had to clear twelve plains, drain the land by making twelve rivers and give Ailill Étain's weight in silver and gold. Aonghus Óg received help from his father, the Dagda, and finally brought Étain to Midir.

Étain went to live with Midir in Brí Leith where his first wife, Fuamnach, was jealous of the beautiful maiden. She enlisted the aid of her druid foster father Etarlann (sometimes given as Bresal), and with his help Étain was turned into a pool of water. The pool was then turned into a worm and the worm into a fly in order to confuse Midir who was searching for Étain. Midir found Étain in the guise of a fly and the fly became his constant companion. Fuamnach, still jealous, prevailed on Etarlann to create a strong wind which blew the fly away. After seven years the fly came to Bruigh na Boinne, the *sídhe* of Aonghus Óg. The love-god recognised her and went to seek Midir. Fuamnach, hearing that Étain was found, blasted her with another wind which lasted for a further seven years. See **Fuamnach**.

Ultimately, in the time of Conchobhar Mac Nessa of Ulster, the fly alighted on the roof of a house in Ulster belonging to the hero Etar. The fly fell through the roof into a golden cup which the wife of Etar was drinking from. The fly was swallowed and eventually Etar's wife became pregnant. A daughter was born called Étain who, although the reincarnation of Midir's wife, had no knowledge of her past. When she grew up she, too, was beautiful. The High King Eochaidh Airemh, hearing of her beauty, came to see her, was captivated and married her. Eochaidh's brother, Ailill, also fell in love with her. See **Ailill** 3. Midir the Proud then found her. See **Eochaidh** 5. He took her back to Brí Leith but Eochaidh followed and forced Midir to give her up. She returned to live with Eochaidh until his death ten years later and gave birth to his daughter Étain Óig. See **Étain** 3.

3. **Étain Óig**. Daughter of Étain (**Étain** 2) and Eochaidh (**Eochaidh** 5). She married Cormac of Ulster and bore him a daughter but Cormac was so embittered that the child was not a boy that he ordered his servants to throw her into a pit. The baby was saved because it captivated the hearts of its would-be assassins and they left it with the cowherd of the High King Eterscél to look after. See **Mess Buachalla** and **Eterscél**.

4. **Étain** daughter of Olc Acha the Smith. Art, son of Conn, was on his way to the battle of Moy Muchruinne to fight the rebel Lugaid Mac Con. He rested for the night at the house of Olc Acha. There was a prophecy that great honour would derive if Art slept with his daughter, Étain. Art, knowing that he was to die in battle the next day, slept with Étain and told her that if she conceived she must take her child to be fostered by Lugna of Connacht. Étain did become pregnant and set out to Lugna's fortress, but just as she reached the Connacht borders her labour pains overtook her and she gave birth to a son. Exhausted, she fell asleep and while she slept a she-wolf came and stole the baby. Lugna had received word of Étain's coming and set out in search of her. He found her distraught and took her back to his fortress where he announced a reward for the recovery of the child. It was Grec, one of Lugna's warriors, who discovered Cormac being raised by wolves and crawling about on all fours. Grec rescued the child and returned him to Étain. Lugna named him Cormac Mac Art. See **Cormac** 3.

Etar, of Echraidhe, a champion of Ulster at the time of Conchobhar Mac Nessa. His wife swallowed a fly which was Étain the wife of the god Midir. His wife thereby became pregnant and gave birth to a girl, **Étain Echraidhe**. See **Étain** 2.

Etarlann. Also given as Bresal or Bresal Etarlam. The foster father of Fuamnach, he assisted her in changing Étain into a pool, a worm and a fly. See **Étain** 2. He was eventually slain by Aonghus Óg, Midir's foster son.

Eterscél. Sometimes Eidirseál, among many other variants. High King of Ireland and husband of Mess Buachalla. It was prophesied that Eterscél would have a son by a woman of an unknown race and when he saw the beautiful Mess Buachalla, his cowherd's foster child, and heard how she had been raised by the cowherd, not knowing her origins, he said: 'This is she that has been prophesied to me.' He married her and she gave birth to Conaire Mór who succeeded him as High King. See **Étain** 3, **Mess Buachalla** and **Conaire Mór**.

Ethal Anubhail. A Dé Danaan, ruler of the *sídhe* of Uaman in Connacht. Aonghus Óg, the love-god, fell in love with his daughter Cáer Ibormeith. In one version of the tale he refused to reveal where his daughter was and only did so when he was taken prisoner and threatened with death by the Dagda, Aonghus Óg's father. See **Cáer Ibormeith** and **Aonghus** 1.

Ethlinn. Sometimes given as Ethniu and Ethnea. Daughter of Balor of the Evil Eye. When Balor, the Fomorii ruler, heard a prophecy that he would be slain by his grandson, he had his only child Ethlinn imprisoned in a crystal tower on Tory Island that she would know no man. She was placed in the charge of twelve matrons with strict instructions to prevent her seeing any male. She grew up as a beautiful maiden. It happened that Balor stole a cow, Glas Gaibhnenn, which Cian, son of Dian Cécht, the god of medicine, was looking after. To retrieve the cow, Cian and a druidess, Birog, followed Balor back to Tory Island. Birog disguised Cian as a woman and in this guise he entered Ethlinn's tower and was struck by her beauty. Birog sent the twelve matrons to sleep while Cian and Ethlinn made love. Cian and Birog then returned to Ireland, having retrieved the cow.

Ethlinn became pregnant and, at first, her attendants tried to keep this a secret from Balor of the Evil Eye. Ethlinn gave birth to three sons, the mystical trinity occurring once again. Balor discovered this and ordered them all to be drowned in a whirlpool. The children were rolled up in a sheet and carried to the appointed place. However, a pin securing the sheet dropped out, letting one of the babies fall out at a spot called Port na Delig (Haven of the Pin). While the other two children were drowned, Birog the druidess found the third, a boy, and conveyed him to the sea-god Manannán Mac Lir to foster. In another version Cian's brother, the smith-god, Goibhniu, fosters the child. He was called Lugh Lámhfada, and became god of arts and crafts. See **Cian** and **Lugh**.

Ethlinn eventually wed Nuada of the Silver Arm and conceived a line through which Murna of the White Neck and her son Fionn Mac Cumhail claimed descent.

Ethné. Sometimes given as Eithne and Eithniu.

1. First wife of Ronán of Leinster and mother of Mael Fhothartaig. See **Mael Fhothartaig**.

2. Daughter of Dichu from the Maigue.

3. Daughter of Eochaidh Féidhleach. When she was pregnant she was drowned by her sister Clothra. Her child had to be cut from her womb, which shows the Caesarean operation was known and practised, and he was called Furbaide.

4. Daughter of Roc, steward of Aonghus Óg, the love-god. She was born at the same time the sea-god Manannán Mac Lir took his daughter to be fostered by Aonghus Óg. Ethne was given the task of being handmaiden to Manannán's daughter and she grew into a lovely and gentle maiden. It was discovered that she took no nourishment, neither food nor drink. On investigation Aonghus Óg discovered that a Dé Danaan chieftain had attempted to rape Ethné while he was staying in Bruigh na Boinne and this had awoken in her a pure spirit and moral nature. She now existed as pure spirit, although Aonghus Óg and Manannán Mac Lir went on a voyage and returned with two enchanted cows whose milk never ran dry and thenceforth Ethné lived on their milk.

One day Ethné accompanied Manannán's daughter to the river Boyne to bathe, became separated from her and found that she had lost her Veil of Invisibility which not only hid the Dé Danaans from mortal gaze but gave them entrance into the world of immortality. She was unable to find her way back to Bruigh na Boinne. In this sad myth, the Christian scribes placed the birth of Ethné in the time of Eremon, the first Milesian king, but they then made her encounter St. Patrick who gave her the rites of Christian baptism. She became a pious Christian. One day she was praying in a little church by the Boyne when she heard a rushing sound in the air and innumerable voices seeming from a great distance which lamented and cried her name. It was her Dé Danaan kindred searching for her in vain.

She tried to reply but she was overcome and fainted. When she came to she was struck with a mortal sickness and St. Patrick administered the last rites. He ordained that the church be named after her, Cill Ethné. The tale is a typical example of the bowdlerisation of early myths by Christian scribes; however the composition is done in such a way that it reveals the tenderness, almost regret, with which some early Christians in Ireland looked back on their lost world of pre-Christian tradition.

Ever Living Ones, The. A synonym for the gods of the Tuatha Dé Danaan.

F. *Fern* (alder) in the Ogham alphabet.

Fachtna. 1. Physician to the High King Eochaidh Airemh. He diagnosed the illness of Ailill, Eochaidh's brother, as 'one of two deadly pangs that no doctor can cure: the pang of love and the pang of jealousy'. Ailill had fallen in love with Eochaidh's wife Étain Échraidhe.

2. Fachtna Fathach, the giant. A king of Ulster who married Nessa, daughter of Eochaidh Sálbuidhe. She bore him a son, Conchobhar Mac Nessa, although some versions give Cathbad the druid as the real father. When Fachtna died his half-brother Fergus Mac Roth succeeded him to the kingship and married Nessa.

3. Fachtna Mac Senchad, a hero of the Red Branch.

Fafne. Brother of Aige. Their father was Broccaid Mac Bric. After his sister's death at the hands of the High King Meilge's warriors, he composed a satire about Meilge so that three blotches appeared on him and for this affront Fafne was executed.

Fáil Inis. A hound whelp owned by the king of Ioruiadh which was invincible in battle. It was one of the prizes which the sons of Tuireann had to bring back to Ireland as reparation for the slaying of Cian.

Falga. A synonym for the Isle of Man. See **Mannin.**

Falias. One of the four great mystical cities from where the Dé Danaan originated.

Fand. Pearl of Beauty. The wife of the sea-god Manannán Mac Lir. She lived with Manannán in Tír Tairnigiri (the Land of Promise). Once she quarrelled with Manannán and he left her. During this period her Otherworld kingdom was attacked by three Fomorii kings. Fand sent for Ireland's greatest hero, Cúchulainn, to protect her and promised him her love if he defeated her enemies. Cúchulainn sent

Fathad Canaan. He obtained dominion over the entire world by taking hostages from the birds, streams and the languages.

Faylinn, The Kingdom of. A country of diminutive people, to whom even dwarfs appeared as giants, ruled over by Iubdan and Bebo.

Fé. An aspen rod used for measuring corpses and graves which had Ogham inscriptions on it. It was regarded with horror and no one would touch it apart from the person whose job it was to do the measuring. According to one ancient verse:

> Sorrowful to me to be in life
> After the king of the Irish and foreigners:
> Sad is my eye, withered my clay,
> Since the *fé* was measured on Flann.

Fea. The Hateful. Said to be wife to Nuada and regarded as another goddess of war.

Febal. Father of Bran. See **Bran 2.**

Fec's Pool. Perhaps synonymous with Brec's Pool. A pool in the Boyne in which dwelt the Salmon of Knowledge. See **Fintan 2.**

Feda. The first Partholónian to die in Ireland.

Fedelm. 1. A female *sídhe* dweller who fell in love with Cúchulainn.
2. Fedelm Noichride, daughter of Conchobhar Mac Nessa. She was wife to Laoghaire Búadach and mother of Fiachna.

Fedelma. A woman of the *sídhe* Cruachan who prophesied to Medb that the invasion of Ulster to obtain the Brown Bull would be defeated. She is described as a young maid with tresses of yellow hair that fell below her knees and wearing a green mantle.

Fedilimid. 1. Fedilimid Chilair Chétach, a champion of the Red Branch.
2. Fedilimid Mac Dall. See **Felim.**

Fe-Fiada. Also called *ceo-druidechta* (druid's fog). A supernatural fog or mist which is frequently mentioned. The Tuatha Dé Danaan covered themselves in it during their invasion, and both Conall Cerneach and Laoghaire encountered it.

Feinius Farsaidh. See **Fenius Farsa.**

Féis. A feast or festival. In the sagas there were three great festivals: Féis Temrach (Tara), Féis Cruachan (Croghan) and Féis Emna (Emain Macha). The gatherings at Tailltenn, Tlachtga and Uisneach were fairs or *aenach.* There were also four pre-Christian religious festivals in the ancient Celtic world, those of Brigit (1 February),

his charioteer Laeg to Tír Tairnigiri to ascertain the situa
Laeg returned, he told Cúchulainn of the wonders he had
Land of Promise. Cúchulainn went there and defeated
emies and became her lover. He dwelt there for a mo
returning to Ulster. Before he left he made an assignatio
Fand again on the strand of the yew tree. Emer, Cúchulai
found out and determined to kill Fand. She said of the
'There is nothing the spirit can wish for that she has not g
argued with Emer over Cúchulainn. Emer, realising that
love him, offered to give Cúchulainn up thereby proving
love. Manannán then arrived and demanded Fand choose
him and Cúchulainn. Fand said: 'In truth, neither of you is
nobler than the other, but I will go with you, Manannán, for
no other mate worthy of you, but Cúchulainn has Emer.' M
shook his cloak between Fand and Cúchulainn to ensure t
would never see each other again and Cúchulainn and Em
later given draughts of forgetfulness by the druids.

Fannel. Son of Nechtan Scéne. With his brothers Foill and T
he boasted that there were not more of the Ulster champio
than those they had slain. Cúchulainn slew them.

Faolan. A member of the Fianna. His sister became Fion
Cumhail's mistress.

Faruach. Son of the king of Innia. He could make a ship by s
three blows with his axe.

Fasting. The ritual fast, *troscad*, or hunger strike, occurs freque
the sagas and tales. It is an ancient custom laid down in the B
Laws as a means of compelling justice and establishing one's rig
has a parallel in the Hindu practice of *dharnia*. The person wish
compel justice would notify the person complained agains
would then sit before their door and remain without food unt
wrong-doer accepted the administration of justice. It is fascina
as well as sad, that the ritual fast continues to have a tradition in
political life. One of the most notable Irish political hunger st
was that of the Lord Mayor of Cork, Terence MacSwiney, als
elected Member of Parliament, who died in a London gaol in 1
after seventy-four days without food. Perhaps even better know
the hunger strike in Long Kesh prison camp in Northern Irelan
1981 when ten Irish political prisoners died, among them Bo
Sands, Member of the British Parliament, and Kieran Doherty T
Member of the Irish Parliament.

Beltaine (1 May), Lughnasa (1 August) and Samhain (1 November). Each of these festivals commenced the evening before, lasting evening to evening, as the Celts measured their units of day in this fashion. The word is not cognate with the Latin *festus* (hence the English, festival) but is derived from *fo-aid* – to spend the night or sleep, therefore meaning food or entertainment for the night.

Felim. Sometimes Fedilimid. Son of Dall and father of Deirdre. He was the bard of Conchobhar Mac Nessa and was entertaining the Ulster king when the news of her birth came. Cathbad the druid was asked to cast her horoscope and prophesied: 'The infant shall be fairest among the women of Ireland and shall wed a king but because of her shall death and ruin come upon the province of Ulster.'

Female champions. Because in ancient Irish society, as indeed in all early Celtic societies, women had an equality of rights with men, being able to be elected to any office, inherit wealth and hold full rights of ownership under law, many prominent female warriors or champions are to be found among the myths and sagas. Perhaps one of the most famous women in Irish saga, who was both queen and warrior, was Medb of Connacht. In one of the *Táin* battles she slew the hero Cethren with her spear. Conchobhar's own mother, Nessa, is described in one passage as a champion. The principal instructor of martial arts to Cúchulainn was Scáthach, the great female champion of Alba. Scáthach's sister, Aoife, was also a champion and Cúchulainn, as great as he was, had to resort to a trick to distract her attention in order to overcome her. There was also Creidne, the female champion of the Fianna, and Coinchend, the monstrous warrior woman, who was slain by Art. The 'Life of St. Mochua of Balla' refers to two female warriors named Bec and Lithben. It is significant that the battlefields are presided over by goddesses of war.

In ancient history one of the most famous Celtic warrior queens was Boudicca (Boadicea) of Britain who rose against the Romans in AD60. She was queen of the Iceni tribe (in what became East Anglia) and her name means 'Victorious' (in Irish Buadach, in Welsh Buddogal). In Irish history, the tradition continued with women like Éabha Ruadh Mac Murchú who was said to have wound iron bars in her long red braids before a battle. She lived in the thirteenth century. In the fifteenth century Máire Ó Ciaragáin led her clans into battle against the English and was believed never to have spared a man overthrown in battle. In the following century there lived one of the most famous Irishwomen, Gráinne Ní Maillie. She was not only chieftain of her clan but became an insurgent leader and sea captain. According to Sir Richard Bingham, she was 'a nurse of all rebellions in Connacht'; she trod on English sensibilities so much that, according to Lord Justice Drury, she was 'a woman who has overstepped the part of womanhood'.

The tradition continued to modern times with the indomitable Countess Markievicz (née Constance Gore-Booth) who was known as the Red Countess because of her avowed socialism. She was the only uniformed and armed female insurgent officer who fought in the Easter Rising of 1916 and she became a national heroine. She was sentenced to death by firing squad for her part in the uprising, and was reprieved 'solely and only on account of her sex'. In December 1918 she was elected to the British House of Commons for the St. Patrick's Division of Dublin, the first woman ever to be so elected, but refused to take her seat and joined the separatist parliament, Dáil Éireann, in Dublin. She was appointed Minister for Labour on 2 April 1919 in De Valera's first revolutionary cabinet.

Fenian Cycle. Sometimes known as the Ossianic Cycle. The cycle concerning the deeds of Fionn Mac Cumhail and his Fianna, thought to date from the third century AD. The first bold synthesis of the eight major parts of the cycle into a cohesive whole appeared in the twelfth-century tract *Acallm na Senórach* (Colloquy of the Ancients). Next to the *Táin* it is one of the longest medieval compositions. The Fenian Cycle became very popular with the ordinary people during the medieval period.

Fenians. See **Fianna, The**.

Fenius Farsa. King of Scythia who was ancestor of the Gaels. His son Niul went to Egypt and married Scota, daughter of the Pharaoh, and their son was Goidel.

Feradach Fechtnach. A king of Ireland whose two sons Tuathal and Fiacha divided Ireland between them.

Feramorc. Alternative for **Fir Morc**. The kingdom in Gaul of which Scoriath was king.

Ferann. A son of Partholón.

Fer Caille. Man of the Wood. A monstrous black man with one eye, one hand and one foot, accompanied by a huge loathsome woman who was his wife. He overtook Conaire Mór on the High King's way to Da Derga's hostel. Fer Caille carried a squealing black pig on his back. It is obvious that he was a seer for he said ominously to Conaire Mór: 'Long has your coming been known,' before continuing his way.

Fer Cherdne. Sometimes Ferchertnae.

1. A bard of Cú Roí, king of Munster. After Cúchulainn had attacked and sacked Cú Roí's fortress and slain the king, Fer Cherdne was taken hostage by Cúchulainn. He discovered that Cúchulainn's victory had been achieved with the help of Cú Roí's wife, Blathnát, who was in love with the Ulster champion. Fer Cherdne sought vengeance for his king. In an unguarded moment, as Blathnát was standing by the cliffs on the Beara Peninsula, Fer Cherdne ran forward, seized her round the waist and leapt with her to their doom over the cliffs.

2. A bard of Móen who accompanied him and the harpist Craiftine in his exile to Gaul.

Ferchertnae. See **Fer Cherdne**.

Fer Chertnae. See **Cairbre 6**.

Fer Cuailge. A warrior at Da Derga's hostel.

Ferdia. Son of Daman the Firbolg. He became a friend of Cúchulainn and was taught his skill in arms with Cúchulainn at the school of the female warrior Scáthach of Alba. During the war of the *Táin* he took the side of Ailill and Medb. He tried to avoid open conflict with his friend, Cúchulainn, but Medb goaded him into single combat with the Ulster champion. On the fourth day of the fierce combat Cúchulainn killed him. It was Cúchulainn's greatest combat and he fell exhausted. 'Rise up, Cúchulainn,' cried Laeg, his charioteer. Cúchulainn replied wearily: 'Why should I rise again now he that lies here has fallen by my hand?' Cúchulainn fainted and was given up for dead while Ailill, Medb and their warriors poured across the ford rejoicing with war songs. Laeg rescued him from falling into their hands. The exultant army of Ailill and Medb paused by the ford to bury Ferdia and raised a pillar stone inscribed in Ogham to his memory.

Fer Doirich. The Dark Druid. A shadowy figure who changed Bodb Dearg's daughter Sadb into a fawn. Having met Fionn Mac Cumhail, Sadb was able to change back into a human shape but, after a while, when Fionn was away, Fer Doirich reappeared and changed her back into a fawn.

Fer Febe. Father of Fiachna. See **Fiachna 5**.

Fer Ferdiad. A druid of the Dé Danaan sent by Manannán Mac Lir to lure the beautiful woman Tuage for him. Disguised as a woman, Fer Ferdiad lulled Tuage to sleep and brought her to Inbhear Glas where he left her to search for a boat. In his absence, she drowned. In anger, Manannán slew the druid for his neglect of the object of his love.

Fer Fogel. A chieftain who appears at Da Derga's hostel.

Fergal. Son of Mael Dúin, a hero who is defeated at the Battle of Allen. See **Allen, Hill of**.

Fer Gar. Son of the champion Donn Désa. See **Désa**.

Fer Gel. Alternative of **Fer Fogel**.

Fergiman. A champion of the Fianna.

Fergna. 1. One of Partholón's three sons.

2. The owner of a great hostel.

3. A physician of Cond who was sent for by Aonghus Óg to interpret his dream in 'The Dream of Aonghus'. He tells the love-god: 'You have the divine illness' (i.e. love).

Fergus. Sometimes given as Feargus.

1. Son of Nemed who slew Conann, the Fomorii leader, on Tory Island.

2. Son of Fionn Mac Cumhail, also known as 'Fairmouth' as he was the bard, diplomat and ambassador of the Fianna.

3. Blacktooth, the High King, defeated by Cormac Mac Art who succeeded him as High King.

4. Long Hair, the brother of Blacktooth.

5. The Fiery, brother of Blacktooth and Long Hair.

6. Lethderg or Redside. A leader of the Nemedians who escaped from the victorious Fomorii in a ship.

7. Mac Erc, an historical king of the Scottish Dál Riada who was brother of the High King of Ireland Murtagh Mac Erc (AD512–533). He asked his brother to send the coronation stone, the Lia Fáil, to Alba so that he could be crowned on it and then refused to send it back to Ireland. See **Lia Fáil**.

8. Mac Léide. A king of Ulster who encountered the Muirdris (a sea monster) beneath Loch Ruaraidh. His face became twisted in fright, a state of affairs which was permanent. Such a blemish should have deprived him of the throne but he was so popular that his subjects hid all the mirrors so that he would not discover what was the matter with him. A servant girl unwittingly revealed the truth and Fergus, in rage, returned to the loch to kill the monster before his own death. Fergus Mac Léide also features in the story in which his court encounter Iubdan, the king of the Faylinn, or little people. See **Aedh 5**, **Bebo**, **Eisirt** and **Iubdan**.

9. Mac Roth. The name is given variously as Mac Roich, Mac Roy

and Mac Roi. He was the half-brother of Fachtna Fathach and succeeded him as king of Ulster. He was in love with Nessa, Fachtna Fathach's widow. Nessa would only marry him if he would give up the throne of Ulster for one year to allow her son Conchobhar Mac Nessa to rule in his place. Fergus Mac Roth agreed to this condition and when Conchobhar reached the age of maturity, Fergus gave up the throne. After a year he went to reclaim it but Conchobhar had ruled so wisely, under Nessa's guidance, that when he refused to give it up the people of Ulster supported him. This was, of course, as Nessa had planned things. Fergus Mac Roth appears to have served Conchobhar for some time afterwards.

Conchobhar sent him as his ambassador to Naoise and his brothers to invite Deirdre and Naoise back to Ireland, following their self-exile in Alba. Fergus gave his solemn word that no harm would befall them, little dreaming of the vengeance that Conchobhar intended (see **Conchobhar Mac Nessa**, **Deirdre** and **Naoise**). Fergus was tricked into leaving Deirdre, Naoise and his brothers to proceed without him to Conchobhar's capital, Emain Macha. Fergus sent his two sons Buinne and Iollan to guard them. When he learnt that Conchobhar had had them all murdered, including his son Iollan while Buinne has been bribed to desert them, Fergus Mac Roth led a dissident group against Conchobhar. With Dubhtach and Cormac he slaughtered three hundred of Conchobhar's champions and burnt Emain Macha.

Fergus and the dissident Ulstermen went into exile in Connacht, seeking refuge with Ailill and Medb. It is said that these exiles numbered three thousand. 'For sixteen years they made sure that weeping and trembling never died away in Ulster; there was weeping and trembling at their hands every single night.' In the war of the *Táin*, Fergus and his followers naturally took the side of Connacht against Conchobhar. Fergus, however, in the days when he was friendly with Cúchulainn, had given a solemn undertaking that he would never fight in single combat with the 'Hound of Ulster'. During the final battle of the *Táin* Cúchulainn recalled this oath and Fergus had to pretend to run away from Cúchulainn on the understanding that the next time they met Cúchulainn would have to run away from him. This episode set the seal on the defeat of Ailill and Medb's army. Tradition has it that it was Fergus Mac Roth who first set down the events of the *Táin* saga in Ogham and that this version was lost when a bard took the Ogham wands to Italy. Fergus was eventually slain by Ailill with a cast of his spear as he bathed in a lake with Medb.

10. Truelips. A champion of the Fianna rescued from an enchanted cave by Goll Mac Morna.

Fer Lé. A son of Donn Dési.

Fer Logs. Charioteer of Ailill of Connacht. He managed to capture Conchobhar Mac Nessa but was persuaded to release the Ulster King when Conchobhar promised to entertain him at Emain Macha with women sent to him every evening. Fer Logs stayed at Emain Macha for a year before returning to his home at Áth Lúain (Athlone) with a personal gift from Conchobhar of two of his horses with gold bridles for each of them.

Fernmag. A kingdom ruled by Durthacht whose son Eogan became a Red Branch warrior.

Fer Rogain. Son of Donn Dési.

Feron. A survivor of the Deluge in Ireland.

Fiacha. 1. Son of Firaba. He fought with Ailill and Medb against Ulster during the *Táin* war. Nevertheless, he felt compassion for Cúchulainn when the members of the Clann Calatin were about to kill him. He cut off the hands of the children of Calatin and rescued the Ulster champion. In another tale the same Fiacha is said to be a follower of Cumal, the father of Fionn Mac Cumhail. After Cumal's death he kept his magic spear which filled a man with strength and battle fury when it was laid against his forehead. Fiacha eventually gave this to Fionn.

2. Broadcrown. Son of Eochaidh of Munster. His mother was the daughter of a druid. It had been told that a child born on a certain day would have great fortune. His mother, in order to prevent the birth occurring before the auspicious time, sat astride a rock in a stream and this flattened his head and gave him his name.

3. The son of Fergus Mac Roth. He tried to prevent Eoghan Mac Durthacht from killing Naoise. When Eoghan thrust his spear through Naoise and broke his back, Fiacha threw his body across the Ulster champion but Naoise was finished off through Fiacha's body.

4. Fiacha Finailches. 'It was by this king that earth was first dug in Ireland in order that water might be in wells,' records the *Annála Ríoghachta Éireann*.

Fiacail Mac Conchinn. A champion of the Fianna who went to the Paps of Anu on the eve of Samhain and saw two *sídhe* opening. Even though he had prepared himself by carrying twelve lead balls to stop him from running away, he was so frightened that he fled, casting the balls as he ran.

Fiachadh. High King of Ireland in 300BC who first organised the Fianna Éireann as the royal bodyguard.

Fiachna. 1. Son of Laoghaire Buadach.

2. Son of Retach. His wife and daughter were abducted and while he slew their abductor, Goll Mac Golb took them and defeated him in seven battles. Fiachna eventually regained his wife with the aid of Laoghaire of the Red Branch who married his daughter Dér Gréine.

3. Fiachna Finn. A king of Dál nAraidi. One version of the tale is that he was sorely pressed while fighting in Lochlann when a tall warrior appeared and offered him victory. The warrior is identified as Manannán Mac Lir. The condition was that Manannán should change his shape into Fiachna and sleep with Fiachna's wife who, Manannán prophesied, would bear a son, Mongán, who would be a great champion. Fiachna assented and a son was born whom Manannán then took to the Land of Promise to foster until he obtained maturity. See **Mongán**.

4. Mac Dáiri. He fished a water worm from a river in Cuailgne and this was swallowed by one of his father's cows which gave birth to the Brown Bull of Cuailgne. The worm was one of the reincarnations of the swineherd of the Bodb Dearg. See **Donn** 6.

5. Son of **Fer Febe**. A Red Branch warrior who recited one of 'The Boyhood Deeds of Cúchulainn'.

Fiachra. 1. Son of Lir, the ocean-god, who was turned into a swan, with his brother and sisters, by his stepmother.

2. Son of Conchobhar Mac Nessa. When Conchobhar ordered the attack on the Red Branch Hostel, Fiachra led the attack. He was bested by Iollan in combat but he was carrying his father's shield, which moaned when its bearer was in danger. This alerted Conall Cearnach who mortally wounded Iollan. Dying, Iollan told Conall of Conchobhar's treachery and Conall, in rage at what he had done, slew Fiachra.

Fial. The elder sister of Emer, Cúchulainn's wife.

Fianchuibhe. See **Finchory**.

Fianna, The. Popularly called Fenians. A band of warriors guarding the High King of Ireland, said to have been founded in 300BC by the High King Fiachadh. They consisted of twenty-five battalions. It has been suggested that historically they constituted a military caste or élite. They consisted mainly of members of the Clan Bascna and the Clan Morna, and Fionn Mac Cumhail was their most celebrated leader. The stories of his adventures are called the Fenian Cycle or, sometimes, the Ossianic Cycle. During the nineteenth century the term 'Fenians' was revived and used as a synonym for members of the Irish Republican Brotherhood. The Fenian Uprising was that of 1867. The word *fianna* is the modern Irish word for soldiers and is also used in the title of one of the main Irish political parties, Fianna Fáil (Soldiers of Destiny).

Fidchell. Wooden wisdom. An ancient Irish board game, said to be akin to chess, in which a piece, known as a king, attempts to escape to the side of the board, and has to be prevented by the opponent's pieces. It was played extensively in the sagas and tales by heroes, kings and gods. Lugh, the god of arts and crafts, is said to have devised it. Cúchulainn was recognised as a champion of the game and it was necessary that all the heroes had a mastery of it. In Welsh myth *gwyddbwyll* has the same meaning and is obviously the same game. See also **Brandubh**.

Figol. Son of Mamos, a druid of the Dé Danaans, who boasted he would take two-thirds of the strength and valour out of the Fomorii so that they could be beaten in battle.

Filidh. Or Filí. A class of poets whose first duties were to praise their patron, to preserve their genealogy and to be learned in history and literature, as well as to master their craft. The Brehon Laws are particular in prescribing the number of tales a Filidh must know, the metres he must learn and the works he must examine in the course of twelve years of study. The Filidh was both honoured and feared in ancient Irish society and seems something akin to a Brahmin. In pre-Christian times the Filidh was obviously a druid but during the Christian era he retained all the prestige that had been given to the druids.

Finchory. Anglicised form of Fianchuibhe. A sunken island. The sons of Tuireann were asked to fetch a spit from it.

Findbec. Daughter of Eochaidh and wife to Cethren Mac Fintan.

Findbhair. Fair Eyebrows. A daughter of Ailill and Medb who fell in love with Fraoch and helped him kill the water demon. See **Fraoch**. She was offered to Ferdia in order to coax him into single combat with Cúchulainn during the war of the *Táin*.

Findchaem. Sometimes Finchoem. Daughter of Cathbad and sister of Dechtiré, mother of Cúchulainn. She became wife of Amairgen

Íarngiunnach (see **Amairgen** 2) and mother of Conall Caernach. She was foster mother to Cúchulainn.

Findige. Wife of Eoghan, son of Durthacht, king of Fernmag.

Findlám. Herdsman to Eterscél, High King of Ireland. It was he who found Mess Buachalla, the baby daughter of Étain Óig and Cormac, and raised the child. See **Mess Buachalla** and **Eterscél**.

Finé. Loosely applied to almost any subdivision of Irish society from the clan in its largest sense to a small group consisting of the same family.

Finegas. A druid who taught science and the arts to Fionn Mac Cumhail. He also watched for the fabulous Salmon of Knowledge, hoping to catch it so that he could eat it and acquire all the wisdom of the ages. He finally caught the fish and gave it to Fionn, his pupil, to cook. Fionn burnt his thumb on the flesh of the fish while turning the spit and sucked the burn. He thereby gained knowledge. Finegas, realising that it was his pupil and not he who was destined to eat the Salmon of Knowledge and acquire wisdom, allowed Fionn to eat the whole fish.

Finegín. Sometimes Finegeen. Physician to Conchobhar Mac Nessa. He made the diagnosis about Conall's 'brain ball'. See **Conchobhar Mac Nessa** and **Cet**.

Fingal. A synonym in Scotland for Fionn Mac Cumhail, made famous by MacPherson in his *Ossian* (1760–63) and also by the composer Mendelssohn with his overture movement 'Fingal's Cave', although this was not directly inspired by MacPherson but by a visit to Fingal's Cave in Scotland which takes its name from the hero of the Fianna. Fingal, however, is not really cognate with Fionn. Fionn means 'fair' while Fingal means 'fair foreigner'. The name Fingal was borne by a king of the Isle of Man (see **Mannin**); this was Fingal Mac Godred (1070–77), a name which demonstrates the intermarriage between the Manx Gaels and the Vikings.

Fingel. The mother of Noidhiu Naoi mBreathach, or Noidhiu of the Nine Judgements. When he was born, she wanted him killed but the baby spoke and gave nine judgements which thus preserved his life.

Fingín. 1. Mac Aedha, father of Sechnasach. His wife Mór fled from his house hearing voices prophesying evil.

2. Mac Luchta of Munster. He visited a prophetess every Samhain who related all the occurrences in Ireland on that sacred night and the results that would issue for the next twelve months.

Finias, City of. One of the four mystic cities from where the Dé Danaan were said to have come and from where the magic spear of the Dé Danaan was taken.

Finnbhenach. The White Horned Bull of Connacht, born into the herd of Medb of Connacht. The bull was originally the swineherd of Ochall of Connacht and arch-rival of the swineherd of the Bodb Dearg. They went through many reincarnations, fighting as ravens, water beasts, demons, champions, water worms and finally as bulls. Finnbhenach decided that it was unseemly that he should be born into the herd of a woman and so he transferred himself to the herd of Ailill, thus starting the chain of events which led to the war of the *Táin*. He was slain by Donn, the Brown Bull of Cuailgne. See **Donn 6, Cuailgne, Nár Thúathcaech** and **Friuch**.

Fintan. 1. Husband of Cesair, the first 'invader' of Ireland. He abandoned her and survived the Deluge by turning himself into a salmon.

2. The Salmon of Knowledge, a separate entity from Fintan 1. He ate of the Nuts of Knowledge before swimming to a pool in the River Boyne. Here he was eventually caught by the druid Finegas and given to Fionn Mac Cumhail to cook. Fionn burnt his thumb on the flesh of the fish as he was turning the spit, sucked his thumb and thus acquired wisdom.

3. Son of Niall of the Nine Hostages. His son was Cethern, fostered by Conchobhar Mac Ness at Dún Dá Bend.

Fionghal Ronáin. The title of the tale 'How Ronán killed his son'. *Fionghal* is a legal term in the Brehon Laws to denote the killing of a kinsman or relative. This story, imperfectly preserved in a tenth-century manuscript, appears to date back to the seventh or eighth century. The theme finds a parallel in the Greek myth of Phaedra and Hippolytus (which Racine turned into his greatest play). Ronán, an old king, married a new wife, a young daughter of Eochaidh of Dunseverick. The girl fell in love with her handsome stepson, Mael Fhothartaig. He rejected her and she, in rage, accused him of attempting to rape her. The old king, blind with passion, had his son killed, found out the truth and died of grief. His wife died by her own hand. Other versions give a tale of vengeance wreaked by the sons of Mael Fhothartaig on everyone concerned.

Fionn. Sometimes given as Finn, meaning 'Fair'.

1. Fionn Mac Cumhail. Frequently Anglicised as Finn Mac Cool. One of the most celebrated heroes in Irish myth. His father Cumal of Clan Bascna was a leader of the Fianna, the royal bodyguard of the

High Kings. He fell in love with Murna but was opposed by Murna's father. Eloping with her, he sealed his own fate for Murna's father incited Goll of the Clann Morna to kill him. Murna bore Cumal's child – Demna. The child was then entrusted to the care of two women – Bodhmall and Liath Luachra. On growing to early youth Demna slew Lia, lord of Luachtar, and rescued the Treasure Bag of the Fianna. He then sought out his uncle Crimmal and others of his father's clan who had escaped from Goll, who now ruled the Fianna. Demna was sent to get further education from Finegas, a druid who dwelt beside the Boyne. Finegas had been waiting for years to catch the Salmon of Knowledge, Fintan, which lived in a pool in the river. He did so and gave the fish to his pupil, Demna, to cook. The boy burnt his thumb on the flesh of the fish and in sucking it he obtained wisdom. He became known as Fionn, the Fair One, son of Cumal.

Having saved the High King's palace at Tara from the attacks of a demon, after being given his father's magic spear by Fiachra, he was made head of the Fianna, over Goll, by Cormac Mac Art, the High King. Fionn Mac Cumhail's exploits in leading the Fianna are many, involving hunting, fighting and sorcery. His hounds, Bran and Sceolan, were his own nephews, being the offspring of his bewitched sister. His son Oisín was the child of a goddess Sadb, who had been transformed into a fawn. He had many loves during his career but none is better known than his unrequited love for Gráinne. He was elderly when Cormac Mac Art gave his daughter Gráinne to him in marriage. But before the ceremony, Gráinne eloped with one of Fionn's warriors, Diarmuid Ua Duibhne (see **Diarmuid** 3). 'The Pursuit of Diarmuid and Gráinne' is one of the classic love tales and a major epic of the Fenian Cycle. In the story *'Cath Fionntragha'* (Battle of Ventry), or 'Fionn's Strand', Fionn overcomes Daire Donn, the King of the World, in one of the great military exploits of his career. This is described in a fifteenth-century manuscript in the Bodleian Library.

Accounts of Fionn's death are varied. Some tales say he was killed by Aichleach while trying to quell an uprising among his own Fianna. One version contains a typical Celtic motif: the tale concludes that Fionn is not dead but is sleeping in a cave, waiting for the call to help Ireland in her hour of need. This is, of course, paralleled in the tale of Arthur of Britain and the story of Owain Llawgoch of Wales.

2. Son of Oisín, born to Niamh in the Otherworld.

3. Son of Brasal, a member of the Fianna.

4. The name of the three brothers of Medb of Connacht, sons of Eochaidh Feidleach, the High King.

5. Sister of Fergoman. When Fergoman was dying, mortally wounded by his own son, Fionn was standing by the side of a loch and heard the echoes of his cries. She swam towards them but, on reaching the far side of the loch, she heard his cries on the other side. Perplexed she swam back and forth, always hearing the cries on the opposite side, until, exhausted, she was drowned. The loch is called Loch Finne (Co. Donegal) after her.

Fionnbharr. One of the Dé Danaans who was assigned Sídhe Meadha (Knockma, five miles west of Tuam) when the Dé Danaan were driven underground by the Milesians. He had seventeen sons and took part in the fight between Midir the Proud and the rest of the Dé Danaan over the kingship. His wife was Oonagh. In one tale he is said to have carried away the wife of Eochaidh Airemh, but it was clearly Midir who took this role. As the memory of the old gods faded and they degenerated into the fairies, Fionnbharr and his wife, Oonagh, became king and queen of all the fairies in Ireland in popular tradition.

Fionnuala. Daughter of Lir, the ocean-god. She was transformed with her brothers into swans by her evil stepmother Aoife.

Fios. Knowledge. One of Partholón's three druids.

Firbolg. The name seems to signify 'bag men'. They came to Ireland after the Nemedians but before the Dé Danaans and may therefore represent the genuine pre-Goidelic population of Ireland. In some accounts it is said that they descended from the Nemedian survivors who had fled to Thrace where they became enslaved. The name was given to them because they were made to carry bags of earth from the fertile valleys to the rocky hills during their enslavement. They came to Ireland in three groups known as the Fir Bolg, Fir Domnan and Fir Gallion, although all three took the general name Fir Bolg. They play no spectacular part in the myths. It is recorded that one of their rulers, Eochaidh Mac Erc, married Tailtu, daughter of the ruler of the Land of the Dead, and that he founded Tailltinn (Teltown) in her honour. See **Tailtu.**

Fithir. The elder daughter of the High King Tuathal Teachtmhair. See **Eochaidh** 4.

Flaithius. Royalty. A beautiful young woman who prophesied to Niall of the Nine Hostages that he would be the greatest king of Ireland.

Flann Mac Dima. He had an affair with Mughain, wife of the High King Diarmuid. See **Diarmuid** 2. In revenge Diarmuid caused his death by setting fire to the house where he was staying. Seeking to avoid the flames, Flann climbed into a bathing vat where he was drowned. It was prophesied that Diarmuid would meet his end in the same way.

Flidias. Chief figure in the *Táin Bó Flidias*, one of the lesser known cattle raid tales.

Fochmart. Questioner. One of Partholón's three druids, the others being Eolas (Knowledge) and Fios (Knowledge).

Fodla. Also Fódhla and Fótla. Wife of Mac Cécht, sister of Banba and Éire. She asked the Milesians if they would name the country after her. The name was used as a poetic synonym for Ireland. As a place name it also survives in Scotland where Fótla was thought to be one of the children of Cruithne. The province named for her was actually called Áth-Fhótla (New Ireland) which in Anglicised form is Atholl.

Foill. Son of Nechtan Scéne, slain by Cúchulainn with his brothers. See **Fannell**.

Follaman. The youngest son of Conchobhar Mac Nessa who was commander of the Boy Corps of Ulster. When Cúchulainn first arrived in Emain Macha they gave him a rough time. Folloman led the Boy Corps against Medb for, while the warriors of Ulster suffered their debility, the Boy Corps was unaffected. However, Medb's warriors slaughtered every one of them.

Foltor. A member of the Fianna. He was son of the king of Innia who could follow any track on land or sea. He assisted Fionn Mac Cumhail.

Fomorii. Sometimes Fo-Moir and Fomorach. A misshapen and violent people who are the evil gods of Irish myth and whose centre appears to be Tory Island. However, the name seems to mean 'under-sea dwellers'. They reached Ireland about the same time as Partholón and they battled not only with the Partholóns but with the Nemedians and the Tuatha Dé Danaan, sometimes succeeding, sometimes failing. Their leaders include Balor of the Evil Eyre, Conann, Morc and Cical. They often appear with only a single hand, foot or eye. Their power was broken for all time at the second Battle of Magh Tuireadh.

Forbaí. Sometimes Forbay. Son of Conchobhar Mac Nessa. He killed Medb of Connacht while she was bathing in Loughrea (Co. Galway) – *Loch riabhach*, the grey lake. He had practised for weeks with his slingshot in preparation and succeeded in striking her in the centre of the forehead.

Forgall Manach. The Wily Lord of Lusca. Father of Emer. He tried to prevent his daughter marrying Cuchulainn and, rather than face the champion's wrath, leapt to his death from the ramparts of his fortress.

Formenius. A king of Thrace whose name seems unknown outside the Irish legend in which he calls on the gods to strike down Dathi, the king of Ireland who invaded his country.

Fors. Son of Electra, son of Seth, who survived the Deluge to die in Jerusalem.

Fortrenn. The name of a southern kingdom of the Tuatha Cruithne, the Picts, which lasted into historical times and was once an alternative name for Alba, Scotland itself. Fortrenn was also a synonym for Ireland. He is recorded as one of the seven children of Cruithne – Cat, Cé, Círech, Fiobh, Moireabh, Fótla and Fortrenn (sometimes Fortriu) – who divided Alba between them.

Fosterage. An important feature of Celtic society lasting in Scotland until as late as the eighteenth century. Boys entered fosterage at the age of seven when they were sent to the household of a distinguished person, a chieftain, a druid, or later a monk, to be educated. They would live and study with them until they reached the *aimsir togu* (age of choice) which was seventeen years. Fosterage was also given to girls, their age of choice being fourteen years. During the period of fosterage they would be taught many subjects, music, literature, poetry, the art of warfare, the virtue of single combat, the high value of honour, recreational pursuits such as *fidchell* and *brandubh*, and team games. They were also taught to be efficient in hunting. In Christian times they were taught Latin, Hebrew and Greek, in addition to their own language.

Fothad. A king slain by Celta of the Fianna in battle.

Fótla. See **Fodla.**

Fountain of Knowledge. During Cormac Mac Art's journey in Tír Tairnigiri (the Land of Promise), the ramparts of a royal *dún* or fortress were seen. Inside was a shining fountain with five streams issuing from it making a murmur more melodious than mortal music. Five salmon swam in the fountain and nine hazel trees grew around it. Whenever a hazel nut (large purple nuts) dropped in the fountain one of the salmon caught it, rejected the husk and ate the kernel. See **Salmon of Knowledge** and **Nuts of Knowledge.**

Fraich. See **Fraoch**.

Fraoch. Sometimes Fraich and Fróech. The name means 'wrath' or 'fury'. Son of Idath of Connacht and Bé Find of the *sídhe*, a sister of the goddess Boann. He is the hero of the *Táin Bó Fraoch*, Cattle Raid of Fraoch, which has been claimed to be the main source of the English saga of *Beowulf*. Fraoch was the most handsome warrior in Ireland, served by the sons of fifty chieftains. He was in love with Findbhair, the daughter of Ailill and Medb. While she returned his love, he could not persuade her to elope with him nor could he pay the exorbitant bridal price which her parents demanded. Ailill and Medb were not so much against their daughter's marriage to Fraoch but were afraid that the jealousy of the other kings of Ireland who wanted to marry her might bring about their destruction.

Worried by Fraoch's continued attention to their daughter, Ailill and Medb plotted to kill him. They suggested he swim in a lake where a monster dwelt. While he was bathing Ailill told him to bring a rowan branch from the far bank. He did so. The monster did not appear and so Ailill sent him for another branch. This time the monster did attack him. Findbhair came to his rescue by seizing his sword, lying on the bank, and rushing into the water with him. Fraoch took the sword and managed to kill the creature. He was wounded and was taken off by the gods and goddesses to be healed. Fraoch, through the relationship of his mother, was one of their number. The next day he returned and Ailill and Medb were forced to consent to his wedding with their daughter.

In the second part of his story he returned to his fortress to find that his wife, Findbhair, and his three children and his cattle herds had been carried off. Among the cattle were twelve supernatural cows given him by his mother Bé Find. Fraoch set out to track them down, meeting the foster brother of Cúchulainn, Conall Cearnach, on the way. Conall joined him in this quest. They eventually found themselves in the fastness of the Alps, in a country inhabited by truculent warriors who delighted in cattle raids. They overcame these warriors, rescued Fraoch's wife, children and cattle and returned in triumph to Ireland.

Freagarthach. The Answerer. The sword of Manannán Mac Lir, the sea-god. Every wound it made was mortal. It was brought by Lugh Lámhfada from Tír na mBeo as a personal gift to Manannán.

Friuch. Boar's bristle. The swineherd of Ochall Ochne of Connacht. He was in perpetual rivalry with Nár, the swineherd of Bodb Dearg of Munster. They fought through many reincarnations until Friuch was reborn as Finnbhenach, the White Horned Bull of Connacht, while Nár was reborn as Donn, the Brown Bull of Cuailgne. An alternative name for Friuch is Ruch Chnint. See **Donn** 6, **Finnbhenach** and **Nár Thuathcaech**.

Froech. See **Fraoch**.

Fuad. A hero of the Milesians who was slain on the slopes of the mountain named after him – Sliabh Fuad (Slieve Fuad).

Fuamnach. Daughter of Beothach son of Iardanel. She was fostered by Bresal Etarlam, who is sometimes referred to as her father. He was a druid. She became the first wife of Midir the Proud and grew jealous when he took Étain Echraidhe as his second wife. Using the skills Bresal had taught her she turned Étain into a pool, then a worm and finally a fly in order to part her from Midir. Then she raised a tempest which blew Étain, in the guise of a fly, away from Midir's palace. See **Étain** 2. Fuamnach is described as clever and resourceful. However, she was finally bested and slain by Aonghus Óg who was helping Midir track down Étain. Fuamnach was sheltered at the house of Bresal. Aonghus Óg took her head to his palace at Bruigh na Boinne as a trophy after slaying Bresal as well.

Furbaide. 1. Son of Ethné and Eochaidh Féidleach. Like Goll Mac Morna he is recorded as having been born of a Caesarean operation.

2. A son of Conchobhar Mac Nessa and called Furbaide Fur Bend.

Fury. Among the swords of Manannán Mac Lir were two called Fury (Fraoch): Great Fury (Fraoch Mór) and Little Fury (Fraoch Beag).

G. *Gort* (ivy) in the Ogham alphabet.

Gabalgline. An ancient seer of the Clan Dedad who was blind. He was consulted by Ailill and Medb about the prophecy connected with the debility of the men of Ulster.

Gabhra, Battle of. Anglicised as Gowra. The last great battle in which the Fianna took part and in which they were exterminated. Cairbre, the High King, trying to curb the power of the Fianna after the death of Fionn Mac Cumhail, finally provoked a conflict. The Fianna, led by the hero Oscar, fought against the Clan Morna, who sided with the High King. In the battle, Oscar and Cairbre killed each other. The battle is full of melancholy grandeur and a fitting end to the Fenian Cycle. Fionn himself returned from the Otherworld to lament his grandson, Oscar, while Oisín, Oscar's father, and Celta carried Oscar's body from the field on a bier. The site of the battle is identified with Garristown, Co. Dublin. See **Oscar.**

Gabur. He plays a role in 'The Destruction of Da Derga's Hostel' with his companions Fer Ger and Fer Rogain.

Gae-Bolg. 'Belly-spear', the famous spear of Cúchulainn. It was originally owned by Scáthach, the female champion of Alba, who taught him the martial arts. She taught him how to cast it with one foot and gave it to him as a gift. It made one wound when entering a man's body but thirty barbs opened so that 'it filled every limb and crevice with wounds'. Cúchulainn used it to kill his son Conlaí, his friend Ferdia and Medb's champion Loc Mac Mofebis.

Gaedhal. See **Goidel.**

Gael. See **Goidel.**

Gaiar. A son of Manannán Mac Lir who had an affair with Bécuma which caused her expulsion from Tír Tairnigiri, the Land of Promise.

Galian. The ancient name for the province of Leinster. See **Laighin.**

Gálioin. Fir Gálioin, one of three groups identified as Firbolg.

Gall. The oldest meaning of the word was a person from Gaul. In subsequent usage it became the word for a stranger, or foreigner, particularly a Norseman, an Anglo-Norman and, finally, an Englishman. See **Gaul**.

Gamal. A doorkeeper at Tara at the time of Nuada of the Silver Hand.

Gamhanrhide. The Connacht military élite, equivalent to the Red Branch.

Gan-Ceann. 'Without a head', sometimes referred to as 'love talker'. A spirit from the *sídhe* which filled girls' heads with pleasant fantasies when they should be working. The personification of 'daydreaming'.

Gancomer. An amorous member of the *sídhe* who spent his time making love to milkmaids and shepherdesses.

Gann. One of the five sons of Dela who led the Firbolg invasion. Gann and Sengann divided the province of Munster between them. Gann and Sengann also appear as Fomorii leaders fighting against the Nemedians.

Garach, Battle of. The final battle of the *Táin* war where the armies of Ailill and Medb faced Conchobhar Mac Nessa's forces on the Plain of Garach. Fergus Mac Roth, commanding the men of Ireland, was within sight of victory when, about midday, Cúchulainn arrived on the battlefield. Cúchulainn reminded Fergus of an oath they had sworn, never to fight each other, and this caused Fergus to leave the field. His going caused the men of Munster and of Leinster to follow him. By evening the Ulster army defeated the army of Connacht. Ailill and Medb's men flooded backwards to Connacht. In chasing them from the field Cúchulainn came across Medb sheltering under her chariot. He told her that he did not kill women and so allowed her to go back to her kingdom after Ailill.

Garmuin. Wife of Ercol. See **Ercol**.

Gaul. The name of the Continental Celts and their territory, often mentioned in the Irish sagas and tales. Ancient Greek and Roman writers tended to use the term 'Gaul' rather than 'Celt' in their references to the Celtic peoples. As a geographical description, it is rather a loose term. Cisalpine Gaul consisted of the territory of northern Italy which was settled by the Celts around 600BC and stretched down to Senigallia (Senones Gaul) just north of Ancona. A great many northern Italian place names and river names are Celtic in origin. On 18 July 390BC, the Celts conquered Rome. It was not until 349BC that Rome felt strong enough to continue aggressive actions against them. A systematic conquest of the northern Italian Celts was undertaken in 196BC but it was not until 180BC that the last Celtic tribes there surrendered. The Gaulish language lasted long afterwards. Many ancient Latin writers were Celts, for example Virgil, Gallus, Trogus Pompeius and Cornelius Nepos. Livy was raised in Cisalpine Gaul and his histories, epic and fabulous, bear more than a cursory resemblance to Irish sagas.

The main Gaulish territory was, of course, the modern territories of France, Belgium (named from the Celtic tribe, the Belgae) and parts of Switzerland (which still uses the Celtic tribal name Helvetica). Celtic territories stretched to Bohemia (named after the Boii) and as far as Galatia in what is now modern Turkey. They also included parts of Spain.

The Gaulish language survived for a long while after the Gaulish territories had been overrun. Apollinarius Sidonius, Bishop of the Avernii of Gaul (d. AD479), writing to his brother-in-law Ecdicius, comments that 'leading families, in their efforts to throw off the scurf of Celtic speech' were making efforts to learn Latin. Many Celtic words survived in Low Latin and thus into modern French. Gaulish Celtic inscriptions now date back to the fifth century BC. For a long time the most extensive text in Gaulish was the Coligny Calendar, engraved on bronze, and dated to the first century AD. In 1983, however, a more extensive text, written on a lead tablet, was found at La Vayssière, in the neighbourhood of Millau, and is the longest Gaulish text so far discovered.

Many Irish gods have Gaulish equivalents: Lugh was known to the Gaulish Celts as Lugus, and his name occurs in place names in France, Holland, Switzerland, Spain and Silesia. Ogma was known in Gaul as Ogmios and Bilé was Belenus. It is clear, therefore, that had Gaulish mythology survived it would have closely resembled Irish and Welsh myth.

Gebann. Father of Cliodhna, the Irish goddess of beauty. See **Cliodhna**.

Geena. See **Gíona Mac Lugha**.

Geilt. One who goes mad with terror or flees panic-stricken from the field of battle. During Cath Fionntrágha (Battle of Ventry) when Fionn Mac Cumhail fought with Daire Donn, the King of the World, one of his young warriors named Goll fled frenzied from the battle. He made his way to Gleann na nGealt (Co. Kerry), the glen of lunatics, which was the one place in all Ireland to which – so it was said – lunatics left to their own devices would go. In the glen (Glennagalt) he found Tobergalt, the lunatics' well, and by drinking from it and eating the cresses that grew near, and living in seclusion, he recovered his senses. Suibhne, who fled frenzied from the Battle of Moyrath, also made for Glennagalt. See **Suibhne Geilt**.

Geis. A taboo or bond which, when placed on someone, compelled them to obey the instruction. From the sagas as well as the Brehon Laws themselves, the *geis* comes down primarily as a *modus operandi* put at the disposal of the druids to ensure their authority and the efficacy of their edicts. They had two particular powers: the *geis* and the *glam dicín*: see **Glam dicín**. The *geis* tended to be complex. It was primarily a prohibition imposed on a particular person and since it influenced the whole fate of that person it must not be cast or imposed lightly. Anyone transgressing a *geis* was exposed to the rejection of his society and placed outside the social order. Transgression, as well as bringing shame and outlawry, usually meant a painful death. The power of the *geis* was above human and divine jurisdiction and brushed aside all previous rulings, establishing a new order through the wishes of the person controlling it.

Examples of the *geis* in mythology are as follows. When Setanta was given the name Cúchulainn (Hound of Culann) he was also given a *geis* never to eat the flesh of a dog. However, trapped by his enemies, he eventually had to eat dog flesh and the infringement inevitably led to his death. Fergus Mac Roth's *geis* was the prohibition never to refuse an invitation to a feast and on this fact turned the tragedy of the sons of Usna. Conaire Mór was subjected to a whole series of complicated and independent *geise* which led to his downfall and death. The giving of a *geis* was usually reserved for the druids but there are exceptions. In some stories ordinary men and women seem capable of pronouncing the taboo. Perhaps the most famous example of this is that placed by Gráinne on Diarmuid: 'I place on you a *geis* of danger and destruction, Diarmuid Ua Duibhne, unless you take me with you out of this house before Fionn and the chiefs of Ireland wake from their slumber. If you do not come with me you are not only a dead man but dishonoured.' Diarmuid, therefore, has no choice but to accompany Gráinne and thus begins the story of 'The Pursuit of Diarmuid and Gráinne'.

Gelban. A son of the king of Lochlann who, according to one version of the tragic tale of the sons of Usna, went to spy on the Red Branch Hostel. Conchobhar Mac Nessa asked him to ascertain whether

Deirdre's looks had faded. Naoise, playing *fidchell* with Deirdre, glanced up and saw Gelban peering through the window. He threw a *fidchell* piece and knocked out one of his eyes. Gelban, nevertheless, was able to make his report to Conchobhar saying that he would gladly give his other eye to gaze on Deirdre's beauty. The same story is given elsewhere with Conchobhar's servant Trendorm as the spy.

Gentradea. Together with Goltrade and Suantrade of the Uaithne, he was one of a trio of harpists whose sad music caused the death by sorrow of many young men.

Ger. A companion of Gabur. See **Gabur.**

Gerald (Gearóid Iarla) Fitzgerald. Third Earl of Desmond (1359–98) and Lord Justiciary of Ireland. The historical figure of Gerald Fitzgerald takes its place here due to a later legend which connects him with the love goddess Áine. It is obviously based on the story of Ailill Olom and Áine. The story is that Maurice, first Earl of Desmond (d. 1356), raped the love goddess and that Gerald was their son. According to the *Annals of Clonmacnois* (now lost save in a seventeenth-century English translation) Gerald 'was a nobleman of wonderful bounty, cheerfulness in conversation, easy of access, charitable in deeds, a witty and ingenious composer of Irish poetry, a learned and profound chronicler & etc.' Gerald composed *danta gadhra*, courtly love poetry, preserved in the *Book of Fermoy* and the *Book of the Dean of Lismore.* He was instrumental in getting the un-precedented decision which allowed one of the 'mere Irish', the son of Conor Mac Conamara, a chieftain, accepted at Oxford University to study in 1375. When Gerald died he was so popular that numerous legends arose that he was not dead but simply sleeping and would rise again from the waters of Loch Guirr in time of Ireland's danger – a typical Celtic motif best known through the Arthurian legends. Other stories are that he rose every seven years and rode the loch on an enchanted steed. His son John actually drowned nearby in 1400. Loch Guirr is said to be the love goddess Áine's resting place. See **Áine.**

Germane. A companion of Mael Dúin. See **Mael Dúin.**

Giants. Giants occur in the myths and sagas several times. It should be stressed that Fionn Mac Cumhail came to be regarded as a giant only in later legends. The term for a giant in Old Irish was *aithech.* During the second battle of Magh Tuireadh the Fomorii appeared in the guise of giants and, indeed, when Oisín followed Niamh to the Otherworld he had to battle with a Fomorii giant.

Giants' Causeway. The Irish name is Clochán na bhFomharaigh or the stepping stones of the Fomorii. It is one of the world's outstanding geological curiosities, formed by the cooling of lava bursting through the earth's crust in the Cainozoic Period, resulting in the splitting of basaltic rock into innumerable prismatic columns, mostly hexagonal but some pentagonal and others variously sided. It is situated on the west side of Benbane Head, in the north of Co. Antrim.

Giolla. Sometimes Anglicised as Gillie. An attendant, servant or follower, sometimes used as title or name as in Giolla Deacair. See **Abarta**.

Giolla Deacair. See **Abarta**.

Giolla Gréine. The daughter of a human father and a sunbeam. When told of her birth she jumped into Loch Gréine (lake of the sun) and floated to Daire Gréine (oak grove of the sun) and died at Tuam Gréine (tomb of the sun).

Gíona Mac Lugha. A leader of the Fianna. His mother was the warrior-daughter of Fionn Mac Cumhail and he was fostered by a woman called 'Fair Mane' or 'Fair Tresses' (Mong Bán). He was slothful and selfish as well as being boastful. So impossible did he become that eventually his men laid down their weapons by Loch Lena and refused to fight under him. Fionn was sent for and taught him the things necessary to be a good leader. He heeded Fionn's counsel and became one of the Fianna's greatest champions.

Gods. There is a degree of confusion about the gods of the ancient Irish because of the fact that the myths were first set down in writing by Christian monks who often changed things to fit their religious sensibilities. The Tuatha Dé Danaan are clearly the 'immortals' of ancient Ireland. The gods and goddesses are not creators of people, they are the ancestors of the people. They come and go throughout the sagas and myths and can, in fact, die on occasion like Nuada of the Silver Hand. There are no hard and fast rules between gods and mortals; mortals can wound gods. Cúchulainn took out the eye of the goddess of battle, the Mórrígán. Yet the gods are also respected and venerated and given their feast days, as with Lugh, Brigit, Bilé etc. The Irish, like their fellow Celts, made their gods and goddesses into heroes and heroines and their heroes and heroines into gods and goddesses. The gods and goddesses are totally human and subject to all the natural virtues and vices.

Glam Dicín. Like the *geis* this was one of the two particular powers of the druids to ensure their authority and the efficacy of their edicts. The *glam dicín* is a satirical incantation directed against a particular person and having the strength of obligation – it is in fact a curse which can be pronounced for such valid reasons as infringement of divine or human laws, treason, breaking a contract or murder. The men of Ulster had to tolerate the poet Athirne because he placed them under threat of an unjust *glam dicín*. Its pronouncement was feared as it put its victims under a sense of shame, sickness and death. The victim was rejected by all levels of society.

Glas Ghaibhnenn. The magic cow stolen by the Fomorii Balor of the Evil Eye and taken to Tory Island. It belonged to Cian who pursued it. See **Cian**.

Glass Castle. Also known as Conann's Tower. A tower of glass or crystal built by the Fomorii on Tory Island. The Nemedians, led by their king Fergus, stormed it and slew Conann Mac Febar, the Fomorii king, but Morc Mac Dela drove them off. Balor of the Evil Eye is said to have imprisoned his daughter in a glass tower on Tory Island. In the various voyages to the Otherworld, glass towers are often one of the sights encountered. There is a reference in Welsh mythology to Caer Wydyr, a glass castle, which seems a synonym for the Otherworld.

Goibhniu. 1. The smith-god. Founder of artistry and handicraft. He had two brothers, Cian and Samhain – again constituting the Celtic trinity of craft gods. In other texts Goibhniu's brothers are given as Credné Cred and Luchtar. He could make a sword or spear by three blows of his hammer. He also presided over the Otherworld feast Fled Ghoibhnenn at which he served a special ale which rendered all who drank it exempt from disease and death. During the second battle of Magh Tuireadh, Ruadan, son of Bres, a Fomorii spy, came to see how Goibhniu was making spears. Ruadan seized one and drove it through Goibhniu. The smith-god merely pulled it out and mortally wounded Ruadan before making his way to Dian Cécht, the god of medicine, and having his wound healed from the spring of health. He has his counterpart in the Welsh smith-god Govannan. And the word 'smith' in all the Celtic languages has a common provenance: Irish, *gabha*; Scottish Gaelic *gobha*; Manx, *gaaue*; Welsh, *gof*; Cornish, *gof*; Breton, *gof*. In later Irish legend, a figure called Góbhan Saer, the Wright, became a master mason and architect of the fairies.

2. Son of Lorgnech, a hero mentioned in 'The Destruction of Da Derga's Hostel'.

Goidel. Also given as Gaedhal and Gael. Son of Niul and Scota, a daughter of the Pharaoh Cingris. He is acclaimed as the progenitor of the Goidelic or Gaelic people (the Irish, Manx and Scots). In what seems to be a Christian embellishment to the story, Goidel was healed by Moses for his father Niul had befriended Aaron during the Hebrew enslavement in Egypt. Goidel's son was Esru, whose son Sru was father of Eber Scot.

Goidelic. Usually given as Gaelic. The Q-Celtic branch of the Celtic languages spoken by the Irish, Manx and Scots. See **Celt**.

Golamh. The original name of Milesius.

Golden Pillars, Kingdom of the. See **Easal**.

Goll. A name meaning 'blind of one eye' or 'one-eyed'.

1. The Fomorii son of Garb. His wife was Lot, described as having bloated lips in her breasts and four eyes in her back. He was father of Cichol Gricenchos.

2. Described as a stranger from beyond the seas who is defeated by Cúchulainn.

3. A young warrior of the Fianna who fled in a frenzy during the Battle of Fionntragha (Ventry) when Fionn Mac Cumhail fought Daire Donn, the King of the World. See **Geilt**.

4. Mac Golb. The ruler of Magh Mell. He abducted the wife of Fiachna Mac Retach and defeated Fiachna in seven battles. Fiachna offered a reward for the champion who would slay Goll. Laoghaire Mac Crimthann and fifty warriors attacked Magh Mell and Laoghaire slew Goll. He rescued Fiachna's wife and married his daughter Dér Gréine.

5. Brother of Bricriu, a son of Carbad.

6. Mac Morna. The leader of the Fianna before Fionn Mac Cumhail. He killed Fionn's father Cumal, in one account, to gain the leadership of the Fianna. However, when Cormac Mac Art rewarded Fionn with the leadership, he seemed to accept him. He eventually married Fionn's daughter Cebha. He features prominently in the tales of the Fenian Cycle. Fionn quoted one of Goll's sayings: 'A man lives after his life but not after his honour.' Goll eventually slew Cairell, Fionn's son, and when Oscar tried to mediate in the affair, Goll cast his spear at him. He fled, and was pursued and finally trapped by the Fianna. Refusing to surrender, he died after twelve days from lack of food.

Goltrade. A harpist. See **Gentradea**.

Gorias, City of. One of the four great cities of the Dé Danaan – Falias, Finias, Gorias and Murias. It was from Gorias that Lugh brought his invincible sword. Urais of the Noble Nature dwelt in the city said to be steeped in wisdom.

Gorm Glas. 'Blue green'. Conchobhar Mac Nessa's sword.

Gortigern. The language spoken by all mankind before the development of different languages. A parallel tale to the Tower of Babel story.

Gráinne. Daughter of Cormac Mac Art, the High King. She was promised to Fionn Mac Cumhail who, though still a renowned warrior, had grown elderly at this time. Fionn and his Fianna came to feast at Tara on the night before the wedding. Gráinne speculated on the handsome appearance of the warriors of his Fianna. At first she was taken with Fionn's son Oisín and asked him to save her from a marriage to an old man. When he refused she turned her attention on Diarmuid Ua Duibhne. With the help of her druid Daire she prepared a sleeping draught with which she ensured everyone at the feast fell asleep except Diarmuid. She demanded that he rescue her from the marriage and take her from Tara that night. He refused but she placed a *geis* on him. Diarmuid had no course but to obey and they fled.

When Fionn awoke and discovered the elopement he flew into a rage. 'The Pursuit of Diarmuid and Gráinne' begins. Diarmuid had been a friend of Fionn and sought to reassure him that there was nothing between him and Gráinne. At each spot where they had been, the pursuing Fionn found pieces of unbroken bread, or uncooked salmon. The symbolism was a subtle message that he had not slept with Gráinne. But Gráinne was determined to have Diarmuid for herself. When crossing a stream she said mockingly: 'You are a mighty warrior, O Diarmuid, in battles and sieges and forays, yet it seems that this drop of water is bolder than you.' In other words, she mocked him for keeping his distance from her. Eventually Diarmuid grew to love her. The pursuit continued for sixteen years until Aonghus Óg, the love-god, interceded, and, helped by Cormac Mac Art, persuaded Fionn Mac Cumhail to forget his anger. Diarmuid and Gráinne set up residence in Ráth Gráinne where Gráinne bore Diarmuid four sons and a daughter.

Gráinne wanted Fionn and Cormac to show their forgiveness by coming to dine with her and Diarmuid at their fortress. Fionn did so though he still nursed thoughts of revenge. Towards the end of the feasting Diarmuid accompanied him and his Fianna on a hunt near Ben Bulben where Diarmuid was wounded by a magic boar, fulfilling the destiny chosen by the gods at his birth. Fionn, however, could have saved his life but refused to do so. Gráinne, seeing the hunting party coming back without Diarmuid but leading his hound, swooned on the ramparts of the fortress. Diarmuid's body was borne to the Otherworld by Aonghus Óg, the love-god.

Gráinne at first swore vengeance on Fionn when she learnt the truth of the matter. She sent her four sons to learn skill in arms for this purpose. But Fionn Mac Cumhail began to woo her and eventually was able to bear her back to his fortress on the Hill of Allen as his bride thus preventing further trouble from her sons. The Fianna, seeing Gráinne in such circumstance, jeered at her. They would 'not haven given one of Diarmuid's fingers for twenty such as Gráinne'. Gráinne's character is always drawn with consistency in the myths. She is a shallow person, wilful, ruthless and passionate, and what in modern terms would be described as a neurotic.

Grec. A warrior of Connacht who rescued Cormac Mac Art as a baby from a pack of wolves. See **Étain** 4.

Grey of Macha. Sometimes Liath Macha. One of Cúchulainn's two horses which were foaled at the same time as he was born. The other was the Black of Sainglenn. Before Cúchulainn went on his final foray the Grey of Macha refused to be bridled and shed tears of blood. During the last fight the Grey was mortally wounded by Erc, king of Leinster, but still managed to kill fifty warriors with its teeth and thirty more with its hoofs before it died.

Grian. Said to be a queen of a *sídhe*, from *grian*, the sun. Her palace was on top of Cnoc Gréine at Pailis Gréine (Pallas Green) in Co. Limerick.

Grianainech. An alternative name for the god Ogma, meaning 'sunny countenance'.

Grianan. A solarium or sun house which seems to have been a feature of Irish houses mentioned in the sagas. Bricriu had one built at his *ráth* as did Ailill and Medb at Rath Cruachan. It is recorded that Medb's *grianan* had twelve large glass windows.

Grianan Aileach. A tumulus where Nuada of the Silver Hand was buried after Balor of the Evil Eye had killed him during the second Battle of Magh Tuireadh.

Grianan Lachtna. The residence of the rulers of the Dál na gCas of North Munster. It lies two miles north of Killaloe on the western shore of Loch Derg.

Grúacach. Often used as a term for an ogre or monster, also an enchanter or wizard. Grúacach signifies hairy, long-haired or maned.

H. Not found in early Ogham inscriptions and not a 'proper' letter of
the Irish alphabet which had seventeen letters. It is now used only in
conjunction with other letters to denote lenition; e.g. bh, ch, dh, fh,
gh, mh, ph, sh and th. Formerly this sound had been written ḃ, ċ,
ḋ, ḟ, ġ, ṁ, ṗ, ṙ, ṫ.

Hag of Beara. See **Cailleach Beara**.

Hallowe'en. See **Samhain** 2.

Head, Cult of the. The ancient Irish revered the human head as,
indeed, did all ancient Celtic societies. It was in the head and not in
the heart that they seemed to locate the souls of men and women.
In battle they collected the heads of their enemies as trophies.
According to Diodorus Siculus:

> They cut off the heads of enemies slain in battle and attach them to
> the necks of their horses. The blood-stained spoils they hand over
> to their attendants and carry off as booty, while striking up a paean
> and singing a song of victory; and they nail up these fruits upon
> their houses, just as do those who lay low wild animals in certain
> kinds of hunting.
>
> They embalm in cedar oil the heads of the most distinguished
> enemies, and preserve them carefully in a chest, and display them
> with pride to strangers, saying that for this head one of their
> ancestors, or his father, or the man himself refused the offer of a
> large sum of money. They say that some of them boast that they
> refused the weight of the head in gold; thus displaying what is only
> a barbarous kind of magnanimity, for it is not a sign of nobility to
> refrain from selling the proofs of one's valour.

Livy describes the placing of the head of an enemy chieftain in a
temple by the victorious Celtic Boii in 216BC. He says how 'some

Gallic (Celtic) horsemen came in sight, with heads hanging at their horses' breasts or fixed on their lances and singing their customary song of triumph'.

In the Irish sagas and stories the cult is mentioned often, particularly in the Ulster Cycle. Cúchulainn, returning to Emain Macha after his first battle foray, is described as having three heads on his chariot and 'nine heads in one hand and ten in the other, and these he brandished at the hosts in token of his valour and prowess'. The magic power of the head is demonstrated in 'The Destruction of Da Derga's Hostel' when Conaire Mór, having been slain, has his head taken off. When Conall, the warrior, pours water into the mouth of the head, it speaks and thanks him.

Archaeological finds give full corroboration to this cult.

Heber. See **Eber**.
Heremon. See **Eremon**.
High King. See **Ard Rí**.
Hy-Brasil. See **Breasal**.

I. *Idad* (yew) in the Ogham alphabet.

Iarbanel. Sometimes given as Iarbonel and Íardanél. One of the three sons of Nemed who escaped after the defeat and death of their father. His son was Béothach. Iarbanel is said to be the ancestor of the Tuatha Dé Danaan while his brother Starn was acclaimed the ancestor of the Firbolg.

Ibath. Son of Béothach. A Nemedian who fled to Boeotia after the Fomorii defeated them. He, also, is said to be an ancestor of the Dé Danaan.

Ibcan. Son of Béothach.

Ibor. The charioteer who accompanied Cúchulainn during the adventures told in 'The Boyhood Deeds of Cúchulainn'.

Ibor cind tráchta. The spot where the goddess Fand arranged her assignation with Cúchulainn; but Emer, Cuchúlainn's wife, having discovered this, arrived with fifty maidens with sharpened knives to destroy Fand. See **Cúchulainn**, **Emer** and **Fand**.

Id. Son of Ríangabur. He was the charioteer of Conall Cearnach and brother of Cúchulainn's charioteer Laeg.

Idath. A warrior of Connacht who married the goddess Bé Find, the sister of Boann. His son is Fraoch, the handsomest warrior in Ireland.

Ilbreg. Sometimes Ilbhreach. Son of the sea-god Manannán Mac Lir. He was ruler of the *sídhe* Eas Aedha Ruaidh, the mound of Mullachshee near Ballyshannon, Co. Donegal. He was also one of the five candidates for the kingship of the Dé Danaan when the Dagda announced his intention to give up the role. During the subsequent war between the gods, Ilbreg fought for Midir the Proud alongside the contingent of mortals led by the Fenian warrior Caoilte who slew Lir, his grandfather.

Ildánach. A title bestowed on Lugh Lámhfada when he presented himself at the court of Nuada. It meant 'The All Craftsman'.

Iliann. See **Iollan.**

Imbolg. One of the four great annual pre-Christian festivals which was sacred to Brigid, the fertility goddess, and held on 1 February. See **Brigid.** It was subsequently taken over by the Christian Church and became St. Brigid's feastday.

Immrama. Voyages, a class of tales including such famous ones as '*Immram Curaig Maile Dúin*' (The Voyage of Mael Dúin) and '*Immram Curaig Bran Mac Ferbal*' (The Voyage of Bran).

Indech. A Fomorii warrior, son of the goddess Domnu, who was killed by the god Ogma at the second Battle of Magh Tuireadh.

Ingcél Cáech. The one-eyed son or grandson of the king of Britain who had been exiled. He met up with Conaire Mór's three dissident foster brothers and joined forces with them and other Irish dissidents, such as the sons of Ailill and Medb. Together they raided and plundered Ireland and Britain. In Britain they attacked a fortress where Ingcél's father, mother and seven brothers, who were guests there, were destroyed. The final raid of this band was against Da Derga's Hostel in which the High King Conaire Mór was finally slain. Ingcél played a prominent role in this and was sent to spy on Conaire Mór before the attack.

Invasions, The Book of. *Leabhar Gabhála*, sometimes known as *The Book of Takings*. Professor Eoin Mac Neill once referred to it as 'a true national epic'. The book contains the mythical history of Ireland, citing all the invasions of the country from Cesair before the Deluge, through the invasions of Partholón, Nemed, the Firbolg, the Dé Danaan and the Milesians. It then follows the subsequent myth/history of Ireland down to the High King Malachaí Mór (Malachaí II) (AD980–1002). The book survives in various ancient manuscripts, mainly in the Book of Leinster (*Leabhar Laignech*) from the twelfth century. However, the historian Micheál Ó Cléirigh, compiler of the first printed Irish dictionary (published at Louvain in 1643), compiled a version of the *Leabhar Gabhála* drawn from several ancient manuscripts which are now lost. It is Ó Cléirigh's compilation to which people generally refer.

Iollan. The Fair, son of Fergus Mac Roth. He accompanied his father and his brother, Buinne the Ruthless, to Alba to bear Conchobhar Mac Nessa's invitation to Deirdre and the sons of Usna. Conchobhar had said he had forgiven Naoise and his brother for eloping with his bride-to-be, Deirdre, and asked them to return to Ulster. While Iollan and Buinne were guarding them in the Red Branch hostel in

Emain Macha, Conchobhar betrayed his word and ordered them killed. At first, Buinne and Iollan defended them. Buinne was then bribed with a gift to stop fighting. Iollan, however, continued to fight. He ran out to meet the attackers and wounded Fiachra, son of Conchobhar Mac Nessa, who was leading the attack on the hostel. Fiachra was carrying Conchobhar's enchanted shield, Ochain (Moaner) which moaned when its bearer was in danger. The hero Conall Cearnach, hearing its cry, rushed up and mortally wounded Iollan. Before he died, however, Iollan told Conall, who had been his friend, of Conchobhar's great treachery. Conall, in rage, then slew Fiachra. It is significant in this tale that both Iollan and Fiachra are said to have been born on the same day.

Ioruaidhe. A kingdom whose ruler possessed a hound-whelp called Fáil Inis who was irresistible in battle, turned any running water it bathed in into wine and caught every wild beast it encountered. In reparation for killing Cian, Lugh's father, the sons of Tuireann had to bring it back to Ireland. They fought with the king of Ioruaidhe, took him captive and demanded the hound in return for his life and freedom.

Ir. A son of Milesius. He was killed by a storm conjured by the Dé Danaan to prevent the Milesian landing in Ireland.

Irgalach. Son of Lách. He commanded 'three fifties' of elderly warriors of Ulster who were no longer of military age. They volunteered to accompany Conchobhar Mac Nessa in the war against Ailill and Medb in order that they might give advice to the younger warriors.

Irnan. One of the three sorceress daughters of Conaran the Dé Danaan who dwelt at Dún Conaran. With her sisters she was sent to capture some numbers of the Fianna. This was accomplished by spinning a magic web with which to capture the warriors. Goll Mac Morna, coming along later, saw what the three 'hags of Conaran' were about and he killed two of them. Irnan begged for mercy and promised to release the warriors. While they were being released Fionn arrived. Irnan then changed into a monster and laid a *geis* on Fionn or his warriors to accept single combat. Oisín, Oscar and Celta all refused to fight the monster. Fionn decided to accept but Goll, still tired from his previous combat, said it was not seemly for Fionn to fight the hag even if she was disguised as a monster. Goll fought and killed Irnan and for this Fionn gave his daughter Cebha in marriage to him.

Iron. Appears frequently in the myths as a valuable and magical property. At the start of the first millennium BC the Celtic peoples were possessed of great skill in metal work, especially in the use of iron, a metal only then becoming known to craftsmen of the classical world. By the sixth century BC their formidable armaments of spears, swords, axes and agricultural implements rendered the Celts militarily superior to their neighbours and they were able to open roadways through the previously impenetrable forests of Europe. An ancient Irish word for a road, still in use today, is *slighe* from the word *sligim*, I hew. The iron swords of the Celts were particularly devastating and enabled them to sweep across Europe, conquering Rome itself in 390BC and defeating the armies of Thrace, Macedonia and the other Greek states including the Athenian army. The very word 'iron' is derived from the Celtic *iarn*, spreading from that source into most European languages including Latin and the Old Germanic languages. Iron bars of certain weight were used in ancient Celtic society as currency. In the story of the *Táin*, Ailill and Medb, counting their treasures, list *iarn-lestair* or iron vessels. Sliabh-an-Iairinn (Mountain of Iron), east of Lough Allen, Co. Leitrim, was said to be where Goibhniu the smith-god worked.

Irusan. A monstrous cat which dwelt in a cave near Knowth on the Boyne. It was said to have seized the poet Senchan in its jaws and run off with him.

Islands. Islands are usually used as representations of aspects of the Otherworld. They appear as fabulous places. Good examples of this occur in the 'Voyage of Mael Dúin', the 'Voyage of Bran', etc.

Ith. Son of Bregon. He was said to have dwelt in a great tower which his father had built in Spain. Spain is a synonym for the Land of the Dead in early Irish literature. From this tower, Ith saw Ireland and resolved to go there. He embarked with ninety of his followers and they landed at Corca Duibhne (Corkaguiny, Co. Kerry). The Dé Danaan had just defeated the Fomorii at the second Battle of Magh Tuireadh and Nuada had been killed. Mac Cécht, Mac Cuill and Mac Gréine were attempting to divide Ireland between them. Ith was asked to make a judgement as to how this should be done. His panegyric was interpreted as an indication that Ith wanted the island for himself. He was killed by the Dé Danaan and his body was taken back to 'Spain' where his children resolved to take vengeance by conquering Ireland: thus began the Milesian invasion.

Iubdan. King of the Faylinn, a kingdom of diminutive people. His wife was Bebo. His poet Eisirt told him that Ulster was a land of giants, in order to quell Iubdan's constant boasting. To prove it he went there and returned with Aedh, the dwarf of the Ulster king Fergus Mac

Léide. Eisirt then placed a *geis* on Iubdan to go to the Ulster court and be first to taste the porridge of the king on the next morning. Accompanied by Bebo, Iubdan went to Ulster and, in making the attempt, fell into the porridge and was made prisoner. This had actually been prophesied. His people tried to obtain his release by offering a ransom of corn. When this was refused they made the calves of Ulster take all the milk from the cows, defiled the rivers and wells, burned mills and kilns and cut off the hair of the men and women while they slept. Whereupon Fergus Mac Léide threatened to kill Iubdan unless they stopped.

In one version of the story Fergus fell in love with Iubdan's wife Bebo. The story illustrates the free approach to sexual relations enjoyed by the early Irish. When Fergus was making love to Bebo he placed his hand on top of her head. When Bebo asked why, Fergus explained that his penis was 'seven fists long' while Bebo was 'only three fists high' and he was afraid it would go through her head. Bebo told him not to worry as 'it's many a thing that a woman's loins absorb'.

Fergus told Iubdan that he had made love to his wife Bebo. 'She liked that,' replied Iubdan unperturbed. Fergus told him that he made love a second time. 'You liked that,' responded Iubdan. Fergus then said he made love a third time. 'Both of you enjoyed that,' Iubdan commented. However, when Fergus said he made love a fourth time, Iubdan condemned his human passion and lust.

After Iubdan and Bebo had been prisoners for a year and one day, Fergus Mac Léide offered them freedom if Iubdan gave up his most treasured possession. This was his enchanted shoes; whoever wore them could travel over or under water as freely as on dry land. Iubdan gave them up and when Fergus put them on they grew into the size of his feet. Iubdan and Bebo were then released and returned to Faylinn.

Iuchar. The second son of Tuireann. See **Brían** and **Tuireann**.

Iucharba. The third son of Tuireann. See **Brían** and **Tuireann**.

Iunsa. Father of Eibhir, wife of Oisín.

L

L. *Luis* (mountain ash) in the Ogham alphabet.

Labraid Loinseach. Sometimes Labra the Mariner. See **Móen**.

Labraid Luathlam ar Cledeb. Labra Swift Hand on the Sword. Ruler of Magh Mell and husband of Lí Ban. He sent Lí Ban to Cúchulainn with a promise to send the goddess Fand to him in exchange for one day's fighting against the three champions Eochaidh Indber, Eochaidh Iuil and Senach Siabarthe.

Ladra. The pilot of Cesair's ship during her coming to Ireland. When Cesair and her companions decided to divide Ireland between them, Ladra took sixteen of the women but his companions had seventeen women each and so he argued about the fairness of the division. He finally accepted his lot and went off to form his kingdom where it is said he died 'of an excess of women'.

Laeg. Sometimes given as Loeg. A son of Ríangabur and called 'the king of charioteers'. His brother Id was charioteer to Conall Cearnach. He became charioteer of Cúchulainn and his faithful companion in many adventures. Cúchulainn trusted him to go to the Otherworld in the company of Lí Ban to report on Fand's kingdom. When Laeg returned he told Cúchulainn of the wonders he had seen and thus decided the hero on his journey there. During Cúchulainn's famous combat with Ferdia at the ford, during the war of the *Táin*, Cúchulainn told Laeg: 'If I look like being bested you must taunt me and deride me to get my battle anger up.' Laeg performed this so that Cúchulainn emerged the victor. During the final combat at the Pillar Stone, Laeg threw himself in front of a spear cast by Laoghaire and meant for Cúchulainn.

Laighin. The province of Leinster. There are two stories about how this province received its name: first, that it took its name from Liath son of Laigne Lethan-glas, a Nemedian; second, that it was named the province of 'spearmen' after the Gauls who accompanied Móen

(Labraid Loinseach) to Ireland to help him overthrow his evil uncle Cobhthach. The Gauls were said to use a broad pointed spear called *laighen* made of a blue-green iron. The province had anciently been called Galian but after the Gauls settled it was called Laighin. The termination *ster* was added at a time of Norse settlement (*stadr*, a place) hence Laighin-ster (pronounced Laynster, thus the Anglicisation Leinster). See **Provinces**.

Laighlinni. One of the sons of Partholón.

Lairgnen. Son of a Connacht chieftain who was betrothed to Deoca of Munster. She asked him to capture the four singing swans as a bridal present. These were, in fact, the children of Lir.

Laoghaire. Sometimes given as Loegaire, Laery, Leary.

1. Buadach, the Triumphant, son of Ugaine and a Red Branch hero.

2. Lorc, king of Leinster, murdered by Cobhthach. See **Cobhthach Coel**.

3. Mac Crimthann of Connacht. He assisted Fiachna Mac Retach to regain his wife and daughter who were abducted by Goll of Magh Mell. He slew Goll and married Fiachna's daughter, Der Gréine.

Leabhar Gabhála. See *Invasions, The Book of.*

Lebharcham. The nurse of Deirdre who is also a poetess. When questioned by Conchobhar Mac Nessa as to whether Deirdre's beauty had faded during her years in Alba with Naoise and his brothers, she tried to persuade the Ulster king that her beauty had faded. She knew that Conchobhar still harboured thoughts of vengeance against Naoise for eloping with his bride-to-be. Conchobhar sent a spy to check on Lebharcham's story and discovered that she was lying.

Leinster. See **Laighin**.

Leith Cuinn. Conn's Half (of Ireland). See **Eiscir Riada**.

Leith Moga. Mug's Half (of Ireland). See **Eiscir Riada**.

Len. The goldsmith of the god Bodb Dearg who gave his name to Loch Lena (Lough Leane, near Killarney).

Lepers and Leprosy. Leprosy features in several tales and the condition was well known in ancient Ireland by various names: *clam, samthrusc, trosc* etc. The Brehon Laws provided for special leper hospitals and several of the medieval Irish medical tracts have sections of information on leprosy and its forms. Slieve Loughter in Co. Kerry was known as Luachair na Lubhair (Loughter of the Lepers). When Ron Cerr attempted to enter an enemy camp he disguised himself as a leper so that none would challenge him.

Leprechaun. See under **Lugh**.

Lí. Son of Dedad, or Degad, who founded the Degad or military caste of Munster (equivalent of the Ulster Red Branch). Traigh Lí Mic Dedad, the strand of Lí son of Dedad (Tralee, Co. Kerry), was said by the *Annals of Connacht* to be named after him.

Lia. Lord of Luachtar, treasurer of Clan Morna and father of Conan Maol. He became treasurer of the Fianna when Goll Mac Morna became their leader after deposing Cumal, father of Fionn. The treasure bag of the Fianna was made from the skin of Aoife (while in the shape of a crane – see **Aoife** 3) and in this (see **Treasure bag of the Fianna**) were kept great jewels and magical weapons. Lia was slain by Fionn Mac Cumhail who took the treasure bag and subsequently had to fight against Lia's son for several years.

Lia Fáil. The Stone of Destiny. There seem to be two separate stones called the Lia Fáil: first, that used at Temuir (Tara) which roared with joy at the touch of the foot of a rightful king, and second, that used at the coronations of the Dál Riada kings of Alba, and subsequently the Scottish kings until it was stolen by Edward I of England (1272–1307) and taken to London. Legend has it that the stone at Temuir, mentioned in the coronations of monarchs such as Conn of the Hundred Battles, was in fact the same as the one taken to the Dál Riada kingdom. According to Irish sources Fergus Mac Erc, of the Scottish Dál Riada, requested that his brother, Murtagh Mac Erc (High King AD512–533), send the Lia Fáil to Alba so that he could be crowned on it. This request was granted but, after the coronation, Fergus Mac Erc refused to return the stone. However, some scholars have claimed to have identified the Lia Fáil as a six foot high pillar stone that still stands at Tara.

The tradition of the Scottish Lia Fáil is that this was Jacob's Pillow, taken out of Egypt by Goidel, son of Scota, daughter of the Pharaoh Cingris. St. Colmcille crowned Aidan on it and it was kept at the Dál Riada capital, now Dunstaffnage, Argyll, until the Dál Riadans united with the Tuatha Cruithne to form the united kingdom of Alba. Then in AD848 the High King of Alba, Kenneth Mac Alpin, took it to Sgáin (Scone) which became capital of the country until the overthrow of MacBeth (1040–57).

After Edward I stole it, it was placed in Westminster Abbey under the English throne and every English monarch since Edward has been crowned on it. A new legend grew up, this time among the English, that should the stone be taken away from Westminster

Abbey, it would mark the end of the English monarchy. The Lia Fáil was removed from Westminster Abbey in 1951 by four Scottish patriots, its successful removal delighting Scottish public opinion which had long felt that the ancient and sacred relic should be returned to the country from which it had been plundered. Some months later the Lia Fáil was found wrapped in a Scottish flag in Arbroath Abbey, site of the Scottish Declaration of Independence in 1320. A second attempt was made to remove it to Scotland in 1967.

Liadin. A poetess with whom the poet Cuirithir fell in love. The story of Liadin and Cuirithir is a tale of sorrowful love which survives from a ninth-century text. It reminds one of the tragic story of Héloise and Abélard of Brittany. The story is not really part of Irish myth although it tends to be accepted as such and hence this entry is appropriate. Liadin and Cuirithir of the Dési were in love. For some reason, instead of waiting for Cuirithir to marry her, Liadin spurned him and became a nun. In despair, Cuirithir took holy orders in a monastery. But they both regretted their actions. Religion prevented a happy outcome. Cuirithir was exiled from Ireland and eventually Liadin lay down and died of grief on the stone at which Cuirithir used to pray. She laments:

> *Cen áinius*
> *in gním í do-rigénus*
> *an ro-carus ro-cráidius* . . .

> No pleasure
> that deed I did, tormenting him,
> tormenting what I treasure.

Liagan. 1. A member of the Fianna and a powerful runner.

2. A chieftain killed by Conan Maol after he had challenged any member of the Fianna to meet him in single combat.

Liath. Son of Laigne Lethan-glas, a Nemedian, who cut down the tangled woods around Tara so that the corn grew rich there. The site was named after him as Druimm Leith but later renamed Temuir (Tara). It is also claimed that the province of Leinster was named after him.

Liath Macha. See **Grey of Macha**.

Lí Ban. 1. Beauty of women. Wife to Labraid Luathlam ar Cledeb (Labra of the Swift Hand on the Sword), the ruler of Magh Mell. Her sister was Fand the Pearl of Beauty. She brought a message from Fand to Cúchulainn inviting the Ulster champion to return to her in Tír Tairnigiri (the Land of Promise) where, if Cúchulainn would help fight against the enemies who were attacking it, the evil Fomorii, Fand would become his lover. Cúchulainn sent his charioteer Laeg back to Tír Tairnigiri to report on it and then Cúchulainn decided to accept Fand's invitation. After the affair was over, Lí Ban brought another message to Cúchulainn, this time from her husband, promising Cúchulainn that Fand would be sent to him if Cúchulainn would slay three champions.

2. A mermaid living in Lough Neagh. The mermaid, according to the *Annals of the Four Masters*, was captured there in AD558.

Linné. A friend of Oscar who was accidentally slain by him when he was in a battle fever.

Lir. The ocean-god, cognate with Llyr in Welsh myth. His greatest son was Manannán who took over the role as the god of the seas. Lir married Aobh and had three sons and a daughter who were changed into swans by his second wife Aoife, who was Aobh's sister. As a deity, his name appears in many place names not only in Ireland but in other countries, for example Leicester in England (Llyr-caster). Geoffrey of Monmouth's mention of him as a king, King Leir, caused him to be immortalised as King Lear in the Shakespeare play.

Lir, Children of. See **Aobh** and **Aoife** 2.

Lobais. A Fomorii druid.

Loch. 1. Son of Mofebis, a champion of Medb of Connacht, who was sent against Cúchulainn during the combat of the ford, succeeded in wounding him but was then slain by Cúchulainn's fabulous Gae-Bolg spear.

2. Lake. Lakes contain several monsters and hold mystic virtues both in myth and in early Irish chronicles. There was a great monster in Loch Derg which was slain by Conan. The Loch Gráinne monster appeared once every seven years while Loch Ree contained not only a monster but an underwater city. Loch Gur also had a supernatural creature in it but is said to have gone dry once every seven years. The most famous loch monster, mentioned in early Irish sources as well as Scottish ones, is the world-famous Loch Ness monster. The first mention of this mythical beast occurs in a *Life of St. Colmcille* by Adamnan, the Abbot of Iona (679–704).

Lochlann. The country of the Norsemen, i.e. 'land of lochs'. Cognate with the Welsh Llychlyn. In some tales it may well be a synonym for the Otherworld while others have interpreted it as a synonym for Alba.

Loch-Lethglas. A Fomorii poet killed by Lugh Lámfhada at the second Battle of Magh Tuireadh.

Lodan. Son of Lir and father of the goddess Sinend.

Lomna. Fionn Mac Cumhail's jester who wrote Fionn an Ogham message informing him of his wife's infidelity. He was then murdered by her lover but Fionn avenged him.

Lon. See **Lúin**.

Lot. A Fomorii. The wife of Goll and mother of Cichol Gricenchos. She had bloated lips in her breast and four eyes in her back. She equalled in strength all the warriors who fought under her, leading them into battle against Partholón.

Love spot. *Ball seirce.* See **Diarmuid** 3.

Luchad. Father of Luchtar.

Luchtar. God of carpentry among the De Danaans. Brother of Goibhniu and Credne.

Lugaid. 1. Son of Ailill Mac Máta. At his father's behest he cast a spear at Fergus Mac Roth while Fergus was swimming in a lake with Ailill's wife Medb. Fergus was killed.

2. Mac Con. He usurped the High Kingship and fought against Art (see **Art**) whom he killed at the Battle of Moy Muchruinne. The kingship lists say he ruled from AD250 to 253.

3. Mac Cú Roí, the son of Cú Roí of Munster who was killed by Cúchulainn. It was Lugaid that killed Cúchulainn's charioteer Laeg in the final combat.

4. Riab nDerg. Of the Red Stripes. He was the son of Clothra (see **Clothra**) by her three brothers. It was said his body was divided into three sections by red stripes, each section resembling that part of each father. According to the kingship lists he was High King from AD65 to 73. He begot a son from his own mother Clothra named Crimthann Nía Náir who also became High King (AD74–90).

5. Mac Daire. When told in a prophecy that one of his five sons would be High King of Ireland, he gave the name Lugaid to all of them. The sons were out hunting when an ugly crone begged a kiss from each. When the youngest, Lugaid Laigde, kissed her she turned into a beautiful goddess and called herself Sovranty, proclaiming him to be the chosen one. A similar story is told of Niall of the Nine Hostages.

Lugh. One of the most important of the Irish gods, cognate with the Welsh Lleu and the Gaulish Lugos. He was son of Cian and Ethlinn, daughter of Balor of the Evil Eye. He is clearly a sun god, known for the spendour of his countenance, and god of all arts and crafts. Rescued from death as a baby, when Balor tried to destroy him because of a prophecy that his grandson would kill him, Lugh was fostered by Manannán Mac Lir. In some versions, it is Cian's brother Goibhniu, the smith-god, who fosters him. After his fosterage he presented himself to the court of Nuada of the Silver Hand. Nuada let him be ruler of the Dé Danaans for thirteen days. During the second Battle of Magh Tuireadh, Lugh fulfilled the prophecy that he would kill his grandfather for he slew Balor of the Evil Eye. He became ruler for a short time after Nuada's death at the hands of Balor. Then Mac Cécht, Mac Cuill and Mac Gréine decided to split the country between them. When the sons of Tuireann killed his father, Cian, he imposed an *eric* (fine) on them in which they had to perform certain tasks in reparation. See **Brían** and **Tuireann** 3.

Lugh was the father of the hero Cúchulainn by the mortal woman Dechtiré. When Cúchulainn grew weary during the combat against Ailill and Medb's warriors in the war of the *Táin*, Lugh appeared and fought beside him. Lugh's last appearance seems to have been in a magical mist when Conn of the Hundred Battles (High King AD177–212) saw him. Lugh foretold how many children Conn would have and the length of his reign.

When the old gods were driven underground, Lugh was given the *sídhe* of Rodrubán by the Dagda. Over the years this mighty god's image diminished in popular folk memory until he became simply a fairy craftsman named Lugh-chromain, 'little stooping Lugh', which became Anglicised as Leprechaun. The leprechaun is now all that survives of this potent patron of arts and crafts whose name is remembered in the place names of many lands, not just Ireland: Lyons, Léon, Loudan and Laon, in France; Leiden in Holland; Liegnitz in Silesia; Carlisle (Luguvalum in Roman times) in England as well as the capital city of England itself which, like Lyons, was named the 'fortress of Lugh' – Lugdunum, hence the Latin Londinium and London.

Lughnasadh. The feast of the god Lugh which was introduced by Lugh to commemorate his foster mother Tailtu. It was one of the four major pre-Christian festivals and was basically an agrarian feast in honour of the harvesting of crops. Early records claim the festival was celebrated for fifteen days. Christianity took his feast over as Lammas, the feast of first fruits. The name survives in modern Irish

(Lúnasa) and Manx (Luanistyn) for the name of the month of August. In Scottish Gaelic, Lùnasad is still the name of the Lammas festival.

Lughlocht Loga. The Cradle of Lugh. A fortress in Bregia which belonged to Forgall, nephew of Tethra the Fomorii.

Lugna. A king of Connacht who fostered the son of Art and Étain, Cormac Mac Art. See **Étain** 4.

Lúin. The enchanted spear of Celtchair. It belonged to a god of the Dé Danaan but was left discarded on the battlefield after the second Battle of Magh Tuireadh. It became the property of the Red Branch hero Celtchair and it is said that when it felt the blood of an enemy it twisted and writhed in the hands of whoever held it and if blood was not spilt a cauldron of venom was the only means to quench it before it turned on its holder. It could kill a man without reaching him.

Lycanthropy. Shape-changing often occurred in the myths. Gods and even mortals could change their shapes into many forms, mostly animals. Sometimes it was a druid who changed the shape of his victim, such as the Dark Druid who changed the goddess Sadb into a fawn. Often death would come to the victims while they were in animal shape, as happened to Aoife, changed into a crane for daring to love the son of the sea-god Manannán Mac Lir. Some sorceresses could change shape into fearsome monsters. The whole idea of lycanthropy is in keeping with the old Celtic belief that everything, even inanimate objects such as stones, was possessed of an indwelling spirit and that the human spirit, which was immortal, could dwell within other creatures or objects just as well as within the mortal form.

M. *Muin* (vine) in the Ogham alphabet.

Mac An Daimh. A companion of Mongán during his attempts to rescue his wife Dubh Lacha from Brandubh of Leinster.

Mac An Lúin. The sword of Fionn Mac Cumhail which is 'Son of the spear'. In MacPherson's *Ossian* it is referred to as 'Son of Luno'.

Mac Cécht. 1. A son of Ogma, the god of eloquence. After the death of Nuada of the Silver Hand at the second Battle of Magh Tuireadh, Mac Cécht and his two brothers, Mac Cuill and Mac Gréine, took Nuada's body for burial at Grianan Aileach (on the Inishowen Peninsula). They decided to divide Ireland between them. In this matter they sought advice from a stranger named Ith, a Milesian who had just arrived in Ireland. Ith gave a judgement which made them suspicious that he wanted Ireland for himself and so they killed him. It was to revenge Ith's death that the later Milesian invasion took place. During this invasion Mac Cécht was slain by Eremon, Milesius' son. He was the husband of Fótla, one of the three goddesses (with Banb and Éire) who asked that their name be given to Ireland. 2. Son of Snade Teched. A champion of Conaire Mór who accompanied the High King on his last fateful journey to Da Derga's Hostel. In one version of the tale it is Mac Cécht and not Conall Cearnach who takes Conaire Mór's golden cup and goes in search of water when the High King is thirsty. The story is basically the same with the gods against Conaire Mór, causing the water to conceal itself until Mac Cécht finally reaches Loch Gara, Co. Roscommon. The gods could not hide the lake in time and so Mac Cécht filled his cup and returned to Da Derga's Hostel. But all was lost. He found a warrior making off with the head of Conaire Mór and he slew the man. Taking the head he poured the water into his mouth whereupon the head praised him and thanked him for his valiant deed.

Mac Conmara. Sometimes given as Macnamara. A scoundrel who obtained supernatural powers by stealing eggs from a raven's nest, boiling them and returning them to the nest. The raven brought a magic stone to the nest to revive its offspring and it was this stone that Mac Conmara sought. He stole it and rubbed himself with it, thus acquiring a number of extra-sensory powers, including those of foretelling the future and forcing others to do his will. He also rubbed his mare, Fínis, and she acquired human intelligence. When she died, however, Mac Conmara lost his powers.

Mac Cuill. A son of Ogma who was husband of Banba. He was slain by the Milesian Eber. See **Mac Cécht** 1.

Mac Da Réo. The owner of one of the most famous hostels in Ireland, a place in Breifne mentioned in the 'Tale of Mac Da Thó's Boar'.

Mac Da Thó. Mesorda Mac Da Thó was a king of Leinster who had two possessions which others coveted. The first was a hound, variously called Ailbe and Ossar, which could outrun all others in Ireland. The second was a boar which was the greatest size of any in the country. Conchobhar Mac Nessa of Ulster and Ailill and Medb of Connacht made offers for these possessions. Each made a veiled threat pointing out the advantages of Leinster being allied with either Ulster or Connacht. After discussing the matter with his wife Buan, Mac Da Thó agreed to sell the hound to both Connacht and Ulster, inviting Conchobhar and Ailill and Medb with their retinues to a feast in order that they might collect it. He slaughtered his famous boar as the prize dish of the feast.

As he suspected, an argument then broke out. Bricriu of Ulster pointed out that the boar should be divided according to the martial accomplishments of the warriors gathered there. Cet of Connacht at once contended that he was the greatest warrior there and challenged anyone to disprove it. Conall Cearnach of Ulster then arrived and claimed he was a greater warrior than Cet. Cet admitted that this was so but said that his brother Anluan was better than Conall. Whereupon Conall produced the head of Anluan and flung it at the Connacht champion. This started a bloody battle in the hall of Mac Da Thó in which the Ulster warriors finally put the Connacht warriors to flight. The hound of Mac Da Thó chased the chariot of Ailill until Ailill's charioteer struck off the hound's head. Neither side won possession of the hound. Yet, while Mac Da Thó had slaughtered his boar and lost his hound, he had kept his kingdom.

However, in a later story the Ulster druid and poet Áthairne the Importunate arrived to stay with Mac Da Thó. He was offered hospitality and demanded that he sleep with Mac Da Thó's wife, Buan. Although breaking the laws of hospitality, Mac Da Thó refused this request. Áthairne returned to Ulster and demanded that Conchobhar Mac Nessa make war on Leinster for this affront to him. Although Áthairne was not liked, Conchobhar reluctantly agreed so as not to rouse the druid's ire. Conall Cearnach slew Mac Da Thó and offered himself to Buan, Mac Da Thó's wife. But, rather than go with him, she died of grief.

Mac Glas. Mael Fhothartaig's jester who was killed by Aedh at the same time Mael Fhothartaig was murdered.

Mac Gréine. A son of Ogma, brother of Mac Cécht and Mac Cuill. He was husband of the goddess Éire who gave her name to Ireland. He was slain by the Milesian druid Amairgen. Significantly, the name means 'son of the sun'.

Macha. A triune goddess, she appears as at least three distinct person-alities. She is certainly one of the goddesses of war (see **Mórrígan**), a personification of battle and slaughter, hovering over warriors and inspiring them with battle madness. Heads cut off in battle were known as 'Macha's acorn crop'.

1. Wife of Nemed, leader of the Nemedians, who died and was buried on one of the twelve great plains of Ireland cleared by Nemed.

2. Wife of Nuada of the Silver Hand who was killed by Balor of the Evil Eye at the second Battle of Magh Tuireadh. She is said to have consorted with the Dagda a year before this battle.

3. The mysterious wife of Crunniuc Mac Agnomain of Ulster. Crunniuc's wife had died when, one day, a beautiful woman arrived at his fortress and took on the role of his wife and became pregnant by him. While attending a royal gathering Crunniuc became involved in a boasting match. The king's horses and chariot were winning all the races and Crunniuc claimed that his wife, pregnant as she was, could win a race on foot against the king's horses. The king demanded that the boast should be fulfilled. Macha was brought before the king and refused to race as she was pregnant. The king said he would kill Crunniuc if she refused. Macha said: 'A long-lasting evil will come out of this on the whole of Ulster.' When the king demanded who she was she spoke her name for the first time: 'Macha daughter of Sainraith Mac Imbaith.' She raced against the king's horses and as she reached the end of the field she gave birth to twins. In one version the place was named Emain Macha, or Macha's Twins. As she gave birth she screamed and with her dying breath proclaimed that all who

Magog. A Biblical character who slips into the myths and is given three sons: Banbh, Iobath and Fathnachta, who became the ancestor of Partholón, Nemed and, surprisingly, Attila the Hun.

Maine. There are several persons who bear this name in the sagas and stories, mostly minor characters. Among the more prominent are:

1. A Norse prince who, according to one version of the tragic tale of Deirdre and the sons of Usna, was the man who killed the sons of Usna because Naoise had killed his father and brothers. This role is more popularly given to Eoghan Mac Durthacht of the Red Branch. See **Eoghan** 3.

2. The seven sons of Ailill and Medb were all called Maine. They were: Maine Mathramail (the Motherlike), Maine Athramail (the Fatherlike), Maine Mórgor (the Strongly Dutiful), Maine Míngor (the Sweetly Dutiful), Maine Mo Epirt (Above Description, also known as Maine Mílscothach, of the Honeyed Tongue), Maine Andoe (the Swift) and Maine Gaib Uile (of All the Qualities). They were all outlawed and joined Ingcél Cáech, the one-eyed son (or grandson) of the king of Britain, who raided Ireland and took part in the raid on Da Derga's Hostel in which the High King, Conaire Mór, was killed. They all responded to their mother's call to join her army in its attack on Ulster during the war of the *Táin*.

Man, Isle of. See **Mannin**.

Manannán Mac Lir. The son of Lir. The major sea-god. He is cognate with the Welsh sea-god Manawyddan, son of Llyr. He ruled from Emain Ablach (Emain of the Apple Trees) in Tír Tairnigiri (the Land of Promise). He was a shape-changer and could drive his chariot over the waves as if they were a plain. His wife was Fand, the Pearl of Beauty. His appearance is always as a noble and handsome warrior. Although he sired children among the gods, such as his son Gaiar, whose affair with Bécuma caused Bécuma's expulsion from the Land of Promise, Manannán also sired human children and he is the father of Mongán.

There are two accounts how this came about. First, he appeared to the queen of the Dál nAraidi of Ulster while her husband was away at war and foretold her husband's death unless the queen would permit him to sleep with her. Second, he appeared to the king, Fachtna, while he was being worsted in battle and said he would help turn the tide of the affray if he could go, disguised as Fachtna, and sleep with his wife. To this Fachtna agreed. The outcome of both versions is the birth of Mongán whom Manannán took to Tír Tairnigiri for fosterage, returning him when he reached the age of choice. Mongán became king and a great warrior. The second version of the tale is remarkably similar to the conception of Arthur in the Brythonic Celtic myth.

Manannán appears more frequently than most gods, creating storms to wreck Milesian ships, appearing to Bran at the start of his epic voyage or conducting Cormac Mac Art around Tír Tairnigiri. When the Dagda resigned the leadership of the gods, Manannán refused to accept the succession of the Bodb Dearg. However, unlike Midir who fought with the Bodb Dearg, Manannán left the gods and retreated into seclusion.

Mannin. The Isle of Man. In Manx, Ellan Vannin, and in Irish, Inish Manannán. The island is mentioned several times in the sagas and stories but little is known of it before the fourth century AD. It was originally thought to be a Brythonic Celtic-speaking kingdom but in about the fourth century Goidelic-, or Gaelic-, speaking Celts arrived from Ireland and began to settle. Several Ogham inscriptions survive on the island. According to *Cormac's Glossary*, Senchán Torpéist, the chief bard of Ireland (d. AD647) visited the island and found a high degree of literary knowledge there, including a knowledge of the Irish epics.

The last independent king of the island died in 1266 and it was ceded to Alexander III of Scotland. The English kings wanted the island and thus begсn a series of conflicts and occupations while the Manx continued to govern their own affairs through their ancient parliament known as Tynwald (Thing-völlr). The ruling house was the House of Keys (from Manx *kiares-es-feed* – twenty-four, the number of elected members). In 1346 the English finally landed an army, drove out the Scots and established a permanent rule. Henry VII instituted a 'Lordship of Man'. In 1736 this lordship was inherited by the Duke of Atholl who sold it to the English Government to pay his debts. In May 1866 the island was given self-government with the House of Keys reconstituted as a democratic parliament. The status of the island is that of a British Crown Dependency which is not part of the United Kingdom.

Manx. The Gaelic language of the Isle of Man, closely akin to Irish and descending from a common root. Manx seems to have become a distinct language from Irish and Scottish Gaelic in about the fourteenth century. As an independent literary language, it does not appear to have taken written form until the early seventeenth century. The sagas and myths were kept alive by oral tradition on the island. In the seventeenth century, however, antiquarians began to copy them down. A fisherman recited some of the Ossianic Cycle to the scholar Heywood in 1789 and his manuscript version of this is retained by the British Museum. In spite of receiving self-government in 1866, the island adopted an English education policy, which added to the decline of the language. By 1901 only 8.1 per cent of the islanders spoke Manx. The last census (1971) showed only 284 people able to speak Manx on the island, although there is a strong revivalist movement. See **Celt**.

Maol. Sometimes Mael. Bald.

1. A druid of Conn of the Hundred Battles.

2. A druid of Laoghaire who, with his brother Calpait, taught Laoghaire's daughters Ethné and Fedelma. The reference to Maol 2 is important in that it gives proof that druids wore a tonsure called *airbacc Giunnae*, which was cut from ear to ear and was similar to the one which later Celtic Christian monks adopted, as opposed to the Roman tonsure which was cut on the crown of the head. The matter of cutting the tonsure was one of the points of contention between the Celtic and Roman Churches.

Maon. See **Móen**.

Marbán. A swineherd who became the chief poet of Ireland having contested with Dael Duiled, the *ollamh* of Leinster. Both men were set riddles to solve. Such contests often occur in the sagas and heroes frequently saved their lives by posing a riddle which their judges were unable to answer.

Marcán. An old chieftain of Connacht and husband of the beautiful Cred, the would-be lover of Cano.

Mathgen. A druid of the Dé Danaan.

May Day. See **Beltaine**.

Meabal. See **Breg**.

Meargach. Of the Green Spears. Husband of Áille, killed by Oscar at the battle of Cnoc-an-Áire. See **Áille**.

Mechi. Son of the Mórrígán, goddess of battles. He was slain by Mac Cécht, son of Ogma, because it was prophesied he would bring disaster to Ireland. He had three hearts in which grew three serpents which, when full-grown, would break out and devastate the land.

Medb. Anglicised as Maeve. It has been contended that Medb was another triune goddess, a goddess representing sovranty, but only two Medbs appear as distinct personages in the myths, the traditions of each being somewhat confused with the other.

1. Queen of Connacht and wife of Ailill. She was daughter of a High King and seems to have married Conchobhar Mac Nessa, Tiride Mac Connra Cas, Eochaidh Dála and finally Ailill Mac Máta, each of whom is significantly named as king of Connacht, although, of course, Conchobhar Mac Nessa was king of Ulster. The point being made by some writers is that Medb represented the sovranty of Connacht and no king was legitimate unless symbolically wed to her. It is recorded that she 'never was without one man in the shadow of another'.

She figures in the famous epic of the *Táin Bó Cuailgne* (The Cattle Raid of Cuailgne) which started when she found her possessions were not as extensive as her husband Ailill's. The White Horned Bull of Connacht had been born into her herd but had betaken itself to Ailill's herd as it thought it not seemly to be in the herd of a woman. Medb heard about the fabulous Brown Bull of Cuailgne and, after attempts to secure it, she persuaded Ailill to help her lead an army into Ulster to obtain it. She also features in several other tales of the Ulster, or Red Branch Cycle. Her affairs were numerous. Finally she was killed by Forbaí, son of Conchobhar Mac Nessa, king of Ulster, while bathing in a lake. Her most famous sons were the seven Maines.

2. Medb Lethderg, of the Red Side. She is daughter of Conán of Cuala, and queen of Leinster. Again she appears as a goddess of sovranty to whom it is necessary for a king to be ritually married in order to reign legitimately. It is recorded that she was wife to nine High Kings, including the father of Conn of the Hundred Battles, Conn himself, Conn's son Art and Art's son Cormac.

Medicine. Much is made of the skills of the ancient Irish physicians and, indeed, in early times the doctors of Ireland were highly regarded. During the Dark Ages the Irish medical schools were famous throughout Europe. The premier medical school of Europe was that founded in the fifth century AD at Tuaim Brecain (Tomregan, Co. Cavan) where the eminent physician Bracan Mac Findloga established his practice. The Brehon Laws of Ireland are very explicit on the rights of the sick and the obligations of doctors. Macha Mong Ruadh is said to have established the first hospital in Ireland in 377BC.

From the medieval medical tracts we can see that skills and knowledge were highly advanced. The oldest medical text surviving heard the scream would suffer from the pangs of childbirth for five days and four nights in times of Ulster's greatest difficulty. The curse would last for nine times nine generations. Only three classes of people were free from the curse: the women, the boys and Cúchulainn himself. Macha died and the men of Ulster were afflicted from that time to the time of Furc Mac Dallán, son of Mainech Mac Lugdach.

4. Macha Mong Ruadh, or Macha of the Red Tresses. Daughter of Aedh Ruadh. She is listed as the seventy-sixth monarch of Ireland, reigning in 377BC. Significantly, it is claimed that she built Emain Macha. Her father, Aedh Ruadh, ruled Ireland alternately with his brothers Dithorba and Cimbaeth. In some versions these brothers are made into cousins. When her father died Macha was elected ruler in his place. Dithorba and Cimbaeth disagreed with the decision and raised armies against her. She defeated Dithorba, killing him, and taking his five sons captive, making them build the ramparts of Emain Macha. She persuaded Cimbaeth to marry her and thus give her claim to rule a greater authority.

The annals say that Macha built Ard Macha (Macha's Height, which is Anglicised as Armagh). Macha is also said to have established the first hospital in Ireland, which was called Bron-Bherg (House of Sorrow) and was in use until its destruction in AD22. It is generally acknowledged that St. Fabiola established the first (Christian) hospital in Rome in AD400. While Macha's establishment is placed among the myths and sagas, it must be pointed out that ancient Ireland did have an astonishingly advanced medical system (see **Medicine**) which was carefully laid out in the Brehon Law texts.

Mac Ind Óg. See **Aonghus 1.**

Mac Moincanta. When Manannán Mac Lir left Ireland, at the time of the disagreement among the gods as to who should succeed the Dagda as their ruler, Mac Moincanta took his place. In folklore he became a short-lived 'king of the fairies' to be succeeded by Fionbharr to whom the Dagda allotted the *sídhe* of Meadha.

MacPherson's *Ossian*. Although he is not part of Irish mythology in the strictest sense, nonetheless it is necessary to mention James MacPherson of Kingussie, Scotland (1736–96). In 1760 MacPherson published *Fragments of Ancient Poetry Collected in the Highlands* which he claimed was a translation of authentic Gaelic poetry written by Oisín constituting the Fenian sagas. MacPherson extended this with *Fingal* (1762) and *Temora* (1763), the three volumes constituting what is popularly known as *Ossian*. In spite of the work being denounced as a literary forgery by Dr Samuel Johnson in 1770, it had a tremendous impact on the literary world causing numerous Ossianic Societies to be established. While MacPherson was reviled by the Irish literati, his work did 'rediscover' Irish myth and bring it to a wide audience, being translated into many European languages. The German poet Goethe classed it with Shakespeare; it had a deep impression on Blake, Byron and also Tennyson in a later generation. Napoleon Bonaparte is known to have carried the volume with him on his campaigns and took it with him into his exile on St. Helena. Marshal Bernadotte of France, who became king of Sweden, named his son Oscar after the Fenian hero.

Mac Riagla. Features in a later Christian tale called 'The Voyage of Snedgus and Mac Riagla' which is a fabulous voyage with similarities to the pre-Christian voyage tales. See **Snedgus.**

Mac Roth. Medb's steward who was asked by her to supply details about the Brown Bull of Cuailgne. During the campaign against Ulster he was sent to reconnoitre the Plain of Garach and the visions which he saw there were interpreted by Medb's druids. He is not to be confused with Fergus Mac Roth.

Mael. See **Maol.**

Mael Dúin. Sometimes given as Maeldun. One of the major heroes of the myths whose fabulous voyage, the oldest so far identified, is thought to have been the inspiration for the later Christian epic *Navigatio Brendani* (The Voyage of Brendan). Alfred Tennyson made the hero popular with his epic poem 'The Voyage of Mael-dune'. The earliest extract of *Immram Curaig Maile Dúin* is found in a tenth-century manuscript but the orthography places it in the eighth century.

Mael Dúin was the son of Ailill Edge-of-Battle of the sept of the Eoghanachta of Aran. Raiding the Irish mainland, Ailill came to a church, looted it and raped a nun. He then went on to meet his own death at the hands of raiders from overseas. The nun gave birth to a boy, Mael Dúin, who was taken to be fostered by the nun's sister (who was queen of the territory) after the nun died in childbirth. Mael Dúin grew to manhood and learnt the truth of his parentage. He set out in a quest to revenge the death of his father. He took with him sixty warriors and his subsequent voyage has been considered as the 'Irish *Odyssey*'.

He came to an island where his father's killers were but was blown away by a storm before he could attack them. Then he came to an island of giant ants; an island of beautiful birds; an island with an equine monster with dog's legs and bird's claws; an island of demon horses; and an island of fighting horses. The voyage continued with adventures on a walled island with a monster which could turn itself around inside its own skin; then to an island of fiery creatures; an island with a palace and a curious cat; an island divided by a brass wall with white sheep on one side and black sheep on the other; and an island with a river of boiling water guarded by a giant. Mael Dúin continued to the dwelling of the Miller of the Otherworld; to an island of weeping black folk; and on to an island with walls of gold, silver, copper and crystal. On again to an island with a crystal bridge, an island of talking birds, an island with a hermit and birds which contain the souls of his children. The adventures continued on an island of giant smiths, across a transparent sea to a country where a stream arced into the air. Beyond was a silver pillar set in the sea, which supported a country called Aoncos. Further on lay an island whose queen tried to make love to Mael Dúin and bade him stay. Then on to an island of intoxicating fruit and to another where a bird renewed his youth by telling him to bathe in a magic lake. On to an island protected by a wall of fire and, finally, nearing home again, Mael Dúin caught up with his father's killers, the purpose of his voyage. They asked to make peace with him and Mael Dúin agreed.

Mael Fhothartaig. The son of Ronán, king of Leinster, and Ethné. His stepmother tried to persuade him to make love to her. When he rejected her advances she had him falsely accused of attempting to rape her. Ronán had his son killed but later learnt the truth. Mael Fhothartaig's sons later avenged their father. See **Ronán.**

Maeltine. A Dé Danaan celebrated for his judgements.

Maen. See **Móen.**

Maer. Although the wife of someone else, she fell in love with Fionn Mac Cumhail and sent him nine charm nuts to make him reciprocate her sentiments. Fionn refused to eat them, guessing their purpose.

Maeve. See **Medb.**

Maga. Daughter of Aonghus Óg, the love-god. She wed Ross the Red. Their son Fachtna wed Nessa.

Magh. Sometimes Anglicised as Moy or Mag. A plain. Plains frequently occur in the myths as euphemisms for the Otherworld as in Magh Da Cheo (Plain of the Two Mists), Magh Mell (The Pleasant Plain) or Magh Mon (The Plain of Sports).

Magh Indoc. The Plain of Indoc features in a Christian embellishment
to the myths. The story is contained in *Leabhar na hUidhre* (Book of
the Dun Cow) compiled in the early twelfth century. Cúchulainn was
conjured back from 'Hell' to face St. Patrick. St. Patrick and St.
Benen were walking on the plain with Laoghaire Mac Néill, High
King of Ireland (AD428–63), trying to convert him to Christianity. St.
Patrick summoned Cúchulainn to prove the truth of Christianity and
the horrors of damnation. A blast of icy wind swept them off their feet
and a dense mist descended on the plain. Through it came a phantom
chariot drawn by one black and one grey horse. It galloped up to them
driven by Laeg. Behind him stood Cúchulainn in battle array. To
prove who he was to Laoghaire, Cúchulainn recounted his famous
deeds. He urged Laoghaire to believe in Christianity.

> Great was my heroism,
> Hard as was my sword,
> The Devil crushed me with one finger
> into red charcoal.

Cúchulainn ended his appearance by beseeching Patrick to intercede
so that he might leave the Otherworld (Hell) and go to the Christian
Heaven. The writer says that Patrick's prayer was granted and that
Laoghaire was converted.

Magh Slecht. Sometimes Moyslaught. The Plain of Adoration, said to
be located in the north of Co. Cavan, where the idol Crom Cruach was
erected.

Magh Tuireadh. Sometimes Moytura. The Plain of Towers. Two
famous mythological battles were fought at Magh Tuireadh.
1. The first Battle of Magh Tuireadh is said to have been fought in the
south of Co. Mayo around Cong, between the Firbolgs, led by their
king Erc, and the Dé Danaan, led by Nuada. The Dé Danaan won
but Nuada had his hand struck off. Its replacement with a silver one
by Dian Cécht, god of medicine, resulted in Nuada's name – Nuada
of the Silver Hand.
2. The second Battle of Magh Tuireadh took place in the north of Co.
. Sligo between the Fomorii and the Dé Danaan. Again, the Dé
Danaan won but their leader Nuada of the Silver Hand was slain
by the Fomorii Balor of the Evil Eye. Balor was slain by Lugh
Lámhfada.

Mag Nuadat. See **Eoghan** 4.

Magog. A Biblical character who slips into the myths and is given three sons: Banbh, Iobath and Fathnachta, who became the ancestor of Partholón, Nemed and, surprisingly, Attila the Hun.

Maine. There are several persons who bear this name in the sagas and stories, mostly minor characters. Among the more prominent are:

1. A Norse prince who, according to one version of the tragic tale of Deirdre and the sons of Usna, was the man who killed the sons of Usna because Naoise had killed his father and brothers. This role is more popularly given to Eoghan Mac Durthacht of the Red Branch. See **Eoghan** 3.

2. The seven sons of Ailill and Medb were all called Maine. They were: Maine Mathramail (the Motherlike), Maine Athramail (the Fatherlike), Maine Mórgor (the Strongly Dutiful), Maine Míngor (the Sweetly Dutiful), Maine Mo Epirt (Above Description, also known as Maine Mílscothach, of the Honeyed Tongue), Maine Andoe (the Swift) and Maine Gaib Uile (of All the Qualities). They were all outlawed and joined Ingcél Cáech, the one-eyed son (or grandson) of the king of Britain, who raided Ireland and took part in the raid on Da Derga's Hostel in which the High King, Conaire Mór, was killed. They all responded to their mother's call to join her army in its attack on Ulster during the war of the *Táin*.

Man, Isle of. See **Mannin**.

Manannán Mac Lir. The son of Lir. The major sea-god. He is cognate with the Welsh sea-god Manawyddan, son of Llyr. He ruled from Emain Ablach (Emain of the Apple Trees) in Tír Tairnigiri (the Land of Promise). He was a shape-changer and could drive his chariot over the waves as if they were a plain. His wife was Fand, the Pearl of Beauty. His appearance is always as a noble and handsome warrior. Although he sired children among the gods, such as his son Gaiar, whose affair with Bécuma caused Bécuma's expulsion from the Land of Promise, Manannán also sired human children and he is the father of Mongán.

There are two accounts how this came about. First, he appeared to the queen of the Dál nAraidi of Ulster while her husband was away at war and foretold her husband's death unless the queen would permit him to sleep with her. Second, he appeared to the king, Fachtna, while he was being worsted in battle and said he would help turn the tide of the affray if he could go, disguised as Fachtna, and sleep with his wife. To this Fachtna agreed. The outcome of both versions is the birth of Mongán whom Manannán took to Tír Tairnigiri for fosterage, returning him when he reached the age of choice. Mongán became king and a great warrior. The second version of the tale is remarkably similar to the conception of Arthur in the Brythonic Celtic myth.

Manannán appears more frequently than most gods, creating storms to wreck Milesian ships, appearing to Bran at the start of his epic voyage or conducting Cormac Mac Art around Tír Tairnigiri. When the Dagda resigned the leadership of the gods, Manannán refused to accept the succession of the Bodb Dearg. However, unlike Midir who fought with the Bodb Dearg, Manannán left the gods and retreated into seclusion.

Mannin. The Isle of Man. In Manx, Ellan Vannin, and in Irish, Inish Manannán. The island is mentioned several times in the sagas and stories but little is known of it before the fourth century AD. It was originally thought to be a Brythonic Celtic-speaking kingdom but in about the fourth century Goidelic-, or Gaelic-, speaking Celts arrived from Ireland and began to settle. Several Ogham inscriptions survive on the island. According to *Cormac's Glossary*, Senchán Torpéist, the chief bard of Ireland (d. AD647) visited the island and found a high degree of literary knowledge there, including a knowledge of the Irish epics.

The last independent king of the island died in 1266 and it was ceded to Alexander III of Scotland. The English kings wanted the island and thus began a series of conflicts and occupations while the Manx continued to govern their own affairs through their ancient parliament known as Tynwald (Thing-völlr). The ruling house was the House of Keys (from Manx *kiares-es-feed* – twenty-four, the number of elected members). In 1346 the English finally landed an army, drove out the Scots and established a permanent rule. Henry VII instituted a 'Lordship of Man'. In 1736 this lordship was inherited by the Duke of Atholl who sold it to the English Government to pay his debts. In May 1866 the island was given self-government with the House of Keys reconstituted as a democratic parliament. The status of the island is that of a British Crown Dependency which is not part of the United Kingdom.

Manx. The Gaelic language of the Isle of Man, closely akin to Irish and descending from a common root. Manx seems to have become a distinct language from Irish and Scottish Gaelic in about the fourteenth century. As an independent literary language, it does not appear to have taken written form until the early seventeenth century. The sagas and myths were kept alive by oral tradition on the island. In the seventeenth century, however, antiquarians began to copy them down. A fisherman recited some of the Ossianic Cycle to the scholar Heywood in 1789 and his manuscript version of this is retained by the British Museum. In spite of receiving self-government in 1866, the island adopted an English education policy, which added to the decline of the language. By 1901 only 8.1 per cent of the islanders spoke Manx. The last census (1971) showed only 284 people able to speak Manx on the island, although there is a strong revivalist movement. See **Celt**.

Maol. Sometimes Mael. Bald.

1. A druid of Conn of the Hundred Battles.

2. A druid of Laoghaire who, with his brother Calpait, taught Laoghaire's daughters Ethné and Fedelma. The reference to Maol 2 is important in that it gives proof that druids wore a tonsure called *airbacc Giunnae*, which was cut from ear to ear and was similar to the one which later Celtic Christian monks adopted, as opposed to the Roman tonsure which was cut on the crown of the head. The matter of cutting the tonsure was one of the points of contention between the Celtic and Roman Churches.

Maon. See **Móen**.

Marbán. A swineherd who became the chief poet of Ireland having contested with Dael Duiled, the *ollamh* of Leinster. Both men were set riddles to solve. Such contests often occur in the sagas and heroes frequently saved their lives by posing a riddle which their judges were unable to answer.

Marcán. An old chieftain of Connacht and husband of the beautiful Cred, the would-be lover of Cano.

Mathgen. A druid of the Dé Danaan.

May Day. See **Beltaine**.

Meabal. See **Breg**.

Meargach. Of the Green Spears. Husband of Áille, killed by Oscar at the battle of Cnoc-an-Áire. See **Áille**.

Mechi. Son of the Mórrígán, goddess of battles. He was slain by Mac Cécht, son of Ogma, because it was prophesied he would bring disaster to Ireland. He had three hearts in which grew three serpents which, when full-grown, would break out and devastate the land.

Medb. Anglicised as Maeve. It has been contended that Medb was another triune goddess, a goddess representing sovranty, but only two Medbs appear as distinct personages in the myths, the traditions of each being somewhat confused with the other.

1. Queen of Connacht and wife of Ailill. She was daughter of a High King and seems to have married Conchobhar Mac Nessa, Tiride Mac Connra Cas, Eochaidh Dála and finally Ailill Mac Máta, each of whom is significantly named as king of Connacht, although, of course, Conchobhar Mac Nessa was king of Ulster. The point being made by some writers is that Medb represented the sovranty of Connacht and no king was legitimate unless symbolically wed to her. It is recorded that she 'never was without one man in the shadow of another'.

She figures in the famous epic of the *Táin Bó Cuailgne* (The Cattle Raid of Cuailgne) which started when she found her possessions were not as extensive as her husband Ailill's. The White Horned Bull of Connacht had been born into her herd but had betaken itself to Ailill's herd as it thought it not seemly to be in the herd of a woman. Medb heard about the fabulous Brown Bull of Cuailgne and, after attempts to secure it, she persuaded Ailill to help her lead an army into Ulster to obtain it. She also features in several other tales of the Ulster, or Red Branch Cycle. Her affairs were numerous. Finally she was killed by Forbaí, son of Conchobhar Mac Nessa, king of Ulster, while bathing in a lake. Her most famous sons were the seven Maines.

2. Medb Lethderg, of the Red Side. She is daughter of Conán of Cuala, and queen of Leinster. Again she appears as a goddess of sovranty to whom it is necessary for a king to be ritually married in order to reign legitimately. It is recorded that she was wife to nine High Kings, including the father of Conn of the Hundred Battles, Conn himself, Conn's son Art and Art's son Cormac.

Medicine. Much is made of the skills of the ancient Irish physicians and, indeed, in early times the doctors of Ireland were highly regarded. During the Dark Ages the Irish medical schools were famous throughout Europe. The premier medical school of Europe was that founded in the fifth century AD at Tuaim Brecain (Tomregan, Co. Cavan) where the eminent physician Bracan Mac Findloga established his practice. The Brehon Laws of Ireland are very explicit on the rights of the sick and the obligations of doctors. Macha Mong Ruadh is said to have established the first hospital in Ireland in 377BC.

From the medieval medical tracts we can see that skills and knowledge were highly advanced. The oldest medical text surviving in Ireland is a manuscript dated 1352 in the Royal Irish Academy but it is obviously a copy of an older text. Some older texts are kept in the British Museum. The majority of surviving medical texts are from the fourteenth and sixteenth centuries, such as the books of the O'Hickeys, O'Lees, O'Shiels and the 1512 *Book of Mac Anlega* (Son of the Doctor). In the myths and sagas, physicians are skilled with herbs as well as having surgical ability: they perform Caesarean operations, amputations and even brain surgery.

Meilge. A High King whose warriors slew Aige when in the form of a deer. Her brother Fafne composed a satire about Meilge and the truth caused a blemish in the form of three blotches on his face. For this Fafne was put to death.

Mend. King of Inis Fer Falga. Father of Bláthnat.

Meng. See **Breg**.

Merban. A champion of Partholón.

Mermaids/Mermen. As in many other cultures mermaids and mermen (*muirgen*, sea-child) were fairly common in the sagas and tales. They appear as sea-dwelling females and males, half-human and half-fish. Most of the mermen were not as attractive as their female counterparts, having pig's eyes and red noses to go with their green hair. As well as being sea-dwellers they are also found in the lochs and are both benevolent and malevolent. Muiris Ó Conchúir, chief of the Munster pipers, is recorded as leaving his home to live beneath the waves with a mermaid, while St. Patrick is supposed to have turned some women into mermaids because they would not be converted to Christianity.

Mess Buachalla. The cowherd's foster child. She was the daughter of Étain Óig and Cormac, king of Ulster. Cormac ordered the infant child to be destroyed because he wanted a son. The two men who undertook this task were captivated by the baby's smile and so they left the child in the barn of the cowherd of the High King Eterscél. It had been prophesied to Eterscél that a woman of an unknown race would bear his son who would be famous. When the High King heard of the wondrous beauty of his cowherd's foster child and learnt how she was found, no one knowing from whence she came, he decided that she was the woman of the prophecy and arranged to marry her. However, on the evening before the wedding, Mess Buachalla was visited by Nemglan, the bird-god, and they slept together. From their union was born Conaire Mór although Mess Buachalla, now married to Eterscél, brought the child up as the son of the High King.

Miach. Son of Dian Cécht, the god of medicine. He proved a better physician than his father by replacing Nuada's silver hand (given by his father) with one of flesh and blood. One of his accomplishments was an eye transplant, giving a human the eye of a cat. Dian Cécht grew jealous at his accomplishments and murdered him. Herbs grew from Miach's grave which could cure all ills and also give a person eternal life. These were gathered by Miach's sister, Airmid, who laid them out on a cloak in the order of their curative values. Dian Cécht, however, shook the cloak and so jumbled them that their secrets vanished for ever.

Mide. Eponym of Meath, the Middle Province. In the days of the Ulster Cycle, Ireland consisted of only four kingdoms or provinces – Connacht, Leinster, Munster and Ulster. But already the word for a province had become *cóiceda*, a fifth (modern Irish, *cúiga*). The fifth province was Mide, established in the reign of the High King Tuathal Teachtmhair (the Acceptable), AD130–160. He established the province as the territory for the High Kings, in order that they might be independent from the politics of the four provinces. The name, and territory, survives in Co. Meath and Co. Westmeath, and hence the term 'Royal Meath'. See **Provinces** and **Tuathal Teachtmhair**.

Midir the Proud. Son of the Dagda and a powerful god of the Dé Danaan. He was always splendidly dressed and his features were beautiful. He was chosen as the foster father of Aonghus Óg, the love-god. His palace was the *sídhe* of Bri Leith, Slieve Callory, west of Ardagh, Co. Longford. His first wife was Fuamnach. But he fell in love with Étain Echraidhe and married her. Fuamnach, in jealousy, turned Étain into a pool, a worm and finally a fly to keep her separated from Midir. Midir and Aonghus searched for Étain but, in the form of a fly, she was swallowed by the wife of Etar, an Ulster warrior, and was reborn in human guise. She grew up to marry the High King, Eochaidh Airemh. Midir found her and stole her away. Eochaidh led an attack on Bri Leith and finally Midir released the human Étain to the High King.

When the Dagda resigned the leadership of the gods, Midir refused to accept the choice of Bodb Dearg as the new leader. He made a war on Bodb Dearg and in this 'civil war' among the Dé Danaan he was aided by Fionn Mac Cumhail and the Fianna. The war seems to be inconclusive, although it meant the end of the power of the gods. They retreated further into their underground palaces and eventually, in popular folklore, became fairies in the minds of the people.

Milesians. The term is applied to the last group of invaders of Ireland before the historical period. Medieval mythographers saw in them the ancestors of the Goidelic Celtic inhabitants of the country. See **Milesius**.

Milesius. Sometimes given as Míl. In Irish his name is given as Golamh, a warrior, but he has become popular under the Latin form Milesius, signifying a soldier. The name is also given as Míle Easpain, a soldier of Spain. It was his children who led the Milesians in their conquest of Ireland. Milesius' ancestry goes back through twenty-two Irish names and thirteen Hebrew names to Adam. He is described as a Scythian of Spain who took service with King Reafloir of Scythia and married his daughter Seang. After Seang died, Reafloir grew fearful of Milesius and plotted to kill him. Discovering the plot, Milesius fled to Egypt with his sons, Donn and Airioch Feabhruadh, and his followers, and took service with the Pharaoh Nectanebus. He was successful in conducting a war against the Ethiopians for the Pharaoh. There were, in fact, two Pharaohs of the Thirtieth Dynasty named Nectanebus but their dates are 380–363BC and 360–343BC. Milesius married Scota (see **Scota** 2), the daughter of the Pharaoh, and two sons Eber and Amairgen were born in Egypt. A third son Ir was born on the island of Irena near Thrace after Milesius and his followers quit Egypt. A fourth son Colpa was born on the island of Gotia. Milesius eventually returned to Spain. Here he learnt of the death of Ith, given as his nephew, slain by the three sons of Ogma (Mac Cécht, Mac Cuill and Mac Gréine), and decided to take revenge by conquering Ireland. He did not reach Ireland although his wife, Scota, did so. She was killed fighting the Dé Danaan and was buried in Kerry. It was his sons who carried out the conquest.

Military organisations. Several élite military organisations appear in the myths, most famous being the Red Branch warriors of Ulster and the Fianna, the bodyguard of the High Kings. There are also the Degad of Munster and the Gamhanraide of Connacht. Ulster also has its famous Boy Corps as well as a Corps of Veterans, elderly warriors above military age.

Miodchaoin. Sometimes Mochaen. A fierce warrior who dwelt on Cnoc Miodchaoin (Miodchaoin's Hill) with his three sons, Aedh, Corca and Conn. Their task was to prevent any man raising his voice on the hill which was said to be located somewhere north of the land of Lochlann. It became one of the tasks of the children of Tuireann to go to the hill and raise three shouts on it to exonerate themselves from the guilt of Cian's death. It was their last task. They slew Miodchaoin and his sons and raised three shouts, thus fulfilling the reparation asked of them by Cian's son Lugh. However, in slaying Miodchaoin and his sons, they were all mortally wounded and returned to Ireland to die.

Móen. Sometimes given as Maon and Maen. The word signifies dumb. Móen later became known as Labraid Loinseach (the Mariner Who Speaks). He was the son of Ailill Áine, king of Leinster, who was poisoned by his uncle Cobhthach after Cobhthach had murdered Ailill's father Laoghaire Lorc, king of Leinster. Cobhthach compelled the boy to eat his father's heart and the boy was struck dumb in disgust, hence receiving his name. He was taken out of Ireland to save him from a worse fate at the hands of his evil great-uncle and resided in Britain and then Gaul. He regained his voice after being struck by a hurly stick in a game.

He came to the Gaulish kingdom of Fir Morc whose ruler was Scoriath. Scoriath had a beautiful daughter named Moriath but Moriath's mother guarded her daughter well, sleeping always with one eye open and on her daughter. Moriath, however, fell in love with Móen and it was she who taught Móen's harpist, Craiftine, a special piece of music which would send her father and mother to sleep. Craiftine played this music and, indeed, Scoriath and his wife fell asleep while Móen and Moriath met and made love.

On waking, Moriath's mother realised what had happened. However, both parents liked Móen and accepted him as the husband of their daughter. Further, Scoriath promised Móen an army of Gauls to accompany him back to Ireland to overthrow his evil great-uncle. Móen and his army set sail and, as they neared Ireland, they were seen. Fearful of the boy's return and not knowing that he had been cured of his dumbness, Cobhthach sent an envoy to ask if the leader of their army spoke. On being told he did, the envoy returned to tell Cobhthach that the leader was Labraid Loinseach (the Mariner Who Speaks).

Móen's army attacked and Craiftine played his sleep-music which sent Cobhthach's men to sleep while the Gauls stormed Dinn Rígh, the fortress of the king. There are two versions: first, Cobhthach surrendered and Móen became king of Leinster and made a peace with his great-uncle. Subsequently Cobhthach's treachery forced him to kill Cobhthach. Second, in the storming of Dinn Rígh

Cobhthach and thirty warriors were shut into a hall and burnt to death.

Móen himself was not without faults for in an addition to his story it is said that he had horse's ears and everyone who cut his hair was killed in order to keep this fact a secret lest the blemish preclude him from kingship. The mother of one barber pleaded for her son's life and Móen spared him on the oath that he would hold his tongue. The barber, unable to keep the secret, told a tree. The tree was cut down and made into a harp for Craiftine and, on being played, the harp revealed Móen's secret. We are reminded of the Brythonic Celtic myth about King Mark of Cornwall, husband of the ill-fated Iseult, who had horse's ears and thus earned his name M'arch. See **Craiftine**.

Moling. 1. 'The Swift'. A foster brother of Fionn Mac Cumhail.

2. A Christian saint whose real name was Tairchell, who encountered a demon but escaped by taking three giant strides.

Mongán. The son of Manannán Mac Lir, the sea-god, by the queen of the Dál nAraidi. He was born in circumstances which resemble the conception of Arthur of Britain. Manannán Mac Lir was attracted by the beauty of the queen of the Dál nAraidi, the wife of Fiachna the Fair. There are two versions of the tale: see **Manannán Mac Lir**. When Mongán was three nights old, Manannán came again and took the boy back to Tír Tairnigiri (the Land of Promise) where Manannán raised him until he reached the age of choice.

There is yet another version: that he was a reincarnation of Fionn Mac Cumhail. Fionn's foster brother Caoilte appeared from the Otherworld to announce this fact at the fortress of Moylinny.

There was an historical personage, Mongán, who ruled Ulster and whose death is recorded in AD625. History and myth become one here.

Mongán married the beautiful Dubh Lacha, who had been born on the same night as himself. One day Mongán, in a burst of emotional friendship for Brandubh, king of Leinster, promised him anything he desired which it was within Mongán's power to give him. Brandubh had secretly desired Dubh Lacha and seized the chance to demand her. It was, of course, dishonourable to refuse. Dubh Lacha had to go to Brandubh's palace. However, Mongán possessed supernatural gifts from his sea-god father, including that of shape-changing. He called at Brandubh's palace in the guise of a monk named Tilbraide, and slept with his wife under Brandubh's roof.

Eventually he tricked Brandubh by turning up in the shape of the son of a king of Connacht, accompanied by an old hag named Cuimne whom he had turned into the beautiful daughter of a king of Munster. To Cuimne also he had given a love charm so that Brandubh became enamoured of her. He then offered Brandubh an exchange of Cuimne for Dubh Lacha. Eagerly, Brandubh agreed. Mongán and Dubh Lacha departed from Brandubh's palace and after they were gone Cuimne returned to her normal, ugly shape.

Mongfhinn. Sometimes Mongfind. Daughter of Fidach of Munster and wife of the High King Eochaidh Muigmedon (said to have reigned from AD358 to 366). She became the hostile and bitter stepmother to Niall of the Nine Hostages and made several attempts to kill the boy. Finally she died by accidentally taking poison which she had prepared for him. The deed was said to have been committed on Samhain Eve and, in later tradition, this was known as the Festival of the Mongfhinn when her evil spirit stalked the countryside in search of children's souls. In Munster women particularly used to address prayers to her to ward off her evil presence.

Moonremur. See **Muinremur.**

Morann. Chief judge and druid of Ulster during the Red Branch Cycle. He was born with a caul on his head and his father, judging him to be a monster, gave an order for him to be drowned in the sea. Two servants went to perform the task and, as he was dropped into the waves, a surge broke the helmet and the baby immediately spoke. The servants then rescued the boy and left him at the door of a smith. The smith raised him and eventually returned him to his father. Morann's most famous judgement was on who should foster Cúchulainn. The matter was referred to him by Conchobhar Mac Nessa when the king's advisers quarrelled amongst themselves. Morann decreed that Sencha should teach Cúchulainn to speak, Fergus Mac Roth should play with him and Amairgen should instruct him on all other matters.

Morca. Son of Dela and a king of the Fomorii. When the Nemedians defeated and killed Conann on Tory Island, Morca arrived with sixty warships and defeated the Nemedians, annihilating them except for thirty survivors who fled from Ireland.

Morgan. King of the Land of Wonder, husband of the monstrous warrior woman, Coinchend, and father of the beautiful Delbchaem. He was slain by Art at the end of his voyage in search of Delbchaem. See **Art** and **Delbchaem.**

Moriath. Daughter of Scoriath, king of the Fir Morca of Gaul. She became lover and then wife of Móen. Her mother's two eyes never slept at once: one was always watching the girl so that she would know no man. Moriath told Craiftine how to play special music which would put her mother and father to sleep so that she could meet Móen. In one version of the story, she also composed a special song for Craiftine to play which would restore Móen's speech. See **Móen.**

Mór Muman. Daughter of Aedh Bennan. Although Aedh was an historical king of Munster, Mór Muman is presented as a manifestation of a sun goddess.

Mórrígán. Sometimes Mórrígú. The major goddess of war, of death and slaughter. The name seems to signify 'great queen' and she appears as another of the typically Celtic triune goddesses. She seems interchangeable with Macha, Badb and Nemain. Her favourite shape was that of a crow or raven. She embodied all that was perverse and horrible among the supernatural powers. She helped the Dé Danaan at the battles of Magh Tuireadh. Having first tried to incite Cúchulainn to make love to her, she fought with him and he managed to wound her. For this his fate was sealed. When he was eventually killed she settled on his shoulder in triumph in the form of a crow and watched while a beaver drank his blood. She also appeared to Conaire Mór before his death at Da Derga's Hostel. The famous whirlpool, Corryveckan, between the northern end of Jura and the Isle of Scarba in the Inner Hebrides (Coire-Bhrecain, the cauldron of Brecan), was referred to as the Mórrígán's Cauldron in some tales.

Mountains. According to the sagas there are twelve chief mountains of Ireland. These are: Sliabh-liag (mountain of flagstones), Slieve League, Co. Donegal; Sliabh Bladhma (mountain of the hero Bladh), Slievebloom; Sliabh Denna Ulaidh; Bri-ruadh (the red hill); Blai-Slaibh: Sliabh Snechta (mountain of snow); Sliabh-Mis (mountain of Mis), Sleemish, Co. Antrim; Mughdhorna (the Mourne mountains); Nephon; Sliabh Maccu Belgodon; Sliabh Segais (Curlieu) and Cruachan Aigle (Croagh Phádraig).

Moytura. See **Magh Tuireadh.**

Mug Eime. The first lapdog to be introduced into Ireland from Britain in spite of the laws forbidding the export of small dogs to Ireland.

Mughain. 1. A matriarchal queen of Munster also referred to as Mór.

2. She bore a child by her own father. The old text says: 'This Mughain was his mother, he to her was brother.'

3. Wife of the High King Diarmuid. She had an affair with Flann

Mac Dima and when Diarmuid had him slain it began a chain of events which resulted in Diarmuid's own death in a like manner according to prophecy. See **Diarmuid** 2.

4. Mughain Attenchaithrech, daughter of Eochaidh Feidlech, and wife to Conchobhar Mac Nessa, king of Ulster. When Cúchulainn returned to Emain Macha still in a battle fever she stripped naked with her handmaidens to shame him and stifle the fever.

Mug's Half. The southern half of Ireland. See **Provinces** and **Eoghan** 4.

Mug Nuadat. See **Eoghan** 4.

Muinremuir. Sometimes Anglicised as Moonremur. Son of Ferrgend. He is described as one of the three greatest heroes of Ulster. He features particularly in the feasting of 'Mac Da Thó's Boar'. In 'Bricriu's Feast' he was the first to step forward and accept the challenge when a churl appeared and invited the warriors to cut off his head if, on the next day, he could return the stroke. Muinremuir cut off the man's head, whereupon the churl picked it up and walked out, leaving the company horrified. The next night Muinremuir failed to appear when the churl arrived to demand his return stroke.

Muirdris. Also called Sineach, a water monster killed by Fergus Mac Léide. 'Sineach' implies a mammal – 'having teats or paps'.

Muirenn. The nurse of the hero Cael who composed a poem for him praising the possessions of the beautiful Credhe, on the strength of which Credhe married him.

Muirthemne, Plain of. Part of Co. Louth between Dundalk and the Boyne which, although mentioned in other tales, is associated mainly with the hero Cúchulainn, who lived there in his fortress of Dún Dealgan (Dundalk). Lady Gregory's re-telling of the Cúchulainn saga was entitled *Cuchulain of Muirthemne* (John Murray, 1902).

Mumhan. See **Munster**.

Muncnican. One of Partholón's champions.

Munster. A province. The Anglicised name is derived from the Irish Mumhan with the addition of the Norse *ster*. Early forms are given as Mumu and Muma. It stands apart from the other provinces of Ireland and current academic opinion is that the Munster kings did not recognise the High Kingship of Ireland at Tara until as late as the ninth century AD. It is thought that Munster itself was divided into five provinces at one time: certainly there is evidence that there were two Munster provinces. There are several aspects which single Munster out from the other provinces. It is associated with the dead:

Tech Duinn, the gathering place of the dead, lies just off its coast. And it is not without significance that the ruling house of Munster was called 'The House of Donn'. The province is associated with more female gods than any other place. It appears in the ancient stories as a primeval world, a place of origin. It is the place where several of the mythical invaders landed. The chieftains and kings of Munster did not trace their ancestry back to the sons of Milesius, as did the chieftains of the other provinces, but to Lugaid, the son of Ith. In Munster the occult powers are supreme. In one text the famous king of Munster Cú Roí is referred to as 'King of the World'.

Murias. One of the four great cities of the Dé Danaan (Falias, Gorias, Finias and Murias). It was from Murias that the magic cauldron of the Dagda, a gift from Lugh, was taken.

Murna of the White Neck. She was a descendant of Nuada and Ethlinn, the daughter of Balor of the Evil Eye. Cumal son of Trenmor, chief of the Clan Mascna and leader of the Fianna of Ireland, fell in love with her. Her father, Tadhg, a druid, refused to allow them to marry so Cumal eloped with Murna. In revenge, her father incited Goll Mac Morna to kill Cumal, which he did, assuming the leadership of the Fianna. Murna fled into the forests around Sliabh Bladh (Slievebloom) and there she bore Cumal's son named Demna. The boy grew up and was called 'The Fair One' – Fionn Mac Cumhail. He went on to revenge his father and become the greatest leader of the Fianna. Murna eventually married a chieftain in Kerry.

Murtagh Mac Erc. High King of Ireland (AD512–33) whose brother Fergus became king of the Dál Riada of Alba. He asked Murtagh to send him the Lia Fáil (Stone of Destiny) so that he could be crowned on it. Murtagh sent it but his brother refused to send it back. See **Lia Fáil**.

Music. Heroes and heroines had to be accomplished in the arts, particularly in music. Various instruments – harps, stringed instruments, bagpipes, and timpani – are mentioned by name. The earliest surviving example of Irish musical notation and composition is contained in an eleventh-century manuscript. Early music would seem to consist of short airs divided into two strains or parts, and it showed a great preoccupation with harmony. Irish musicians were celebrated from earliest times.

N. *Nin* (ash) in the Ogham alphabet.

Naas. Said to be a wife of Lugh Lámhfada who died and was buried at the site of a town which bears her name, Naas, Co. Kildare. The town was the chief residence of the kings of Leinster until as late as AD908 when Cearbhall was slain there by the Norse.

Náir. Modesty. A goddess who consorted with the High King Crebhán and took him to the Otherworld where he obtained fabulous treasures.

Naisii. See **Naoise.**

Naked warriors. References to warriors stripping naked to do battle or to engage in single combat indicate a religious significance in the ancient Celtic world. Polybius recounts how a tribe, which he designated the Gaesatae, went naked into battle, throwing themselves in fury at the Romans at the Battle of Telamon in 225BC. Polybius did not realise that the name, which he thought was just a tribal one, was the word for 'spearmen'. *Gae* for a javelin or spear occurs in Old Irish, and Cúchulainn's spear was, of course, the Gae-Bolg. The Gaesatae were probably a group of warriors akin to the Fianna.

Naoise. Sometimes Noisiu, also given as Noise. The eldest of the three sons of Usna and his wife Elbha, daughter of Cathbad the druid. With his two brothers, Ainlé and Ardan, he was a champion of the Red Branch. While in the service of Conchobhar Mac Nessa he met Deirdre, who was due to wed the Ulster king. They fell in love and resolved to run away together. Naoise took Deirdre and his brothers and they fled to Alba, taking service with the king of the Tuatha Cruithne (the Picts). After some years it seemed that Conchobhar had mellowed for he sent Fergus Mac Roth as his emissary to invite Naoise, Deirdre and Naoise's brothers to return to Ulster. Although Deirdre foresaw disaster, Naoise decided to return with Fergus Mac Roth.

Fergus was tricked into allowing the party to go on to Emain Macha, the capital, under the protection of his two sons, Buinne and Iollan. Conchobhar asked Deirdre's old nurse, Lebharcham, if Deirdre was as beautiful as ever. The nurse, realising what Conchobhar had in mind, said that she was withered. However, Conchobhar sent a spy, Trendom in one version and Gelban in another, and ascertained that Deirdre was still as beautiful as ever. Naoise saw the spy peering through the window of the Red Branch Hostel where they were staying as he played *fidchell* with Deirdre. He threw a *fidchell* piece and struck out the eye of the spy.

Conchobhar then attacked the Red Branch Hostel. At his request Cathbad the druid cast a spell creating a green slime which bogged the brothers and Fergus's sons down, making their fighting difficult. Then Fergus's son Buinne was persuaded to stop fighting by a bribe. Iollan continued and he was killed as were Ainlé and Ardan, Naoise's brothers. Finally Eoghan Mac Durthacht seized the magic sword of Manannán Mac Lir, which the sea-god had given to Naoise during one adventure, and slew him. (Another version gives Maine, a Norse prince, as killing Naoise.) Conchobhar was then able to take Deirdre by force. See **Conchobhar Mac Nessa** and **Deirdre**. From Naoise's grave grew a pine tree. When Deirdre was buried on the opposite side of the lake to Naoise, a similar pine tree grew from her grave. The branches twisted and entwined across the water.

Nár Thúathcaech. The name signifies 'shame'. He was the swineherd of the Bodb Dearg. 'He has never attended a feast where he does not shed blood,' comments a warrior during 'The Destruction of Da Derga's Hostel'. He was a rival of the swineherd of Ochall Ochne of Connacht. They fought together through many reincarnations until Nár was reborn as Donn, the Brown Bull of Cuailgne. See **Donn 6**, **Finnbhenach** and **Friuch**.

Natchrantal. A Connacht champion in Medb's army. While Cúchulainn was engaged in single combat, Natchrantal took a third of his army and made a swift raid into Ulster, penetrating as far as Dunseverick on the northern coast. He found the Brown Bull of Cuailgne in the great glen of Antrim and drove it and its herd back to the Connacht army in triumph. See **Buic**, to whom this adventure falls in another version.

Nath Í. See **Dathi**.

Navan. See **Emain Macha**.

Neamhuain, Clan. Fionn Mac Cumhail's trackers. They tracked down Diarmuid and Gráinne to a hut which had a fence around it with seven doors. However, Diarmuid managed to extricate himself for Fionn's siege.

Nechtan. An early water-god and husband of Boann. Sídhe Nectain, or Nectan's Hill (Hill of Carbery, Co. Kildare) held a sacred well, the secret Well of Segais which was the source of knowledge. See **Nuts of Knowledge**. Only four persons were privileged to go there, Nechtan and his three cup-bearers. Boann disobeyed this taboo and went to the well which rose and chased her, thus forming the river Boyne named after her. See **Boann**.

Nechtan Scéne. The mother of three supernatural sons – Foill, Fannell and Tuachell. In Cúchulainn's first battle foray he came to their fortress. He was told that they had boasted 'that more of the men of Ulster have fallen by their hands than are yet living on the earth'. He challenged them to single combat and slew first Foill, then Fannell and then Tuachell. While Nechtan Scéne set up a lament, he cut their heads off and tied them to his chariot before returning to Emain Macha.

Nectanebus. Pharaoh of Egypt who emerges in Irish myth by virtue of the fact that his daughter Scota married Milesius and was killed fighting the Dé Danaan in Co. Kerry. She is not to be confused with Scota, the daughter of the Pharaoh Cingris and mother of Goidel, the progenitor of the Gaels. It is interesting that there were two Pharaohs named Nectanebus in the Thirtieth Dynasty; the first ruled from 380 to 363BC and the second from 360 to 343BC. The name, in the form of Nechtan, was apparently popular in Ireland and several historical personages bore it.

Neide. A Red Branch poet. He was the son of Adna, chief Ollamh and poet of Ireland in the days of Conchobhar Mac Nessa. Having learnt all he could from his father, Neide went to Alba to study under Eochaidh Ech-bel (Horse Mouth). One day he went down to the sea for 'poets believe that the place where poetry was always revealed to them was at the edge of the water'. He composed a lament to the rhythm of the waves and wondered why this mood was upon him; a wave answered and told him that his father, Adna, was dead. Neide returned to Ireland to claim the *tugen* or mantle in succession to his father. He had to fight a contest with Fer Cherdne who also claimed the honour of being chief poet. This story is featured in 'The Dialogue of the Sages', which has survived in three different manuscripts, the principal being in the *Book of Ballymote*, composed in 1391 from earlier texts.

Neimed. See **Nemed**. Old Irish for a 'sanctuary' or 'sacred grove'. In view of the closeness to the names Nemed and Nemain it is worth pointing out that a war goddess named Nemetona was worshipped as the goddess of the sacred grove at Aquae Sulis (Bath, in England) during the Romano-Celtic period. The name is found in Celtic place names in many spots: Nemetacum (north-east Gaul), Nemetobrigia (Galicia, Spain), Nemetodurum (Nanterre), Nemeton (Vaucluse), Vernemeton (Nottingham), Medionemeton (on the Antonine Wall, Scotland) and so on. Drunemeton was the chief settlement of the Galatian Celts near Ankara in Turkey.

Néit. Sometimes **Net**. A god of war. His wife appears as Nemain, who seems part of the triune goddess Mórrígán. See **Nemain**. Néit occurs in some manuscripts as the father of Mac Cécht, Mac Cuill and Mac Gréine, instead of Ogma. He is said to have been slain in the second Battle of Magh Tuireadh after which his sons divided Ireland between them. As it was Nuada's death which caused this division, and as Nemain is sometimes confused with Nuada's wife Macha, it may well be that Néit is merely a synonym for Nuada himself.

Nem. One of the three doorkeepers of the palace of Conchobhar Mac Nessa. The others were Dall and Dorcha.

Nemain. A war goddess and wife of Néit. She is listed as one of five goddesses who hover over battlefields inspiring battle madness: Fea (Hateful), Badb (Fury), Nemain (Venomous), Macha (Personification of Battle) and the Mórrígán (Great Queen or supreme war goddess). Nemain is sometimes referred to as Nuada's wife, as is Macha, and it may be that she and Macha are one entity or part of the triune goddess Mórrígán. Néit himself is often confused with Nuada. See **Néit**.

Nemanach. The radiant one. A son of Aonghus Óg, thought to be cognate with Nemglan.

Nemed. A descendant of Magog and Japhet who sailed to Ireland from Scythia with thirty-two ships. They spent a year and a half on the sea and most of his people perished from hunger, except for Nemed and four women. After they landed in Ireland, their numbers increased again and Nemed was able to defeat the Fomorii three times in battle and clear sixteen plains. He finally died on the Great Island in Cork Harbour.

Nemedians. The followers of Nemed. After Nemed's death, the

Nemedians, groaning under the rule of the Fomorii, rose up and attacked the Fomorii stronghold on Tory Island. Fergus, the new Nemedian ruler, killed the Fomorii king Conann. But Morca Mac Dela arrived with a new Fomorii battle host and slaughtered 16,000 Nemedians leaving only thirty alive and these left Ireland in despair, searching for a new land. It is said that half went to the 'northern world' while half went to 'Greece'.

Nemglan. A bird god (perhaps the same as Nemanach) who appeared to Mess Buachalla and made love to her. The son of this union was Conaire Mór. When the High King Nuada Necht died a flock of birds descended over Conaire Mór's chariot. They had such marvellous plumage that Conaire Mór took out a sling but they immediately turned into armed warriors. One, more handsome than the rest, came forward and introduced himself as his father Nemglan. Nemglan laid a *geis* on Conaire Mór, telling him to walk naked along the road to Tara with only a stone and his sling. If he did so, and presented himself to Tara, he would be High King. Conaire Mór obeyed and the prophecy was fulfilled.

Nera. A servant of Ailill of Connacht. One Samhain Ailill offered a prize of a gold-hilted sword to whoever would go to the gallows outside Ráth Cruachan on which two captives had been executed the previous day and encircle the foot of one with a *withe* or band of willow twigs. It being Samhain, it was a time when the Otherworld became visible to mortal men and the spirits set out to wreak vengeance on the living. Several of Ailill's warriors set out but all returned frightened. Nera accepted the challenge.

As he was placing the band on the foot of the dead man, the corpse spoke, asking Nera to take him down and carry him to the nearest house for he needed a drink. Nera obeyed. The first house was encircled by a lake of fire and so they went on; the second house was encircled by a lake of water and so they moved on again; at the third house the corpse was given three cups of water. He drank two of them and spat out the third at the people who had offered him hospitality, whereupon they died. The corpse then instructed Nera to carry him back to the gallows.

Returning to Ráth Cruachan, Ailill and Medb's palace, Nera saw it in flames; the heads of Ailill and his warriors had been cut off and were being taken away by Otherworld dwellers. Nera followed them to the Cave of Cruachan, one of the famous entrances to the Otherworld, and plunged through.

He was in the *sídhe* of the Otherworld people and was ordered to serve the king of the *sídhe* by bringing firewood. He was lodged with a woman of the *sídhe* and they became lovers and had a child. The woman then told Nera that what he had seen at Ráth Cruachan was only a vision but it would come to pass unless he went back to Ailill and warned him to destroy the *sídhe*. Nera took the woman and their child and escaped back to Ailill. Ailill sent Fergus Mac Roth to destroy the *sídhe* and the warriors of Connacht took a great plunder from it, including the Crown of Bríon, one of the three wonders of Ireland. The tale seems clearly pre-Christian in origin but *Eachtra Nerai* is said to be dated back to an eighth-century text.

Nerbha. The wife of Partholón's son Er.

Nessa. Daughter of Eochaidh Sálbuidhe of Ulster. She married Fachtna, king of Ulster. According to one version she slept with Cathbad the druid and bore him a son who was called Conchobhar Mac Nessa. Her husband Fachtna died and his half-brother Fergus Mac Roth succeeded to the throne of Ulster. Fergus was in love with her but Nessa would only agree to become his wife if he would let her son Conchobhar rule as king in Ulster for a year. Nessa was a powerful and ambitious woman. Fergus gave up the kingship and during the year she instructed Conchobhar how to be an exceptional monarch. When the time arrived for Fergus to become king again, Conchobhar was thus able to refuse to surrender the kingship with the support of the people. Thus did Conchobhar become king of Ulster and Nessa, initially, the most powerful woman in the land. However, Nessa's power diminished as Conchobhar grew more secure in his kingship.

Nía. 1. The name for a warrior or champion.

2. A king of Connacht, half-brother of Cormac Mac Art and son of Étain (2) by Lugaid.

Nía, Plain of. The spot near Cong which was known as Magh Tuireadh. See **Magh Tuireadh**.

Nía Náir. See **Crimthann** 1.

Nía Natrebuin Chró. A hero of the Red Branch.

Niall Noíghiallach. Niall of the Nine Hostages. The youngest son of Eochaidh Muigl Mheadoin (see **Eochaidh** 12) said to have ruled as High King (AD358–66). Niall became High King from AD379 to 405 and was the progenitor of the Uí Néill dynasty. He is recorded as raiding Britain and Gaul during the time of Theodosius the Great and being forced to retreat by the Roman general Stilicho. While on a raid in Gaul he was assassinated on the shores of the Loire by one of his own Leinster chieftains after he had been distracted by some women. The story of Niall is a typical case in which myth and history are combined in the minds of the medievalists.

Niall was Eochaidh's youngest son; the others were Brían, Fiachra, Ailill and Fergus. His mother died in childbirth and his evil stepmother, Mongfhinn, sought ways to rid herself of the child, at one time abandoning him as a baby naked upon the hill of Tara. He was found by a wandering bard named Torna Éices and returned to the High King. Mongfhinn sent all five boys to Sithchenn the Smith, who was also a prophet, to see who would succeed as High King. He sent the five boys into the forge and set fire to it. The four eldest boys ran out carrying hammers, pails of beer, spearheads and dry sticks. Niall came out with the anvil. By this sign Sithchenn recognised that he would be High King.

Monghfinn attempted to poison Niall but took the poison herself by mistake and so died. See **Mongfhinn**.

There was another sign for Niall. The five boys were out hunting when they developed a thirst. They came across an old hag with grey hair, black skin and green teeth. She offered them water in return for a kiss. The three eldest boys refused but Fiachra pecked her cheek, whereupon she prophesied that he would reign briefly at Tara. When Niall kissed her properly, she demanded that he have intercourse with her. He did so and she turned into a beautiful woman named Flaithius (Royalty) who foretold that he would be the greatest High King of Ireland.

There is a further confusion of myth and history when some saga writers place Niall's son Fintan of Dún Dá Bend as a contemporary of Cúchulainn in the story of the intoxication of Ulster.

Niamh. 1. Daughter of Celtchair. Celtchair married her to Conganchas Mac Daire, the brother of Cú Roí, a warrior whom no one could slay. Celtchair asked her to learn the secret of his invulnerability. She did so and told her father so that he could kill Conganchas. See **Conganchas Mac Daire**. Niamh then married Cormac Cond Longes, son of Conchobhar Mac Nessa, king of Ulster.

2. Wife of Conall Cearnach. She tended Cúchulainn in his sickness and became his mistress during the last period of his life. She tried to prevent him from leaving the fortress until he was well but Badb, the daughter of the druid Calatin, whom Cúchulainn had slain, along with all the male children of Clan Calatin (see **Calatin**), took the

shape of Niamh's handmaiden and enticed her from the sickroom. Badb put a spell of straying on Niamh so that she was lost. Badb then returned to Cúchulainn in the form of Niamh and bade him rise and go out, putting into movement the events that would lead to his death.

3. Of the Golden Hair. A daughter of Manannán Mac Lir. She appeared to Oisín on the shores of Loch Lena and requested him to accompany her to Tír Tairnigiri (the Land of Promise) and live there as her lover. Oisin did so. After three weeks he found that three hundred years had passed. They had a daughter named Plur na mBan (Flower of Women).

Nibe. From the *sídhe* of Breg, considered one of the nine best pipers in the world.

Niul. The son of Feinius Farsaidh. He was so famous as a wise teacher that he was invited by the Pharaoh Cingris to settle in Egypt. He married Cingris' daughter Scota and their son was Goidel, the progenitor of the Gaels. It is said that Niul befriended Aaron and the Israelites during the period of the exodus from Israel and that Moses healed Niul's son Goidel from the bite of a serpent, it being foretold that no serpent could live in the land of the Gaels.

Noidhiu. Son of Fingel who had been kept guarded by her parents to prevent her becoming pregnant. However, one night a god mysteriously appeared and slept with her. After nine years and nine months she gave birth to Noidhiu. Fingel wanted the child put to death whereupon the baby uttered nine judgements and thus obtained the right to live. He was given the name Noidhiu Naoi mBreathach (Noidhiu of the Nine Judgements).

Noinden. The curse put on the men of Ulster by the woman Macha. See **Macha** 3. It is sometimes called 'The Birth Pangs of Ulster'.

Nuada. 1. The chief druid of Cahir Mór, a king and ancestor of Fionn Mac Cumhail who built the fortress on the Hill of Allen, which was covered with lime (*almu*, dative *Almain*) 'until it was all white' – the place taking its name from this. See **Allen, Hill of**.

2. Argetlámh. Nuada of the Silver Hand. He appears as the supreme leader of the gods with a sword from which none could escape. He was the first ruler of the Dé Danaan on their arrival in Ireland but lost his hand at the first Battle of Magh Tuireadh fighting against the Firbolg. He had to give up the kingship as a consequence. Dian Cécht made him a silver hand but Dian Cécht's son Miach made him a hand of flesh and blood with which he was able to regain the kingship. In

displacing Bres, the half-Fomorii, as ruler, Nuada set off the events
which led to the second Battle of Magh Tuireadh against the Fomorii.
In this battle Nuada, and his wife Macha, were slain by Balor of the
Evil Eye. Nuada is cognate with the Welsh Nudd of the Silver Hand.
The name also appears in the form of Llud and Nodons, surviving in
London's Ludgate.

3. Nuada Necht (the White). He was the king who directly preceded
Conaire Mór as High King at Tara and is given in the king lists as the
107th High King of Ireland.

Numbers. It should be noted that numerology plays a significant and
symbolic part in myth. Some numbers can be particularly noted.
Five is significant in that there are five great roads in Ireland, five
celebrated hostels, five paths of law, five prohibitions for provincial
king, five provinces; Fionn Mac Cumhail counts in fives, as do the
people of the *sidhe*; there are five masters of every great art; Cúchulainn has five wheels painted on his shield. The number nine can be
described as a sacred number, the counterpart of the seven of eastern
cultures. There are traces that the ancient Celts reckoned with a
nine-day week; Medb rides off to Ulster with nine chariots; Bricriu's
Hall has nine rooms; Cúchulainn has nine weapons; the curse on
Ulster is for nine times nine generations; there are the nine judgements of Noidhiu, and Niall of the Nine Hostages. Combinations of
nine also play an important part. Twelve is significant; kings usually
have twelve companions. Seventeen is mystic: seventeen kings accept
gifts at Cashel; several events are listed as taking place after periods of
seventeen days or seventeen years; there are said to be seventeen
petty kingdoms in Meath; a youth becomes a man at the age of
seventeen years; a druid suggests Mael Dúin takes seventeen men
with him on his voyage; and on the fabulous Island of Women they
are greeted by seventeen maidens. Lastly, the number thirty-three
crops up as another frequent symbol.

Nuts of Knowledge. They are described as rich crimson in colour and
are inevitably hazel nuts. Nine hazel trees of wisdom grew over
Segais' Well (sometimes Conlai's Well). The hazel nuts dropped into
the well causing bubbles of mystic inspiration. The location of the
well is variously described. One is at the source of the Boyne (see
Nechtan and **Boann**) and the other is at the source of the Shannon
(see **Sionan**). The most popular story is how the Well of Segais
chased the goddess Boann to form the river named after her, taking
the salmon Fintan with it. The salmon had eaten of the Nuts of

Knowledge and settled in a pool on the Boyne where the druid Finegas caught it and gave it to his pupil Fionn Mac Cumhail to cook. Fionn's thumb brushed against the salmon and he sucked at the spot where it was burnt, thus obtaining knowledge.

O. *Onn* (furze) in the Ogham alphabet.

Oak. The oak is mentioned as a tree sacred to the druids. Veneration of the oak was widespread among the British and Continental Celts but not so much among the Irish. The yew, hazel and rowan trees are more frequently referred to. Sacred trees were common. Each clan or confederation of clans had its sacred tree or *bile*. Not infrequently reference is made to a hostile clan invading a territory and felling a sacred tree as a dramatic gesture which would shame and demoralise their enemies for many of these trees were considered as the *crann bethadh*, 'tree of life'. Oaks are mentioned in an early Christian context in Ireland and it has been noted that many early churches were significantly sited by druidic oaks. Most famous are St. Brigid's monastic foundation at Cille Daire (Kildare), 'Church of the Oak', and the great monastic school of Daire Maugh (Durrow), 'Plain of the Oaks', in Wexford. St. Colmcille's favourite church was Daire Calgaich (Derry), 'the oak grove of Calgaich'. However, the popular image associated with the British and Continental Celts, of druids cutting mistletoe in sacred oak groves, does not occur in an Irish context. Mistletoe is not a native Irish plant and was only transported to Ireland in the eighteenth century.

Oak of Mughna. According to the *Leabhar Gabhála* this was the earliest sacred oak tree in Ireland.

Oath. There are many references to oaths being taken by the elements, in particular the sun and the moon. For an oath *in testiculis* see **Geis**.

Ó Brasil. an alternative name for Hy-Brasil. See **Breasal**.

Ocean-sweeper. In Irish *Aigéan scuabadoir*. Sometimes Wave-sweeper. A magical ship which knew a man's thoughts and was propelled without sails or oars wherever he willed it. It was brought from the Otherworld by Lugh Lámhfada and given as a gift to Manannán Mac Lir, the sea-god.

Ochain. Sometimes Acéin or 'Moaner'. The enchanted shield of Conchobhar Mac Nessa, king of Ulster. Whenever its bearer was in danger, it moaned a warning and was answered by the roars of the Waves of Tuaithe, Cliodhna, and Rudraidhe, the chief waves of Ireland. See **Tonn**. It was carried by Fiachra, Conchobhar's son, when he led the attack on the Red Branch Hostel and moaned when Fiachra was in danger, thus bringing Conall Cearnach to his rescue.

Ochall Ochne. King of the *sidhe* of Connacht. He had a swineherd named Friuch who was in perpetual rivalry with Nár, the swineherd of Bodb Dearg of Munster. See **Friuch**.

Octriallach. Son of Indech, a Fomorii, who was killed by Ogma at the second Battle of Magh Tuireadh. During this battle it was Octriallach who discovered how the Dé Danaan god of medicine, Dian Cécht, was able to bring the slain Dé Danaan back to life and cure the wounded by use of a magical 'Spring of Health'. Octriallach led the Fomorii warriors in filling in the spring by placing great rocks over it and erecting the 'Cairn of Octriallach'.

Odras. Daughter of Odarnatan, keeper of the hostel of Buchat Buasach. She tended Buchat Buasach's cow herd. The Mórrígán came with a bull called Slemuin (Smooth) and mated it with one of Odras' cows. The Mórrígán then enticed the cow away with the bull to the Cave of Cruachan, one of the entrances to the Otherworld. Odras, fearing to lose a cow from the herd, pursued the Mórrígán. Becoming tired, she fell asleep in the wood of Falga. The Mórrígán then sang an enchantment over her and turned her into a pool of water.

Oenghus. See **Aonghus**.

Oes. See **Áes**.

Ogham. Sometimes Ogam. The earliest form of Irish writing, frequently mentioned in the myths and sagas. Its invention is ascribed to Ogma, god of eloquence and literature. Its use is varied throughout the myths. In the story of '*Baile Mac Buain*' we hear of a library of 'rods of *Fili*' on which ancient stories and sagas are inscribed. In the 'Voyage of Bran' we are told that Bran writes poetry in Ogham, having written down fifty or sixty quatrains of a poem on Ogham rods. In the *Táin* saga Cúchulainn carves warnings and challenges the warriors of Ailill and Medb on pieces of wood. In a tale from the Fenian Cycle, Lomna writes a cryptic message to Fionn Mac Cumhail informing him of his wife's infidelity. More often Ogham was used to inscribe magic spells. At the funerals of great heroes it was used to inscribe the hero's name on a wand of aspen to be placed in the tomb.

Ogham consists of short lines drawn to, or crossing, a base line in the following manner:

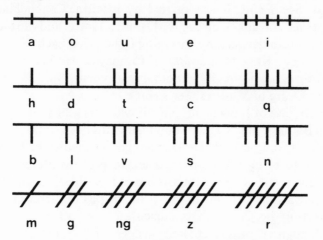

Mention is made of vast libraries of Ogham writing usually inscribed on the bark or wands of hazel and aspen. Over four hundred Ogham inscriptions have survived, the majority being in Ireland, but these have been carved on stone. The language is an archaic form of Irish and most of the surviving inscriptions date from the fourth to the sixth centuries. *The Book of Ballymote*, compiled in the fourteenth century in Co. Sligo, contains a treatise on Ogham. Parts of this book are said to be copied from earlier ninth-century texts. Ogham is sometimes called 'The Tree Alphabet' because each letter takes the name of a tree: e.g. A, *ailim* (elm); B, *beithe* (birch); C, *coll* (hazel).

Ogma. God of eloquence and literature. A son of the Dagda. He was skilled in dialects and poetry as well as being a warrior. Some sources say that he had another role in conveying souls to the Otherworld. He was also called Ogma Grian-aineach (of the Sunny Countenance) and Ogma Cermait (of the Honeyed-Mouth). He is cognate with the Continental Celtic god Ogmios whom Lucian claimed was the Celtic equivalent of Heracles. This god was also known among the British Celts and a piece of pottery found at Richborough bears the name Ogmia and depicts a figure with long curly hair and sun rays proceeding from his head. He also holds the whip of the Sol Invictus.

In Ireland Ogma is credited with the invention of Ogham script. His children appear varied. In some stories he is married to Étain, given as daughter of the god of medicine Dian Cécht, and among their offspring are Tuireann and Cairbre. But Mac Cécht, Mac Cuill and Mac Gréine are also listed as his children. Ogma fought at the second Battle of Magh Tuireadh and slew Indech, son of the Fomorii goddess Domnu. After the battle he claimed the sword of Tethra, the Fomorii king, which was called Orna and could speak, recounting the deeds it had performed. With the passing of the old gods, Ogma retired to the *sídhe* of Airceltrai.

Oillpheist. A fabulous beast. *Oille* signifies greatness or vastness and *pheist* means a beast or monster in the fabulous sense. It features several times in the myths. A late legend has an *oillpheist* learning that St. Patrick was coming to Ireland to drive out its kind. The *oillpheist* fled towards the sea cutting its way through the land and forming the River Shannon. On its way it swallowed a piper named Ó Ruairc who continued to play his pipes to the beast's discomfiture so that it finally threw him back to land.

Oílmelc. 'Sheep's milk'. An alternative name for the feast of Imbolg. See **Brigid** and **Imbolg**.

Oirbsen. An alternative name for Manannán Mac Lir, the sea-god. An ancient name of Lough Corrib, Co. Galway, was Loch Oirbsen in which, tradition has it, Manannán Mac Lir met his death by drowning.

Oisín. Sometimes Ossian. Son of Fionn Mac Cumhail and of Sadb, daughter of the god Bodb Dearg. He was acknowledged to be the greatest poet in Ireland as well as being a warrior of the Fianna. Oisín was found by his father while Fionn was searching Ireland for Sadb, who had been turned into a deer. The shapely young boy had been raised by his mother while in her deer shape. Fionn named him Oisín (fawn). He grew up to be one of the leading champions of the Fianna. He married a yellow-haired stranger from a sunny country named Eibhir and his most famous son was the warrior Oscar. Oisín took part in many of the adventures of the Fianna but he refused to help his father, Fionn, exact vengeance on the ill-fated lovers, Diarmuid and Gráinne.

One day, while Oisín was hunting with the Fianna, a beautiful maiden appeared on an enchanted horse. This was Niamh of the Golden Hair, one of the daughters of Manannán Mac Lir. Oisín fell in love with her and she invited him to accompany her back to Tír Tairnigiri (the Land of Promise). Without further ado, Oisín mounted behind her and they rode off across the sea. Oisín had several adventures, including the rescue of a Dé Danaan goddess from an evil Fomorii giant. Niamh had several children by him, Oscar and Fionn and also a daughter called Plur na mBan (Flower of Women). But Oisín began to pine for Ireland. Niamh gave him her magic horse but warned him not to dismount when he returned to Ireland for three hundred years had passed since last he was there. This version, of course, contradicts the tale where Oisín laments the death of his son Oscar at the Battle of Gabhra. Oisín returned to Ireland to find the Fianna no longer existed and the Christian era had commenced. He fell from the horse by accident, the beast disappeared and Oisín was changed immediately from a divine youth into a blind, grey-haired, withered old man. The tale, obviously a Christian embellishment, has Oisín meet St. Patrick. He is made welcome by the saint and invited to recount all the adventures of the Fianna.

The Fenian Cycle is often referred to as the Ossianic Cycle. The tales were made famous by the Scot, James MacPherson, whose rendering of them under the general title *Ossian* was based loosely on Irish sources and became a European classic. See **MacPherson**.

Olc Acha. A smith and father of Étain. See **Étain** 4.

Ollamh. Sometimes given as Ollave.

1. Of the seven grades of *filí* or poet, the *ollamh* was the highest grade and therefore the highest dignitary among the bards. It took a candidate nine to twelve years of study to memorise the two hundred and fifty prime stories and one hundred secondary stories necessary to claim the title. *Ollamh* is the modern Irish word for a professor.

2. Son of Delbaeth, and grandson of Ogma.

3. Ollamh Fódhla. Recorded as the eighteenth High King of Ireland to reign after the first Milesian king Eremon, according to the *Leabhar Gabhála*. Other texts say he was the fortieth High King after Eremon and reigned in 714BC Ollamh Fódhla is traditionally recognised as founding rule by legislature in Ireland and giving the country a codified system of law. He is claimed as founding the great Feis Temrach or Festival of Tara, which was held every three years. He is said to be buried at Tailltinn (Teltown, Co. Westmeath).

Olloman. Father of Aí. See **Aí**.

Oonagh. Sometimes Onagh. Wife of Fionnbharr, she became relegated in popular folklore from an ancient goddess of the Dé Danaan to 'queen of all the fairies in Ireland'. Oonagh and Fionnbharr dwelt at the *sídhe* of Meadha, five miles west of Tuam. They had seventeen sons.

Oral tradition. Although the ancient Celtic people knew and possessed the use of writing, they preferred to maintain a lively oral tradition. Surviving Celtic inscriptions and texts actually date back to the same period as the earliest surviving Latin literary remains. Celtic tradition, however, was that all knowledge – law, poetry, philosophy, science etc. – should be passed on orally. Julius Caesar comments: 'They commit to memory immense amounts of poetry. And some of them continue their studies for twenty years. They consider it improper to commit their studies to writing.' The epics, such as the *Táin Bó Cuailgne*, may well have been passed down orally for a thousand years before being finally written down during the Christian period. In the myths we learn that the ancient Irish literati had a secret literary language, *bérla na Filied* (the language of the poets), which only the initiated could understand. Both Cúchulainn and his wife Emer, we are told, knew this exclusive literary language. Celtic heroes and heroines were no empty-headed beauties but were always accomplished in the arts and sciences.

Orba. The second son of Partholón.

Orc-Triath. Sometimes Torc Triath. King of Boars. He is listed as being among the possessions of the fertility goddess Brigid, daughter of the Dagda. According to the *Leabhar Gabhála* (Book of Invasions) Brigid owned Fea and Femen, two oxen of Dil, and the Orc-Triath, three powerful Otherworld creatures which symbolised plunder and destruction.

Oriel. The Irish form is Airgialla and signifies 'subject people'. The kingdom of Oriel consisted of the territory of the modern counties of Armagh, Monaghan, Tyrone and most of Fermanagh and Derry. The kingdom was carved from Ulster and the name occurs in some stories even though it was a later development and set in the historical period.

Orlam. A son of Ailill and Medb who was slain by Cúchulainn during the war of the *Táin*. Cúchulainn met Orlam's charioteer repairing his chariot and told the man to warn his masters that he was coming. Cúchulainn met Orlam in single combat and slew him.

Orna. The sword of Tethra, the Fomorii king, which could speak and recount its deeds. Ogma claimed it, having killed Tethra at the second Battle of Magh Tuireadh.

Oscar. 1. Son of Oisín and Eibhir. The name *Os* (deer) *car* (lover)

reflects that of his father whose mother was Sadb, a goddess turned
into a deer by the Dark Druid. He was the mightiest warrior among
the Fianna, a man of hard strength with a heart 'like twisted horn
sheathed in steel'. As a youth, however, he was so clumsy that the
Fianna refused to take him on their expeditions. One day he followed
them unbeknown and found them falling back before their enemies.
He armed himself with a piece of wood and went into the attack with
such a battle frenzy that he slew two kings and his own friend Linné
before the fever left him. Thereafter he was given command of a
battalion of Fianna which had as its banner 'The Terrible Broom'
(*Scuab Uafásach*) because it would not retreat an inch but swept its
enemies from the field. Oscar, like his father Oisín, refused to help
Fionn Mac Cumhail exact vengeance on Diarmuid and Gráinne.
Oscar married 'the fair Aidín'.

At the end of Oscar's life we seem to have entered a period where
Fionn Mac Cumhail is dead and Oisín is on his sojourn to Tír
Tairnigiri with Niamh, Manannán Mac Lir's daughter. Cormac Mac
Art, the High King and patron of the Fianna, is also dead and his son
Cairbre is High King. Cairbre disliked the Fianna and sought a way
of breaking their power. His daughter Sgemih Solais was about to
wed the son of the king of the Dési. The Fianna claimed their
customary tribute of twenty ingots of gold for their attendance at a
royal wedding. Cairbre refused to pay them and summoned the Clan
Morna to help him curb the Fianna, thus resurrecting a long term
enmity between Clan Morna and Fionn's clan, the Clan Bascna.

Cairbre led Clan Morna to meet the Fianna in battle at Gabhra (said
to be Garristown, Co. Dublin). The Fianna were commanded by
Oscar. The battle saw the destruction of the Fianna. Oscar killed
Cairbre in single combat but not before Cairbre had inflicted a mortal
wound on Oscar. In one version we are told that Fionn himself came
to bewail his grandson's death, arriving in a ship, presumably from
the Otherworld. According to another version Oisín came to lament
his son with the hero Celta. Oscar sighed before his death:

No man ever knew
A heart of flesh was in my breast.

Oisín and Celta raised the body of Oscar on a bier of spears and
carried him from the field with his battle flag draped over him. Aidín,
his widow, hearing the news of his death, died of grief. It fell to Oisín

to bury her on Ben Edair (Howth) and build a great cairn over her grave. Oscar's death at the Battle of Gabhra is a fitting melancholy end to the Fenian Cycle.

Lady Jane Francesca Wilde, the nineteenth-century Irish nationalist once prosecuted for sedition, wrote several works on Irish myths and legends including *Ancient Legends of Ireland* (1888). She gave the names of two ancient Fenian heroes to her son Oscar Fingal O'Flahertie Wills Wilde – the playwright Oscar Wilde. Another famous person to bear the name of Oscar was the son of Marshal Bernadotte of France, whose wife Désirée was the daughter of a Dublin merchant Francis Cleary (Clary) who settled in Marseilles. Bernadotte became Charles XIV of Sweden and his wife became Queen Desideria. Their son was Oscar I of Sweden and Norway (1844–59).

2. Oisín had a second son Oscar by the goddess Niamh, born in Tír Tairnigiri (the Land of Promise).

Ossar. The hound belonging to Mac Da Thó which was coveted by Ailill and Medb and also by Conchobhar Mac Nessa. In another version the hound is called Ailbe. At the end of the story of 'Mac Da Thó's Boar' the hound chases Ailill's chariot and is killed by his charioteer. See **Mac Da Thó**.

Ossian. See **Oisín**.

Otherworld. A general term for the various lands of the gods, both good and evil, and for the place where one was reborn after death. The Celts were one of the first European peoples to evolve a doctrine of immortality of the soul. Their basic belief was that death was only a changing of place and that life went on with all its forms and goods in another world, a world of the dead which gave up living souls to this world. A constant exchange of souls was always taking place between the two worlds; death in this world brought a soul to the Otherworld and death in the Otherworld brought a soul to this world. Several Greeks, such as Sotion of Alexandria in the second century BC, and Clement of Alexandria, claimed that their own immortality doctrine was borrowed by the ancient Greeks from the Continental Celts.

It was believed that on one night of the year the Otherworld became visible to mankind and the ancient Celtic world celebrated this as one of their four major feasts of the year. This was the Feast of Samhain (31 October/1 November). On this night all the gates to the Otherworld opened and the inhabitants could set out to wreak vengeance on those living who had wronged them. This ancient pagan belief survived the coming of Christianity and still continues today as Hallowe'en, the evening of the Christian All-Hallows or All Saints' Day on 1 November. It is thought that this is the night when witches and demons and spirits from Hell set out to ensnare unsuspecting souls; it is a direct survival from the old Celtic Otherworld festival.

The concept of the Otherworld in Irish mythology is a very fluid one. It is not just the place where the souls of the dead go. There is a definite 'realm of the dead'. This realm is known as Tech Duinn (House of Donn) which was thought to be a small rocky islet off the south-west coast of Ireland. There were several gods of the dead, such as Bilé and Donn, and Ogma was said to be one of the transporters of souls to this realm.

The other forms of Otherworld range from the dark, brooding purgatories of the Fomorii islands such as Hy-Falga and Dún Scaith to the sunny lands of Tír Tairnigiri and Tír na nÓg. In such exotic places as Tír na nÓg, the god of metal work, Goibhniu, presided over an Otherworld feast, Fledh Ghoibhnenn. Any mortal who took part in the feast and drank the intoxicating liquor which Goibhniu served became an immortal.

Among the synonyms for the Otherworld are: Tír na nÓg (the Land of Youth); Tír Tairnigiri (the Land of Promise); Tír na tSamhraidh (Land of Summer); Magh Mell (Plain of Happiness); Tír na mBeo (Land of the Living); Magh Da Cheo (Plain of the Two Mists); Tír fo Thuinn (Land under the Wave); Hy-Brasil (Breasal's Island); Hy-Falga (Falga's Island) and Dún Scaith (Fortress of Shadows).

Many heroes had adventures in the various lands of the Otherworld. Cúchulainn and his companions went to Hy-Falga and Dún Scaith and fought with terrible serpents. Later he went to live with the goddess Fand in Tír Tairnigiri. Conn of the Hundred Battles was lured away to the Otherworld in a magical mist by Lugh. His son Connla was wooed by a goddess and borne off to the Otherworld in a boat made of glass. The most famous sojurn in the Otherworld was that of Oisín who rode off on a magical horse with Niamh, the daughter of the sea-god Manannán Mac Lir, and stayed for three hundred years.

Owel. See **Eogabaill.**

P. *Pin* (perhaps – dwarf elder) in the Ogham alphabet. The letter 'p' was not found in pre-Christian Irish nor in early Ogham. Consequently words beginning with 'p' in Old and Middle Irish are derivates from Latin, British Celtic, Romance and Scandinavian.

Parthanán. A wraith from the Otherworld who, at the end of the harvest, would thresh any corn left standing. It is suspected that Parthanán may be a folk memory of Partholón.

Partholón. The leader of the third mythical invasion of Ireland. He was a descendant of Magog, son of Japhet. He murdered his father, Sera, and his mother, hoping to inherit their kingdom. When he failed in this attempt he led his followers to Ireland and settled in Munster. On arrival they found Ireland inhabited by the Fomorii led by Cichol Grinchenghos (the footless) and did battle with them. Partholón's wife was Dealgnaid. He left her alone with his servant Todga to go on a journey and they had an affair. When Partholón returned home he accepted blame by saying that it was his fault for leaving her alone. Accounts credit him varyingly with three sons and 'a hireling' and with four sons. His eldest son appears as Eber (the same name as a son of Milesius), the others being Rudraidhe and Laighlinne. He is said to have introduced agriculture into Ireland and among his followers were two ploughmen who had two iron ploughs and four oxen. The Partholónians also hunted, set up the first hostels and cleared plains. During his time new lakes sprang forth and one of these came from the grave of his son Rudraidhe, and was named Loch Rudraidhe. Partholón and his followers were killed by a plague.

Perilous Plain, The. The plain of devouring wild beasts through which Cúchulainn had to cross to get to Scáthach's fortress.

Pharo! Pharo! Occurs as a battle cry. Seathrún Céitinn (d. 1650) believed this to be a corruption of *faire ó!* (look out, ó!).

Picts. Sometimes given as Pictii. In Old Irish, known as Tuatha

Cruithne. An ancient people who appear in the sagas and tales as well as being an historical group. This popular name, which displaced the native Irish word Crutnech, derives from the Latin *pingere*, to paint, and means 'painted people'. They were one of the Celtic groups and, as far back as historical record, were recognised as a Goidelic people. William F. Skene, the Celtic scholar, was one of the first to identify them as Gaelic-speaking although Joseph Loth and Kuno Meyer point to the fact that the names in their king lists show a slight predominance of Brythonic Celtic names. The Picts were found both in Ireland (the *Annals of Ulster* note them still living in the Irish midlands as late as AD809) and in Scotland (Alba). It is said that a warrior named Cruithne settled in Alba and his seven children divided the country into provinces: Cat (Caithness), Cé (Marr and Buchan), Círech (Angus and Mearns), Fiobh (Fife), Moireabh (Moray), Fótla (Ath-fhótla, Atholl) and Fortriu (Strathearn). During the first four centuries of the Christian era the Picts were very prominent as raiders and there are references to their ability as ship-builders and sailors. They were also literate and references occur in chronicles to quotations *in veterrimus Pictorium libris* (in old books of the Picts).

Pigs. Pigs as magical animals have a special place. They have certain properties of enchantment. The pig skin of Tuis, which the sons of Tuireann were asked to bring to Ireland, cured all wounded and sick and if dipped into a stream would turn the water into wine for three days. The seven pigs of Easal of the Golden Pillars provided an inexhaustible feast for, if eaten on one night, they would appear next day ready to be slaughtered for another feast.

Plur na mBan. The Flower of Women. The daughter of Oisín and the goddess Niamh, daughter of Manannán Mac Lir.

Polyandry/Polygamy. Plurality of marriages was permitted in ancient Irish society and was enshrined in the Brehon Laws. The practice continued well into the Christian era. Men and women enjoyed equal rights in pre-Christian Ireland and nowhere is this more carefully demonstrated than in the laws relating to marriage. Divorce could be had by mutual consent as well as for numerous 'offences'. Rights were carefully listed in the law tracts giving protection to both sides.

Pooka. See **Púca**.

Provinces. Irish geography is a special feature of the myths. Today Ireland consists of four historic provinces: Connacht, Leinster, Munster and Ulster, the *ster* ending being a survival from the Norse period. Yet the world for a province is *cúiga* – a fifth. The fifth province was 'the Middle Province' Mide, the name surviving in Co. Meath and Co. Westmeath. See **Mide**. These five ancient provinces met at a central point called the Hill of Uisneach (sometimes Usna) in Westmeath by a great stone called Aill na Mirenn, the stone of divisions, which still stands there. It was at this point that Tuathal raised his royal palace.

The division of Ireland goes back to the sons of Dela, the Firbolg, who also divided Ireland into five. The *Leabhar Gabhála* says: 'And that is the division of the provinces of Ireland which shall endure forever, as the Firbolg divided them.' Another story tells how invaders slew three nobles; their pregnant wives fled to Alba where their sons Conn, Araide and Eoghan Mór were born. The sons returned, chased out the invaders and the provinces of Connachta (for Conn) Ulaidh (for Araide) and Mumhan (for Eoghan Mór) were named after them. Laighin (Leinster) received its name later from Gaulish warriors.

See **Connachta**, **Laighin**, **Munster** and **Ulaid**.

Púca. Anglicised as Pooka. A mischievous spirit or demon who led travellers astray or performed other devilment. It occurs in later legend and seems to have no basis in myth, probably being an import from the Norse *pukí*, an imp, from where it also went into Welsh *pwca* and into English as *puck*. The famous Puck Fair held in August in Killorglin, Co. Kerry, is nothing to do with the *púca*. The Puck Fair is named from *poc* (pronounced puck), a buck-goat. The old song '*An Poc ar Buile*' (The Mad Goat) is associated with the festival which has been held since the seventeenth century and may have its origins in the Feast of Lughnasadh.

Pursuit. In Irish *toruidheacht*. A class of tales of which the most famous is *Toruidheacht Dhiarmuda is Ghráinne* (The Pursuit of Diarmuid and Gráinne). There are numerous pursuit tales.

R. *Ruis* (dwarf elder) in the Ogham alphabet.

Ragallach. A king of Connacht whose death at the hands of his own child was foretold by a druid. Ragallach ordered his wife to kill their baby daughter and the child was cast into a bag and given to a swineherd to destroy. However, the swineherd left the bag at the door of a woman who raised the child. The daughter of Ragallach grew up into a beautiful maiden who became her father's own concubine and eventually fulfilled the prophecy. It is recorded that Ragallach, king of Connacht, was assassinated at Ráth Cruachan in AD645 or 648. The assassin was a male and Ragallach's son Cathal, a student at Clonard, avenged his father by slaying the man.

Raighne. A son of Fionn Mac Cumhail.

Rann. Also *rannaigecht*. A type of verse, the general scheme being a stanza of four heptasyllabic lines but including variations. The form for the verse and for the versifier often appears in Irish texts and is so used in modern Irish.

Rath. He was lulled to sleep by a mermaid singing and then torn to pieces by her and her companions, a fate that occurred to several unwary mariners.

Ráth. A fortress or earthwork, usually circular, surrounding a chieftain's house as in Ráth Cruachan, the fortress of Ailill and Medb of Connacht; Ráth Gráinne at Tara; Ráth Luachara, where Lia, Lord of Luachtar, hid the Treasure Bag of Clan Morna.

Rathand. A son of Conall Cearnach who was fleeing with his father *en route* to Emain Macha when he was drowned in a river at a spot subsequently known as Snamh Rathaind.

Raven. See **Crow**.

Red Branch. The body of warriors who were the guardians of Ulster during the days of Conchobhar Mac Nessa. Cúchulainn was their greatest champion. As far back as Irish tradition goes there is an institute of 'knighthood', the Irish terms being *ridire* (often interpreted as riders) and *curad*. Many scholars feel that the Red Branch (Craobh Ruadh) may be a corruption, the word *ruadh* being confused with *rígh* meaning 'king' (thus Royal Branch). A boy started his 'apprenticeship' in the Red Branch at the age of seven (as did Cúchulainn). There was a Boys' Corps at Emain Macha consisting of 'three fifties' of sons of chieftains and kings. It was led by Follaman Mac Conchobhar and was totally destroyed in the war of the *Táin*.

The Red Branch had their headquarters in Emain Macha and their banner was a yellow lion on a field of green silk. The Red Branch claimed to be founded by Ross the Red of Ulster who wed Maga, daughter of the love-god Aonghus Óg. Near Navan (Emain Macha) is a village called Creeveroe, an Anglicisation of Craobh Ruadh, the Red Branch.

Red Branch Cycle. Also known as 'The Ulster Cycle'. This is the great heroic cycle of Irish mythology, comparable to the *Iliad* in theme and heroic tone. The main stories comprise the famous epic of the *Táin Bó Cuailgne*. Scholars accept that the cycle must have been transmitted orally for nearly a thousand years, preserving, in a remarkable way, faithful descriptions of a remote past. Weapons, crafts, customs, political and social conditions are depicted. The basic texts of the epic survive in the *Leabhar n hUidre* (the twelfth-century Book of the Dun Cow) and in the *Leabhar Laigeneach* (the twelfth-century Book of Leinster).

In addition to the *Táin* itself, the other stories of the cycle consist of enlargements on themes occurring in the *Táin*, preparatory tales leading up to the epic, romances that were added later to fulfil the desire of people to know the later fortunes of the main characters and several entirely independent tales. These stories fall into three main groupings: 1. the prologue to the *Táin*, 'The Debility of the Men of Ulster', 'The Conception of Cúchulainn', 'The Wooing of Emer', 'Conchobhar's reign' etc. 2. 'The Great Rout of Muithemne', 'Cúchulainn's Death', 'Red Rout of Conall Cearneach', 'Battle of Rosnaree' and the Death Tales of Heroes. 3. 'Bricriu's Feast', 'The Intoxication of the Men of Ulster', 'Mac Da Thó's Boar' and 'The Fate of the Children of Usna'.

Red Javelin. In Irish Gae-Ruadh. A spear of Manannán Mac Lir, the sea-god.

Red riders. In Irish *ridire ruadh*. Three horsemen in red, riding red horses, who appeared to Conaire Mór while he was on his way to Da

Derga's Hostel. One of his *geise* (taboos) was that 'no three reds shall go before thee to the house of red'. Of course, Da Derga means 'of the red'. Conaire Mór sent a messenger to the riders asking them to fall behind him but the messenger, lash his horse as he would, failed to catch up with them. He shouted to them but they refused all the rewards offered. They chanted:

> Lo, my son, great the news!
> Weary are the steeds we ride,
> – steeds from the Otherworld –
> Though we are living, we are dead,
> Great are the signs, destruction of life,
>   satiation of ravens, feeding of crows,
>   strife of slaughter, wetting of sword-edge,
>   shields with broken lances after sundown.
> Lo, my son!

They rode up to Da Derga's Hostel, dismounted and fastened the horses to the portal. The red riders were the last of Conaire Mór's taboos to be broken before doom and disaster overtook him.

Reincarnation. A theme occurring frequently. See **Otherworld**. Not only could the gods enter the womb of a woman and be born again, passing through different stages of existence, but people could do so as well. The most interesting reincarnation cycle was that of the swineherds Friuch and Nár who went through various changes to emerge in their final forms as Finnbhenach and Donn, the two massive bulls who had their final clash in the closing stages of the *Táin Bó Cuailgne*.

Remanfissech. A chief of Feden Chuailgne, the father of Uma, a Red Branch champion referred to as 'one of the three battle strays of Ulster'.

Retaliator. In Irish Díoltach. One of the three swords of Manannán Mac Lir which never failed to slay. This was the sword which Manannán gave to Naoise and with which Eoghan Mac Durthacht killed Naoise. There is another version however that Naoise and his two brothers were captured and awaiting execution. Each brother wanted to be killed first so that he would not have to look on his slain brothers. Naoise finally gave the sword to the executioner (in this story a Norse prince named Maine) so that he could slay them all with one blow.

Riada. The ancestor of the Dál Riada (of both Ulster and Alba). In the fourth century AD there was a famine in Munster and its ruler Conaire was driven north with his people. He settled first in Co. Antrim where the first Dál Riada kingdom was established. Then he and his followers quarrelled and he crossed the sea into Scotland, forming a second Dál Riada kingdom on Airer Ghàidheal (Argyll), the seaboard of the Gael.

Ríanbind. A piper of Sídhe Breg named by Fer Rogain as one of the nine best pipers in the world. Also named are Bind, Robind, Nibe, Dibe, Dechrind, Umal, Cumal and Cíalgrind.

Ríangabur. Father of the two most famous charioteers of Ulster: Laeg, charioteer to Cúchulainn, and Id, charioteer to Conall Cearneach.

Ríastarthae. The name given to Cúchulainn's battle fury.

Rib. See **Ébliu** 2.

Ridge of the Dead Woman. See **Aedh** 10 and **Bebhionn**.

Righairled. He introduced war chariots into Ireland and is given as the fourteenth High King after Eber, son of Milesius.

Rinnal. A High King of Ireland in whose time weapons were first supposed to be given points (*rinn*, spear point).

Roc. The steward of Aonghus Óg, the love-god. Roc had a son by the wife of Donn, the father of Diarmuid Ua Duibhne. Donn killed Roc's child by crushing it between his knees. Roc smote his dead child with a magic wand and it revived as a huge boar without ears or a tail. Roc charged this boar to follow the fortunes of Donn's own son, Diarmuid, and encompass his death. The boar then went off to Ben Bulben to await its destiny in destroying Diarmuid. See **Diarmuid** 3 and **Gráinne**. Roc also had a daughter – see **Ethné** 4.

Rochad. Son of Fathemen. A warrior of the Red Branch.

Roech. See **Roth**.

Roitheachtaigh. The innovator of the chariot, confused with Righairled. The name means 'possessor of wheels'.

Rómit Rígoinmít. The jester of Conchobhar Mac Nessa of whom Cú Roí says: 'No want nor sorrow that has ever afflicted the people of Ulster has not departed when they saw Rómit Rígoinmít.'

Ronán. A king of Leinster and father of Mael Fhothartaig. When his wife Ethné died, Ronán decided to marry again to the daughter of Eochaidh, a king of Dunsverick. Ronán's young wife lusted after her stepson but when he refused her love she told Ronán that Mael Fhothartaig had attempted to dishonour her. In a jealous rage, Ronán ordered a warrior named Aedh to slay his son. The warrior transfixed the boy in his chair with a spear. Ronán later learnt the truth and died of grief. His wife took poison while Mael Fhothartaig's children exacted vengeance on Aedh.

Ron Cerr. A young champion of Brandubh, king of Leinster. Before the Battle of Dúnbolg he put on a wooden leg and smeared himself with calf's blood and dough of rye to give himself the appearance of a leper. In this disguise he entered the camp of the High King Aedh, with whom Brandubh was at war, and pulled him from his horse, cutting off his head.

Rosai. Infrequently used as an alternative title to *ollamh* (professor), perhaps from the Old Irish *ros*, knowledge.

Ross the Red. The father of Fachtna, king of Ulster, by Maga, the daughter of the love-god Aonghus Óg. See **Red Branch**.

Rosualt. A mighty and fabulous sea monster who was cast ashore on the plain of Murrish under Croagh Phádraig (Co. Mayo). Murrish seems to take its name from *muir-iasc* (sea-fish). Rosualt is said to have vomited three times in three successive years before its death. The first time it vomited into the sea and in consequence all the fish died and the *curraghs* and ships were wrecked or swamped. The second time it vomited into the air and all the birds fell dead. The third time it vomited on land causing a pestilence to spread killing all men and four-footed creatures.

Roth. Often given as Roy and Roeth and sometimes Roi. The father of Fergus Mac Roth and Súaltaim Mac Roth.

Roy. See **Roth**.

Ruadán. 1. A son of Bres the half-Fomorii ruler of the Dé Danaan and the goddess Brigid. At the second Battle of Magh Tuireadh he was sent to spy on Goibhniu. Ruadán wounded the smith-god but was himself slain in the combat. The goddess Brigid came to the battle-field to bewail her son and it is recorded that this was the first keening (*caoine*, lament) heard in Ireland.

2. Of Lorrha. Sometimes given as Rodán and Ruadhan. Described as 'of the race of Eoghan Mor, son of Ailill Olom'. An early Christian saint, one of the 'Twelve Apostles of Ireland', he sheltered a kinsman guilty of the crime of murdering an officer of the High King. For refusing to give up the kinsman, the High King had Ruadán arrested. For daring to lay hands on the saint, Diarmuid was cursed. Ruadán also cursed Tara and brought about its downfall as the seat of the High Kings of Ireland. 'Let Tara be desolate for ever!' See **Diarmuid 2**.

Ruadchoin. Three heroes of the Uí Briúin from Cuala in Leinster bear
this name. They each commanded twelve score men and a 'frenzied
troop' during the attack on Da Derga's Hostel.

Ruadh. 1. Son of Rigdonn. He voyaged with three ships off the north
coast of Ireland and found himself becalmed. With his crew getting
weaker, he swam to find assistance and came upon a secret island
under the sea on which dwelt nine beautiful women. For nine nights
he slept with them 'without gloom, without fearful hurt, under the
sea, free from waves, on nine beds of bronze'. One of the nine bore
him a son.

2. This Ruadh may well be the same character as Ruadh 1. He, too,
went on a voyage. *En route* his ship was stopped by three goddesses
who took him to the seabed where he slept with them. They told him
that they would bear him a son (collectively) and entreated him to
return to them when he came back from his voyage. When he did not,
they pursued him, with his young son. Seeing their pursuit to be in
vain the three goddesses cut off the young boy's head and threw it
after Ruadh.

Ruadh Rofessa. Thought to be identical to the Dagda, and represented
as a god of druidism among the Dé Danaan. See **Dagda, The**.

Rudraidhe. One of the sons of Partholón and acclaimed as the founder
of the royal house of Ulster. The men of Ulster were known as the
Clan Rudraidhe and sometimes as Rudricans.

Rus Mac Fíachu. One of three brothers (with Daire and Imchad) who
were champions of the Red Branch.

S. *Sail* (willow) in the Ogham alphabet.

Sacra. A name anciently applied to Ireland. It is mentioned by Anvienius (*c.* AD380) in an account of the voyage of Himilco the Phoenician in 510BC. Sacra is apparently a translation of the Greek Ιεϱα, Eiriu.

Sacrifices. Contrary to popular belief, there is no conclusive evidence that druids practised human sacrifice. The prime source for this is Julius Caesar who was, of course, an implacable enemy to the Celts and particularly to the druids. There is a reference to human sacrifices being performed in Ireland in the Book of Leinster, in the *Dinnsenchas* tract which speaks of children being sacrificed to Cromm Cruach, an idol set up by Tigernmas on Magh Slécht. However, the story is put forward as an aberration rather than the norm. See **Cromm Cruach** and **Tigernmas**. Cromm Cruach was quickly overthrown by the normal druidic practices.

Sadb. 1. Daughter of Bodb Dearg. She was turned into a fawn by the Dark Druid. One day, hunting near his fortress on the Hill of Allen, Fionn Mac Cumhaill came across a fawn and his two hounds refused to kill it – although another version says that Fionn killed his hound Bran by crushing him between his legs to prevent it killing the fawn. That night Sadb appeared to Fionn in human form as a beautiful woman, told him her story, and became Fionn's mistress. They lived happily for a while until, while Fionn was away hunting, the Dark Druid caught up with Sadb and turned her back into a fawn and she vanished. Fionn searched Ireland until, near Ben Bulben, he found a naked boy who had been raised by a fawn. Fionn recognised in him his son by Sadb and called him Oisín (Little Fawn).
2. Sadb Subhair, a daughter of Ailill and Medb.

Saidhthe Suaraigne. 'Bitch of evil', one of the hounds of Cromm Dubh.

Sainnth. Son of Imbath and father of Macha 3 who cursed the men of Ulster.

Sál Fhada. Son of a king of Greece who, when his father died, was sent out of the kingdom by a king of Munster who, being related to his father, wanted the kingdom of Greece for himself. In the story '*Seachranuidhe Sál Fhada*', Sál Fhada joined the Fianna of Fionn Mac Cumhaill and they eventually restored him to his kingdom, but not before he had been mortally wounded and then restored to life by use of a magic cup.

Salmon of Knowledge. See **Fintan** 2.

Samaliliath. A Partholón who is said to have introduced ale into Ireland. Irish ale was well known even in Europe from a very early period. An ale-house – *coirmthech* – was a place where it was made.

Samhain. 1. Brother of Cian and Goibhniu who was looking after Cian's magical cow, Glas Gaibhnenn, when Balor of the Evil Eye, disguised as a little red-haired boy, tricked him into parting with it. He was obviously one of the gods but his role does not seem clearly defined although one of the four major Celtic feasts appears to have been named after him.

2. Feis na Samhain. One of the four major pre-Christian festivals. It was held on the evening of 31 October into the following day, 1 November. It marked the end of one pastoral year and the commencement of the next. It was also an intensely spiritual time for it was the period when the Otherworld became visible to mankind and when spiritual forces were let loose on the human world. Christianity took this pagan festival over as a harvest festival. The feast became St. Martin's Mass (Martinmas). The festival also became All Saints' Day or All-Hallows and the evening prior was Hallowe'en, still celebrated as the night when spirits and ghosts set out to wreak vengeance on the living and when evil marches unbridled across the world. In Ireland, as in the other Celtic countries, the fires were extinguished and could only be rekindled from a ceremonial fire lit by the druids at Samhain on Tlachtga (now the Hill of Ward). Significant events always occurred on Samhain in myth. It was the time when the Fomorii oppressed the people of Nemed and when the Dé Danaan defeated the Fomorii at the second Battle of Magh Tuireadh.

Samhair. A daughter of Fionn Mac Cumhail who married Cormac Cas, son of Ailill Olom, of Munster. Cormac Cas is recorded as ruling in the third century AD. He built a palace for his bride and their bed was supported by three pillar stones. Hence the palace was called

Dún-tri-liag, the fortress of the three pillar stones, which is now
Duntryleague, Co. Limerick. It is recorded that Cormac received a
terrible wound in the head from which he recovered.

Scáthach nUanaind. Also known as Scáthach Buanand (Victory). She
was the daughter of Árd-Greimne of Lethra and the most famous of
female warriors. She lived in Scáthach's Island (*scáthach*, shadowy)
which is thought to be Skye and ran a military academy there at which
many heroes of Ireland received their training in the martial arts. Her
most famous pupil was Cúchulainn. She taught him his famous battle
leap and also gave him the Gae-Bolg, the terrible spear. Cúchulainn
trained with her for a year and a day during which time her daughter,
Uathach, became his mistress. Later, he joined her in her expedition
against her sister Aoife, reputed to be the strongest of female
warriors. After her defeat Aoife became Cúchulainn's lover and bore
him a son, Connlaí.

Scéal. Story. In old Irish *sgéal*. Used as a title in many of the tales,
e.g. '*Sgéala Muccee Maic Da Thó*' ('The Story of Mac Da Thó's
Boar').

Sceanb. Wife of the harpist Craiftine. She became the lover of Cormac
Cond Longes. Her husband had him killed in jealous fury. See
Craiftine.

Scena. Wife of Amairgen, son of Milesius. She died on the voyage to
Ireland and was buried at Inbhirscena, said to be an ancient name for
the mouth of the Kenmare River in Co. Kerry.

Scenmed. Sister of Forgall Manach. Following Forgall's death, when
Cúchulainn eloped with Fogall's daughter Emer, Scenmed raised
an army and followed the Ulster champion to exact vengeance.
Cúchulainn defeated and slew her.

Sceolan. A hound of Fionn Mac Cumhail but also his nephew. With its
brother Bran it was born to Fionn's sister (sometimes given as
sister-in-law and even aunt) Tuireann while she had been transformed into the form of a bitch-dog. She was changed into this form
by the jealous mistress of her husband Ullan. See **Tuireann** 1.

Sciathbhreag. A member of the Fianna. The name signifies 'speckled
shield'.

Scoriath. A king of the Fir Morca in Gaul and father of the beautiful
Moriath. He welcomed Móen to his court, allowed him to marry his
daughter and supplied him with an army of Gauls to help him
establish himself as king of Leinster and exact vengeance on his evil
great-uncle Cobhthach.

Scota. 1. Daughter of the Egyptian Pharaoh Cingris. She became wife of Niul and mother of Goidel, the progenitor of the Gaels.

2. Daughter of the Egyptian Pharaoh Nectanebus and wife of Milesius. She was killed fighting the Dé Danaan and was buried in Scotia's Glen, three miles from Tralee in Co. Kerry.

Scotland. See **Alba**.

Scots. In early medieval Latin, the term Scottus meant Irishman. This created confusion when the kingdom of Alba began to be referred to by the same name. The utter confusion it caused is demonstrated by the Würzburg Schottenklöster, which was an Irish Benedictine monastery until 1497. By that time there had been a linguistic change and the terms Scottus, Scotia and Scot now applied to the kingdom of Alba. Scottish clerics demanded that the Pope expel the Irish from Würzburg on the grounds that it was, by name, a Scottish foundation. The Pope did so and Würzburg became a Scottish monastery until as late as 1803. However, Johannes Scottus Eriugena, Sedulius Scottus, Marianus Scottus, Clemens Scottus, etc. were all Irishmen and not from modern Scotland.

Scottish Gaelic. The language of Alba. Irish mythology is very similar to Scottish Gaelic mythology because the literature of both cultures descended from a common root after the myths and sagas had been well established. The first written differences between Old Irish and Scottish Gaelic (Gàidhlig) occur in the ninth century *Book of Deer*, now in Cambridge. Professor Kenneth Jackson has pointed out that the Gaelic language achieved its greatest territorial expansion when Scotland annexed the tiny kingdom of Angles around the mouth of the Tweed in 1018 and 'in consequence of this the whole of Scotland became for a time Gaelic in speech'. Scottish Gaelic did not begin to recede from the 'Lowlands' of Scotland until the fourteenth century. The last Gaelic speakers of Galloway, for example, did not die out until the late eighteenth century when Robert Burns was a child. Today, however, only 1.6 per cent of the people of Scotland speak Gaelic as a first language (79,303 according to the 1981 census). This census is only concerned with Scotland and there are many thousands of Gaelic speakers living outside the census areas as well as outside the United Kingdom itself. Canada's 1971 census gave 18,420 'mother-tongue' Gaelic speakers there. Even before the Union with England of 1707, Gaelic was one of Europe's most persecuted languages. The Reformation particularly dealt it a severe blow. Entire libraries of Gaelic books were destroyed. Literary remains date from the eleventh century. They are sparse but indicative of a greater lost literature. Works such as the sixteenth-century *Book of the Dean of Lismore* show the sophistication of a long tradition of literary endeavour. The first book printed in Gaelic was *Form na hOrdaigh*, a book of common prayer, by Bishop John Carswell, in 1567.

Scuab Uasáfach. Terrible Broom. The name of the battalion of the Fianna commanded by Oscar which swept the enemy from the battlefield and never gave an inch of ground. Its banner was a broom.

Seanchaidhe. *Seanchaí* in modern Irish. A story-teller and historian. The word has now been adopted into English in varying forms as seannachie, seannachy and sennchie.

Seang. Daughter of the king of Scythia and wife to Milesius. She died, and he left Scythia for Egypt where he remarried Scota. See **Scota** 2.

Searbhán. The surly. A one-eyed Fomorii warrior who guarded a magic tree, squatting at its foot all day and sleeping in its branches all night. So terrible was his appearance that none of the Fianna would go near him. During the pursuit of Diarmuid and Gráinne, Diarmuid made friends with him so that the couple could hide in the tree safe from the pursuing Fianna. All went well until Gráinne grew restless and wanted to eat the magic berries from the tree. When Searbhán refused to allow her to do this, Diarmuid slew him.

Sechnasach. Son of Fingen Mac Aedha, whose wife was Mór of Munster. She fled before his birth under the influence of voices prophesying evil.

Segais, Well of. See **Nuts of Knowledge**.

Ségda Saerlabraid. Son of the 'king and queen of Tír Tairnigiri', 'sinless people', according to the medieval scribes, who never slept together except at his conception. Interestingly, this Christian embellishment forgets that the rulers of Tír Tairnigiri (the Land of Promise) were Manannán Mac Lir and his wife Fand.

Semion. Son of Stariat from whom all the Firbolgs were descended.

Senach Síaborthe. A warrior with whom it was suggested that Cúchulainn fight, as a reward for which Fand would be sent to him.

Senboth. Partholón's eldest chieftain and adviser.

Sencha Mac Ailella. Chief judge and poet of Ulster in the days of Conchobhar Mac Nessa. He acted as a foil to Bricriu, the creator of discord, and it was he who taught Cúchulainn how to speak.

Sera. Father of Partholón and Starn. In some versions it was Sera who was married to Dealgnaid and not Partholón.

Sétanta. The original name of Cúchulainn. It is interesting to note that there was a Celtic tribe called the Setantii who inhabited an area in what is now north-west England.

Seth. In Christian-orientated accounts this Biblical character, son of Adam and Eve, and the three daughters of Cain were the first people to see Ireland.

Sgeimh Solais. Light of Beauty. The daughter of the High King Cairbre whose marriage to the son of the Dési started the war between Cairbre and the Fianna which resulted in the eventual destruction of the Fianna.

Shape-changing. A very common motif in the myths and tales. Gods often did it, frequently changing shape to sleep with mortals. Druids and druidesses also were able to change their shape and turn others into various forms of animals.

Sídhe. A mound or hill, the dwelling place of the Dé Danaan after their defeat by the Milesians. The ancient gods, thus driven underground, were relegated in folk memory to fairies, *aes sídhe*, the people of the hills. Most popular is the banshee (*bean sídhe*), the woman of the fairies. Each god was allotted a *sídhe* by the Dagda before he gave up leadership of them. For example, Sídhe Fionnachaidh went to Lir; Sídhe Bodb went to Bodb Dearg; Sídhe Brí Leith went to Midir; Sídhe Airceltrai to Ogma; Sídhe Rodrubai to Lugh; Sídhe Eai Aedha Ruaidh to Ilbreach son of Manannán; Bruigh na Boinne to Aonghus Óg.

Simon Breac. Son of Starn. After the Nemedian defeat by the Fomorii he and his followers fled from Ireland. Arriving in Thrace they were enslaved and became the ancestors of the Firbolg.

Simon Magus. The New Testament character makes a surprising appearance in the myths when his sons are said to have raped the goddess Tlachtga.

Sineach. See **Muirdris.**

Sinend. See **Sionan.**

Sionan. Daughter of Lir's son Lodan. She went to the Well of Knowledge at the source of the Shannon, even though it was forbidden. As with Boann, the water of the well rose up and chased her westward and drowned her. The path of the water became the river Shannon, named after her. The Shannon has its source in Co. Cavan and, at 170 miles in length, is the longest river in the British Isles. The story is a complete parallel to that of Boann and the formation of the Boyne.

Sithchenn. A druid, seer and smith, to whom Niall of the Nine

Hostages and his four brothers were sent by Mongfhinn to see what their futures were. Sithchenn enticed them into his forge and set fire to it to see what items they would rescue. While the others came out with sledge hammers, a pail of beer, bellows, spearheads and dry sticks, Niall came out with the anvil and from this Sithchenn foretold he would be the greatest High King of Ireland.

Sláine. 1. Sometimes Slainge. The name signifies 'health'. He was a son of Partholón who was the first physician in Ireland. His grave is at Dinn Rígh which was also known as Duma Slainge, Sláine's Grave.

2. Son of Dela the Firbolg. He was an antagonist of Nemed and ruled Leinster.

Slemuin. A bull which belonged to the Mórrígán. See **Odras**.

Sliabh Mis. Anglicised as Sleemish. Situated in Corco Duibhne (Co. Kerry), this was the fabulous fortress of Cú Roí. The entrance could never be found at sunset. No matter what part of the fortress he was in Cú Roí only had to utter a spell and the fortress was able to revolve like a millstone. It is not to be confused with a mountain of the same name in Co. Antrim where St. Patrick passed his youth herding swine.

Slieve. In Irish *sliabh*, a mountain. Slieve Fuad, near Newtonhamilton in Co. Armagh, the dwelling place of the god Lir, was where the hero Fuad was slain. Slievebeagh (Sliabh Beatha), the mountain of the hero Bith, is on the borders of Cos. Monaghan, Fermanagh and Tyrone. Slievebloom is the mountain of Bladh (Sliabh Bladhma), a Milesian hero. Slieve Slanga was named after Sláine (Slainge), the physician son of Partholón who was buried on its summit. This is now called Slieve Donard (the highest of the Mourne mountains), renamed from Donart, son of a king of Ulster who became a disciple of St. Patrick. There is also Slieve Eelim (Sliabh Eibhlinne), the mountain range east of Limerick, which took its name from Ebliu (see **Ebliu** 1), the sister of Lugh.

Smirgat. A wife of Fionn Mac Cumhail. She prophesied that if he drank from a horn he would die. He was therefore careful to drink from goblet or bowl.

Snedgus. A cleric in the service of St. Colmcille who enters into myth because of a fabulous voyage – 'The Voyage of Snedgus and Mac Riagla'. While it is preserved in the fourteenth-century *Yellow Book of Lecan*, scholars have dated the tale to the seventh century. Snedgus and Mac Riagla sat in judgement on the men of Ross who had assassinated a tyrannical king. Rather harshly, in view of the circumstances, they said judgement should be left to God and that sixty couples should be cast upon the sea in curraghs. The two clerics, however, decided to join them, and as their own curragh drifted on the sea they visited many marvellous lands, seeing strange beasts, until they came to an island on which they lived in a form of immortality.

Socht's sword. It would cut a hair off a man's head without touching his flesh and would cut a man in two 'so that neither half knew what had befallen the other'.

Somhlth. Sometimes Sowlth. A supernatural without shape.

Sovranty of Ireland. The form of 'sovranty' appears in various myths as a female figure. Invariably she starts off as an ugly crone but turns into a beautiful maiden who bestows the kingship on the man deemed 'rightful'.

Spain. This country is frequently mentioned but is a synonym for 'The Land of Death'. It was probably introduced by Christian monks when they began to record the sagas because of some reticence about pre-Christian terminology. Spain, or rather the Iberian peninsula, was settled by Celts from 900BC, classified as Celtiberians by archaeologists and early historians. They left much archaeological evidence and some of the earliest Continental Celtic inscriptions such as the text found at Botorrita. When the British Celts were moving out of Britain during the settlements of the Angles and Saxons (ancestors of the English) in the fifth and sixth centuries AD, some Celtic tribes settled on the north-west of the Iberian peninsula, mainly in Astruias. The Celtic Church flourished there for a time before accepting Roman orthodoxy at the Council of Toledo in 633. This settlement has given rise to a popular modern myth that Galicia, which received a form of home rule from Spain in 1980, is a Celtic country. This is, of course, not so. Galician is a Romance language deriving from the same Hispanic dialect as Portuguese.

Sreng. A Firbolg who was sent as ambassador to the Dé Danaan when they landed in Ireland. He met with Bres who suggested they divide Ireland between then. Sreng was impressed with the weapons of the Dé Danaan: they were light and sharply pointed compared with the Firbolg heavy and almost blunt weapons. The Firbolg rejected the Dé Danaan offer and the first Battle of Magh Tuireadh took place. Sreng fought in single combat with Nuada and gave him a terrific blow which cut Nuada's shield in two and cut off his hand.

The god Dian Cécht had to give Nuada a silver hand in replacement, thus earning Nuada's name. In Connacht, until the middle of the seventeenth century, people still claimed to trace their descent to Sreng.

Starn. 1. A son of Sera and brother of Partholón.

2. Son of Nemed and father of Tuan, acclaimed the ancestor of the Firbolg.

Stone. Reverence for stones was common among all the ancient Celts. The Celts dwelt in a firm communication with Nature, believing in the consciousness of all things. Trees, fountains, even weapons and implements were but a fragment of one cosmic whole. Stones particularly were thought to have an indwelling spirit, thus could the Lia Fáil (the Stone of Destiny) roar with joy when it felt the touch of a rightful ruler's foot. Another stone could tell if a man lied. See **Lia Fáil**.

Sualtam Mac Roth. Also Sualdaim. The brother of Fergus Mac Roth. He was Cúchulainn's 'mortal father'. The night before his wedding to Dechtiré, the god Lugh took her off and slept with her. She gave birth to Sétanta who was to become known as Cúchulainn. When Ailill and Medb invaded Ulster during the war of the *Táin* he attempted to raise the warriors of Conchobhar Mac Nessa. Unable to wake the men of Ulster he turned his horse, the spirited Grey of Macha, so angrily that the sharp rim of his shield sliced off his head. The severed head continued to cry its warning until the curse of Macha was lifted and the warriors were roused to the danger.

Súantrade. One of the harpists of Úaithne who made such sad music that men died listening to it.

Suibhne Geilt. A king cursed by St. Ronán so that, in spite of his human form, he assumed the characteristics of a bird, leaping from tree to tree. In this Suibhne, interestingly, has a Welsh counterpart in Myrddin Wyllt. He is said to have fled frenzied from the Battle of Moyrath. See **Geilt**.

Sun. Heliolatry or sun-worship, judging from the abundance of solar motifs, was a common Celtic practice, although there is little evidence in the myths and sagas of a sun-cult. There are references, however, to sun-deities, such as Mac Gréine (son of the sun) who was the husband of Éire, who gave her name to Ireland. The god Bel (Irish Bilé) was known as 'the shining one' and his feast of Beltaine (1 May) was obviously connected with a sun-cult. On Mount Callan (near Ennis) there stands a sun altar where the Beltaine festival was celebrated on midsummer's day down to 1895. Near Macroom is a standing stone called 'the stone of the sun' while Seathrún Céitinn (*c.* 1570–1650) claimed that many of the dolmens associated with Gráinne were, in fact, originally connected with Gréine (the sun). Among the various sun references in Irish, we have Giolla Gréine, whose mother was a sunbeam.

Swans. A favourite form among shape-changers. The children of Lir were turned into swans and Cáer, of whom the love-god Aonghus Óg dreamt and went in search, was a human who lived in the form of a swan.

T

T. *Tinne* (holly) in the Ogham alphabet.

Tábhall-lorg. A tablet staff. Frequently mentioned is the fact that records, books of poetry, genealogy and history were kept by druids and *ollamhs* on rods of wood in Ogham. These were variously called *tábhall-lorg*, *taibhli-filidh* (poets' staffs), *tamlorga filidh* and *flesc filidh* (poets' rods). The Brehon Laws say it was only lawful for poets to carry them. They were collections of wooden sticks, usually of beech or birch, which opened into the shape of a fan on which Ogham was recorded. In a few instances other forms of wood are referred to, especially yew. See **Ogham**.

Tabhfheis. The Bull Feast. A ceremony particularly associated with the choosing of the High Kings. A druid would eat the flesh of a bull and drink its blood. He was then put to sleep by four other druids. The person that he dreamed of was the one who was to become High King. If he lied about his vision then the gods would destroy him.

Taboo. See **Geis**.

Tadhg. 1. Son of **Cian** king of Munster, Tadhg allied himself with Cormac Mac Art. He was wounded in the Battle of Crinna, fought against the men of Ulster. Cormac had promised to reward his alliance with any land which he could circumnavigate in his chariot after the battle. But Cormac knew that Tadhg really wanted Temuir (Tara) and therefore the High Kingship. Cormac therefore bribed Tadhg's charioteer and Tadhg was so wounded in the battle that he kept swooning. Therefore his charioteer was able to make a circumnavigation of land which formed an 'L' shape around Tara, excluding it. When Tadhg discovered the trick played on him, he slew his charioteer. The goddess Cliodhna appeared to Tadhg during his voyage in 'The Adventures of Tadhg, son of Cian, son of Ailill Olum'. Standish Hayes O'Grady, translating the story in his *Silva Gadelica*, believed the story to date back to the third century AD.

2. Son of Nuada. He was a druid and father of Murna of the White Neck, the mother of Fionn Mac Cumhail. When Cumal wanted to marry her, he opposed it for it had been prophesied that the marriage would result in his losing his power and estates. Cumal abducted her and so Tadhg persuaded Conn, the High King, to send Goll Mac Morna after him and in the resultant battle Cumal was slain. See **Cumal** and **Murna**.

Taidle Ulaidh. A steward of the household of the High King Conaire Mór. The heroes are told, in 'The Destruction of Da Derga's Hostel', that 'it is necessary to listen to his judgements for he has power over seat, couch and food'.

Taillcenn. The name given by the druids to St. Patrick. The druids prophesied to Laoghaire the High King (AD428–63) of his coming, an incident quoted in 'The Life of St. Patrick' by Muirchiu of Armagh, written before 700, and surviving in the *Book of Armagh*.

The Taillcenn will come over a furious sea,
His mantle head-holed, his staff crook-headed,
His dish in the east of his house,
All his household shall answer – Amen! Amen!

Tailltinn, Battle of. A great battle between the Dé Danaan and the Milesians. It is said that three kings and queens of the Dé Danaan were slain.

Tailtu. Daughter of the Firbolg king of the Great Plain. Eochaidh Mac Erc, another Firbolg king, married her. She became foster mother to Lugh Lámhfada and gave her name to Tailltinn (sometimes Teltin) which is Anglicised as Teltown, midway between Navan and Kells. She cleared the forest of Breg, making it into a plain. As a result of her labours she died and was buried at Tailltinn. Lugh Lámhfhada decreed a feast in her honour which became known as Lughnasadh. See **Lughnasadh**. 1 August was supposed to be the anniversary of the date on which the Firbolg landed in Ireland. The festival became a major event in pre-Christian Ireland. Its games corresponded to the Olympics of ancient Greece. According to Cuan Ó Lathcháin, whose poem on Tailtu survives in the twelfth-century *Leabhair Laighnech* (Book of Leinster), the games were held around the graves on the hill of Tailltinn. Ollamh Fótla is said to be another distinguished personage buried there. According to *Annála Ríoghachta Éireann* (Annals of the Four Masters) the last official games held at Tailltinn were on 1

August 1169, under the jurisdiction of the last High King, Ruraidh Ó Conchobhar. This was almost on the eve of the Anglo-Norman invasion of Ireland.

Táin. A plundering expedition, usually a cattle-raid. Reference to 'The *Táin*' usually means the epic *Táin Bó Cuailgne*, the Cattle-Raid of Cuailgne (sometimes Anglicised as Cooley), the most famous 'cattle-raid' tale. There are, however, several of these tales although the two most quoted are those of Cuailgne and Fraoch. See *Táin Bó Cuailgne* and *Táin Bó Fraoch*.

Táin Bó Cuailgne. The Cattle-Raid of Cuailgne. The most famous epic in mythology. It has been compared with the Greek *Iliad*. Its date of origin is uncertain although we can be sure that it had an oral tradition for many centuries before it was written down. The first reference to it being put in written form is in the seventh century when it is recorded that Senchan Torpeist, the chief *ollamh* of Ireland (d. AD647), committed it to writing. However, surviving texts date from much later. The basic texts are found in *Leabhar na h-Uidhre*, the eleventh-century Book of the Dun Cow, and *Leabhar Laighnech*, the twelfth-century Book of Leinster. Both versions are incomplete but additions are to be found in *The Yellow Book of Lecan*. The *Táin*, as it is popularly known, describes the campaign by Medb, the masterful queen of Connacht, to capture the famous Brown Bull of Cuailgne in Ulster. She led a vast army against Ulster whose warriors were prevented from defending the kingdom by a strange debility inflicted by Macha, perhaps a war goddess. Only the youthful champion Cúchulainn was able to carry on a defence, a long, single-handed resistance, until the Ulster men recovered from their debility and came to his aid. It is the longest, most elaborate and powerful of all the Irish myths and is the central theme of the Red Branch Cycle.

Táin Bó Fraoch. Sometimes *Táin Bó Fróech*. Cattle-Raid of Fraoch. The second most popular cattle-raid tale. The first part of the story tells how Fraoch, the most handsome warrior in Ireland, set out to woo Findbhair, the beautiful daughter of Ailill and Medb. It is famous for the encounter between Fraoch and a water monster in which Findbhair assisted him. It has been suggested by Professor C. W. von Sydow (*Beowulfskalden och nordisk tradition*, Arsbok, 1923) that the story provided the model for the English saga of *Beowulf*. *Beowulf* was, of course, written in Northumbria about the reign of Aldfrith (*c.* AD685). Aldfrith was the son of Osy, born at Druffield on the Humberside, but he was sent for his education to the Irish monastic school at Lisgoole, on the west bank of Loch Erne. He composed poetry in Irish and the authorship of three extant compositions is credited to him. It has been suggested that Aldfrith, with his obvious knowledge of the Irish language and literary traditions, was the 'begetter' of *Beowulf*. Von Sydow's theory is also supported by Professor Gerard Murphy in his work *Duanaire Finn*. It is claimed that there are nine significantly close points of identity between the two compositions.

Tairchell. See **Moling** 2.

Tallaght. A mound near Dublin. Formerly known as Taimhleacht Muintir Partholain, the plague grave of the people of Partholón. According to *Cormac's Glossary*, the term *tamhlachta* was given to plague graves and this occurs in several Irish place names. It is said that 9000 of Partholón's people died of the plague and were buried at this spot. The monastery of Mael Rúain, who founded the Cele Dé (Culdee) order, was also at Tallaght.

Tanáiste. The successor to a king or professional man elected during his predecessor's lifetime. The word means 'second'. His or her position is clearly delineated in the Brehon Laws but Professor Eoin Mac Neill believed that the *tanáistech* (tanistry system) was not an ancient institution but a custom which only spread as late as the thirteenth century. This is disputed by other scholars. The deputy Prime Minister of the modern Irish Republic is called the Tanáiste.

Tara. Also Temuir and Temair. The modern form is Teamhair. A site in Co. Meath generally regarded as the capital of ancient Ireland and the main royal residence of the High Kings. Muirchiu, in his 'Life of St. Patrick' (*c.* seventh century) described Tara as *caput Scotorum* – the Irish capital. The name is derived from the goddess Tea, wife of Eremon, the first Milesian High King. Temair is to be found in other place names, most notably Temair Luchra, the chief royal residence of south Munster at the time of the Red Branch Cycle. The Degads, the Munster equivalent of the Red Branch, had their headquarters there.

Tara is certainly an ancient site and parts of the remains have been dated back to 2000BC. There are two detailed early descriptions of the site extant, one written by Cineth Ó hArtigan in the tenth century, and the other by Cúan O Lathchain in the eleventh century.

The principal fortification was Ráth Rígh (fortress of kings) whose ramparts measured 853 feet in diameter. There were apparently two walls with a ditch in between them. One, at least, of these ramparts was of stone. Within the central enclosure was the *forradh* or public meeting place which also had two outer rings or ramparts. Here stands a remarkable pillar stone, 6 feet high, which is thought to have been the Irish Lia Fáil (Stone of Destiny), an inauguration stone for the High Kings which roared with joy at the touch of a rightful king's foot. See **Lia Fáil**. Within the enclosure also stands Tech Cormaic, Cormac's House, a circular *ráth* which is said to have been erected by Cormac Mac Art. Duma na nGiall, the mound of hostages, is also within the main fortification and was anciently described as a timber house in which the hostages of the High King lived. A little to the side stands Duma na Bó, the mound of the cow. It is 40 feet in diameter and 6 feet high and this is where the celebrated legendary cow of Cian, stolen by Balor of the Evil Eye, is believed to have been buried.

One hundred paces from Ráth Rígh on the north-east side is a well called Nemnach (sparkling or bright), celebrated in the legend of Cormac Mac Art's mill.

Ráth na Senaid, the *ráth* of synods, now called the King's Chair and partly encroached on by the walls of a modern church, was the spot where the major Christian synods were held: the first in 433 when St. Patrick preached to the High King Laoghaire, the second in 560 when St. Ruadán of Lorrha pronounced his curse against Tara, and the last in 697 when Adamnan procured acceptance in Irish law that women could be exempt from military service in time of war. Nearby are the remains of an old Celtic cross called Adamnan's Cross. The Tech Miodhchuarta or banqueting hall (literally, mead-circling house) can be seen on the northern slope. The hall was, according to record, a timber building standing 45 feet high, ornamented, carved and painted in colours. There was an elaborate sub-division of inner space. Entrance was gained by twelve or fourteen doors and this ancient description is supported by the remains.

Ráth Caelchon to the north was named after a Munster chieftain named Caelchu, a contemporary of Cormac Mac Art. He died in Tara and was interred in a *leacht* beside which the *ráth* was raised in commemoration. Next to this rises Ráth Gráinne, 258 feet in diameter, where, it is said, the lady Gráinne, daughter of Cormac Mac Art, entertained her father and Fionn Mac Cumhaill. The *forradh* or meeting place rises next to it. To the north of Ráth Gráinne is Tobar Fionn, or Fionn's Well.

To the south of the complex at Tara stands Ráth Laoghaire, 300 feet in diameter, named after the High King during the arrival of St. Patrick. West of this fortress is a well called Tobar Laegh (signifying a calf) which, according to the seventh-century 'Annotations of Tirechan' is where St. Patrick baptised his first convert at Tara. This was Erc Mac Dego who afterwards became Bishop of Slane.

Significantly, five main roads led from Tara to the provinces of which three are still quite traceable – Slige Dala and Slige Midluachra are covered by modern roads and Slige Asail can also be seen.

Close to Tara there are two other great circular forts which are worth noting. Ráth Medb lies a mile south of Ráth Rígh, 673 feet in diameter, said to be erected by Queen Medb of Leinster when she was wife of Art the Solitary. The other lies one mile north of the banqueting hall, Ráth Miles, 300 feet in diameter. Nothing is known of its history.

The story of the abandonment of Tara as the seat of the High Kings is told in the story of Diarmuid son of Fergus Cearbaill (AD545–568). See **Diarmuid** 2. However, the curse of St. Ronán (or Ruadán) of Lorrha is contradicted by the annals for as late as 786 Tara appeared neither cursed nor deserted. However, shortly after 734, Tara did seem to lack the importance of previous years and, while it was still used, the High Kings tended to take up residence where they pleased, usually in the safety of their own provinces.

Tea. Wife of the first Milesian king, Eremon. She is referred to as a goddess of the Dé Danaan and Eremon named his capital of Tara (Tea-mhair) after her. See **Tara**.

Tech Duinn. The House of Donn. The gathering place of the dead, said to be an island lying to the south-west of Ireland presided over by Donn, god of the dead.

Tech Screpta. Sometimes *Teach Screpta*. Libraries, mentioned in the Book of Leinster, which existed as early as the sixth century AD. As Ireland was the seat of European scholarship and learning during the so-called Dark Ages, vast libraries were common in Ireland presided over by *leabhar-coimdaech* (librarians). Many of these were destroyed during the period of the Viking raids.

Tegmong. One of the three doorkeepers of Tara in the days of Conaire Mór.

Teideach. One of the two sons of Cromm Dubh, the other being Clonach. He appears as a god although the name also occurs as that of a chieftain with whom St. Patrick fought.

Teltown. See **Tailtu**.

Temuir. See **Tara**.

Tethra. A Fomorii who seems to be a sea-god. Like the Dé Danaan Manannán Mac Lir he was known as 'lord of the joyous Otherworld'. He took part in the second Battle of Magh Tuireadh and there lost his sword Orna, which was found by Ogma. See **Orna** and **Ogma**.

Three, Significance of. See **Triads**.

Three gods of craftsmanship. See **Credné Cred**, **Goibhniu** and **Luchtar**.

Three-headed bird. A creature that devastated Ireland but was slain by Amairgen.

Threefold Death. A popular motif where a person fulfils an unlikely prophecy that they would suffer three different types of death. Diarmuid Mac Fergus' multiple death is a typical example. See **Diarmuid** 2.

Tigernmas. Son of Follach. The name signifies 'lord of death'. In king lists he is given as the twenty-sixth High King, being either fifth or eighth after Eremon, the first Milesian ruler. He is said to have found the first gold mine in Ireland, and to have introduced silver-work and variegated colours in the clothing of his people, i.e. the tartan. The number of colours varied and went up according to rank. He is also recorded as having introduced the worship of an idol called Cromm Cróich or Cromm Cruach (Bloody Crescent) which involved human sacrifice. The idol was worshipped on the Plain of Adoration (Magh Slécht) on the feast of Samhain. Tigernmas was mysteriously slain during the frenzied worship of the idol.

Tiobraide Tireach. King of Ulster who slew Conn of the Hundred Battles as the High King was preparing to celebrate the annual festival at Tara.

Tír. The Irish word for 'Land' or 'Country' as in Tír fo Thuinn (Land under the Wave); Tír na mBan (Country of Women), Tír na mBeo (Land of the Living); Tír na nÓg (Land of Youth); Tír Tairnigiri (Land of Promise), etc. All these countries appear frequently in the myths and equate with the Otherworld.

Tlachtga. 1. A goddess who was daughter of the druid Mug Ruith of West Munster. She 'had been with her father learning the world's magic'. It is said that she was raped by the sons of Simon Magus. She produced three sons by three different fathers at one birth, but she died in the process. She gave her name to the Hill of Tlachta.

2. Hill of: now the Hill of Ward near Athboy, Co. Meath, 12 miles

from Tara. The Hill of Tlachtga was associated with the Samhain Festival.

Toba. See **Todga**.

Tobar. Sometimes *tober*. A well. Wells play a significant part in the religion of pre-Christian Ireland as places of worship. Unable to suppress the custom, Christianity designated them as holy wells. Pope Gregory, realising the problems of loyalty to pre-Christian cults, wrote in 601: 'The temples of the idols in that nation ought not to be destroyed; but let the idols that are in them be destroyed; let holy water be made and sprinkled in the said temples; let altars be erected and relics placed. For if those temples are well built, it is requisite that they be converted from the worship of devils to the service of the true God; that the nation, seeing that their temples are not destroyed, may remove error from their hearts and knowing and adoring the true God, may the more familiarly resort to places to which they have been accustomed.' There are many places in Ireland named after the former pagan wells: Toberaheena (Friday's well), Toberbilly (well of the ancient tree), Tobercurry (well of the cauldron), Tobermore (great well), etc.

Tochmarc. Wooing. A class of tales such as '*Tochmarc Emer*' (The Wooing of Emer), '*Tochmarc Ailbe*', '*Tochmarc Étain*', '*Tochmarc Fithirne agus Dairine, dá ingen Tuatháil*' (The wooing of Fithirne and Dairine, the two daughters of Tuathal), etc.

Tochur. One of the three doorkeepers of Tara in the time of Conaire Mór.

Todga. A servant of Dealgnaid, the wife of Partholón. He seized the opportunity of her husband's absence to have an affair with her.

Tógail. Destruction. A class of tale, such as '*Tógail Bruidhne Da Derga*' (Destruction of Da Derga's Hostel), '*Tógail Bruidhne Da Choca*' (Destruction of Da Choca's Hostel), '*Tógail Troí*' (Destruction of Troy), etc.

Toice Bhrean. The guardian of the well out of which rose Loch Guirr. The name implies a guardian of 'fortune' from the Old Irish *toice* (*toicthiu*), fate or destiny. See **Áine**.

Toll Tuinde. Hill of the Wave. Forty days after Cesair's landing in Ireland, Fintan, son of Bochra, Cesair's husband (given in other versions as her husband, not her son), fled to Toll Tuinde, sometimes Tul Tuinde. Cesair and her companions died while he spent a year sheltering there and then, when the Deluge came, he survived it by becoming metamorphosed into a salmon.

Tonn. A wave. 'The Three Great Waves of Ireland' are much celebrated in the sagas and myths. These were: Tonn Tuaithe at the
mouth of the Bann, Co. Derry; Tonn Rudraidhe, Dundrum Bay, Co.
Down; Tonn Cliodhna, Glandore Bay, Co. Cork. See **Cliodhna,
Rudraidhe** and **Tuaithe.** The three waves used to roar in response to
the moan of the magic shield of Conchobhar Mac Nessa, which cried
out when its bearer was in trouble. See **Ochain.**

Tóraigheacht. Rescue. A class of tales such as '*Tóraigheacht an Chairthe
Sgárlóide*' (Rescue of the scarlet cloth), '*Tóraigheacht Duibhe Lacha*'
(Rescue of Dubh Lacha), '*Tóraigheacht Fiacail Ríogh Greag*'
(Rescue of the tooth of the King of Greece), '*Tóraigheachta Ghruaidhe
Grian-Sholuis*' (Rescue of the lady of sunburnt cheeks),
'*Tóraigheachta na hEilite*' (Rescue of the does), etc.

Torc. Torque. An ornament of twisted or modelled gold worn around
the neck (*muin-torc*, the neck torc, being the commonest form). This
was a common adornment to all the Celtic peoples in ancient times
and the famous statue of *The Dying Gaul* (Capitoline Museum,
Rome) depicts a warrior with such a torc around his neck. Numerous
torcs have been found in Ireland as well as in other Celtic areas.
Usually, the terminals of these torcs have animals or other exotic
figures moulded into them. They clearly have a religious connotation
and are often seen on the necks of gods as well as heroes. Significantly, the Old Irish word *torc* signifies a chieftain or hero.

Torc Triatha. See **Orc-Triath.**

Torna Éices. Torna the Learned. A Munster poet who found a baby
abandoned and naked near Tara and fostered him. The baby grew up
as Niall of the Nine Hostages.

Tory Island. Chief island of the Fomorii. The name derives from *torach*
(tower-like) which is an apt description of the island which lies off the
coast of Donegal. Conann's Tower, which the Nemedians attacked,
was built on it. On Tor Mór, a headland, Balor of the Evil Eye
imprisoned his daughter Ethlinn in a tower of crystal.

Tradaban, Well of. Celta the warrior, in a Christian embellishment to
the story of the Fianna, is said to have met St. Patrick and led him to
the well where he uttered an exquisite lyric in praise of its healing
properties.

Traighthren. Son of Traighlethan. A Red Branch champion who,
together with his brother, was slain by Fergus Mac Roth when
Fergus realised how he had been deceived by Conchobhar Mac Nessa
over the sons of Usna.

Transmigration of souls. A basic belief in pre-Christian Ireland. See **Otherworld**. Souls migrated from the Land of the Living to the Land of the Dead and vice versa. They also migrated through various births. People could not only be reborn as other people but could go through various metamorphoses, for example Fintan who survived the Deluge by changing into a salmon, the swineherds of Bodb and Ochall who became various animals before ending as the two great bulls of Connacht and Cuailgne, and Tuan Mac Cairell's varying transformations.

Treasure bag of the Fianna. It contained numerous articles with magical properties such as the knife and shirt of Manannán Mac Lir. The treasures would appear in the bag at full-tide but vanish at ebb-tide. It was made from the skin of Aoife who was killed while in the form of a crane. Lia, lord of Luchtar, was keeper of the bag until slain by Fionn Mac Cumhail. See **Aoife** 3.

Tree of Life. Crann Bethadh. Sacred trees were talismans of all tribes and clans. Each had its own sacred tree standing, usually, in the centre of its territory. Often a tribal raid by a rival clan would simply be for the purpose of destroying the tree and thus demoralising the enemy.

Trendorn. A spy of Conchobhar Mac Nessa sent to inform the Ulster king whether Deirdre was as beautiful as ever. In other versions of the story this role falls to Gelban. Although Naoise put Trendorn's eye out, the spy told Conchobhar that he would gladly give the other to gaze on the beauty of Deirdre.

Tren-fher. Strong man. A champion in the retinue of a chieftain or king. He is sometimes referred to as *cath-míled* (battle soldier). He answers any challenges to single combat on behalf of his chieftain. In some romances he appears as *aire-echtra* (avenger of insults) and the position is actually prescribed in Brehon Law. Even St. Patrick had his personal *tren-fher*. This was St. Mac Carthen, the first Bishop of Clogher. Anglicised, this title is to be found in the Irish name Traynor.

Treon. Father of Bebhionn.

Triads. The concept of three or the trinity seems more or less universal among Indo-European cultures, although nowhere is it more prominent than in Celtic culture. Diogenes Laertius (*c.* second or third century BC) mentions that the druids taught in the form of triads. In both Irish and Welsh myth the gods came in threes, triune gods and goddesses. Three and three times three permeate Celtic philosophy and art. Hilary, who became Bishop of Poitiers about 350, is regarded as the first native Celt to become an outstanding force in the Christian movement. Significantly, his greatest work was *De Trinitate*, defining the concept of a Holy Trinity which is so integral to Christian belief today. As a Celt, Hilary was imbued with the mystical tradition of his people and therefore the Trinity in Christian tradition probably owes its origin more to Celtic concepts than to the Judaic-Greco background of the religion.

Triath. Son of Febal. A foster son of Midir who told Aonghus Óg the truth about his parentage.

Trinity. See **Triads**.

Triscatal. The champion of Conchobhar Mac Nessa. He was a mighty broad-fronted, shaggy-haired man with thighs as thick as an ordinary man's body, wearing a leather apron from his armpit down; his limbs were bare and his aspect so fierce that he killed by his very glance.

Tuage. A woman for whom Manannán Mac Lir lusted. He sent a druid, Fer Ferdiad, to bring her to him. The druid lulled her to sleep and led her to Ibhear Glas. While he went to seek a ship to transport them, Tuage drowned and for this neglect Manannán Mac Lir slew the druid.

Tuaithe. A god of whom little is known save that the Wave of Tuaithe, at the mouth of the Bann, Co. Derry, was named after him.

Tuan Mac Cairell. Son of Starn, brother of Partholón. When a plague destroyed the Partholóns, he survived and found himself transformed into a stag. After living as king of the stags in Ireland until old age, he was then changed into an eagle. Eventually he metamorphosed into a salmon which was caught and eaten by the wife of Cairell who then gave birth to him in human form again with his memory of the whole history of Ireland from the coming of Partholón. The story typifies the Celtic belief in reincarnation.

Tuan Mac Starn. The original name of Tuan Mac Cairell. See above.

Tuatha. A people, tribe or nation. It is also used in the sagas to denote a country or petty kingdom or territory and it later became used as a term for the state or people as opposed to the church.

Tuatha Cruithne. See **Picts**.

Tuatha Dé Danaan. The people of the goddess Dana. The gods of the pre-Christian Irish who inhabited the land before the coming of the Milesians. When Christian monks started to write down the sagas, these gods and goddesses were demoted into heroes and heroines although much remained to demonstrate their god-like abilities. Under their leader Nuada, the Dé Danaan came to Ireland from a northern country where they had four fabulous cities – Falias, Gorias, Finias and Murias. They defeated the Firbolg and then overcame the Fomorii to become rulers of Ireland. They are represented as gods of light and goodness as opposed to the more sinister Fomorii. This is not to say that they were without vice. All human passion was experienced by them. Eventually, they were overcome by the Milesians, regarded as the ancestors of the Gaels, who drove them underground. The gods of the Dé Danaan were common to all the Celtic peoples: their names are cognate with many deities who appear in the Welsh myths. As they were pushed underground they were demoted in the eyes of the people and became merely fairies. However, the argument created by the Christian monks was still raging in the tenth century when the poet Eochaidh Ua Flainn (d. 974) wrote a poem asking whether the Dé Danaans were gods or humans. He concludes that they were humans and emphasises: 'I do not worship them, I worship the one true god.' It is an interesting point to end with. Does it mean that the gods were still worshipped in some parts at that time?

Tuathal Teachtmhair. Tuathal the Legitimate. According to the king lists he was High King from AD130 to 160 and was father of Fedilimid Rechtmar (the Lawgiver, who ruled from AD164 to 174). He was also the father of Fithir and Dairine, whose marriage to Eochaidh of Leinster is the story of the beginning of the famous Bóramha Tribute, the fine placed on the kings of Leinster. Tuathal was of Connacht ancestry and it is said that during a rebellion his mother fled to Britain where he was born. Returning to Ireland, Tuathal rose from provincial king to High King and it was he who formed the new province of Meath as the personal estate of the High Kings. Meath and Westmeath now constitute only half of the original 'middle province'. Tuathal also built palaces at Tara, Teltown, Tlaghtga and Uisneach.

Tugen. Sometimes Taiden or Stuigen. The multi-coloured cloak of bird feathers which was the official robe of the chief *ollamh* of Ireland, described in 'The Dialogue of Two Sages' when Fer Cherdne and Neide debated as to who would fill the office.

Tuirbe. Claimed as the father of Goibhniu the smith-god in some texts. He was the greatest axe-thrower among the gods.

Tuireann. 1. A female – she appears varyingly as the sister of Fionn Mac Cumhail, the sister of Fionn's mother Murna and sometimes as Fionn's sister-in-law. She was married to Ullan who was having an affair with a druidess. In jealousy, the druidess turned Tuireann into a bitch-dog. In this form she gave birth to Fionn's hounds Bran and Sceolan. Ullan promised the druidess that he would leave Tuireann and go to live with her if she turned her back into a human being.

2. A male – he had three sons by the goddess Brigid, Brían, Iuchar and Iucharbha. He was the son of Ogma and Étain 1.

3. Children of: Brían, Iuchar and Iucharba slew Cian the father of Lugh Lámhfhada. In compensation they were ordered by Lugh to obtain for him the following items: three apples from the Orient Garden; the healing pig-skin of King Tuis of Greece; the Lúin or spear of King Pisear of Persia; the chariot and horses of King Dobhar of Siogair; the magic pigs of King Easal of the Golden Pillars; Fáil-Inis, the whelp of the king of Ioruaidh; and the cooking spit of the women of Fianchuibhe. Finally they were to give three shouts on the Hill of Miodchaoin. This saga is said to be the Irish equivalent to the voyage of Jason and his quest for the Golden Fleece. See **Brían**.

Tuis. King of Greece who had a magical pig-skin which had the property of healing all battle wounds and illnesses. It was one of the items which the children of Tuireann had to bring back to Ireland.

U. *Ur* (blackthorn) in the Ogham alphabet.

Úaig Búana. Búan's Grave. See **Búan 1**.

Uaithne. 1. Sometimes Uathe. The harp of the Dagda. It was enchanted and would only sound when summoned to do so by the Dagda. It was stolen by the Fomorii but the Dagda traced it to their feasting house and called it. It leapt forward, killing nine Fomorii, and began to sing a paean praising the Dagda.

2. The Dagda's harpist who had an affair with Boann. They had three sons, Goltrade, Gentrade and Suantrade, who played such sad music that it was said twelve men once died listening to it and weeping for sorrow.

Uaman. The name of the *sídhe* in Connacht which was ruled by Ethal Anubhail, the father of Cáer with whom Aonghus Óg, the love-god, fell in love.

Uan. One of the six servers of the High King at Temuir (Tara).

Uar. The name signifies 'cruel'. He and his sons, Ill-Omen, Damage and Want, dwelt in Munster but appear to be Fomorii. They clashed with Fionn Mac Cumhail. Uar's three sons were described as 'three foemen – lame-thighed . . . left-handed of the race of wondrous evil, and from the gravelly plain of Hell below . . . venom on their weapons, and venom on their dress, and on their hands and feet and on everything they touched'.

Uarad Garad. Sometimes Uarán Garaid. A river in Connacht where Conall Cearnach (in other versions Mac Cécht) filled his cup to take water back to Conaire Mór at the time of 'The Destruction of Da Derga's Hostel'.

Uath Mac Imoman. The name signifies 'Horror, son of Terror'. During the story of 'The Feast of Bricriu' the heroes Cúchulainn, Laoghaire and Conall were sent to Uath's Lake, where Uath dwelt, so that he should judge which of them was the greatest warrior in

Ireland. Uath is said to have been able to transform himself into any shape that pleased him. Uath asked the warriors to submit to a test. They could take his axe and cut off his head provided that he could cut theirs off the next day in turn. There are two versions as to what happened next. In one, both Laoghaire and Conall refused on the grounds that they had not the power to remain alive when Uath cut their heads off, but they knew Uath, being a *sirite* (elfman), had such power. The other version says that they did cut off Uath's head but when he picked it up and replaced it, they refused to return the next day to receive Uath's stroke. In both versions only Cúchulainn agreed to the conditions. When Uath came to cut off Cúchulainn's head, the blade of the axe reversed whereupon Uath hailed Cúchulainn as the true champion of Ireland. However, Laoghaire and Conall refused to accept this judgement. There are other variants of this tale in which a nameless churl presents himself at Bricriu's hall and challenges all the warriors of Ulster along the same lines.

Uathach. Daughter of Scáthach, the female champion who ran a school of martial arts in Alba where Cúchulainn trained. As Scáthach's name means 'shadow', so Uathach's name means 'spectre' and she is usually referred to as Uathach of the Glen. When Cúchulainn arrived at Scáthach's fortress, it was Uathach who let him in. While she served him food, Cúchulainn forgot his strength and broke her finger in taking a dish from her hand. Her scream brought the champion Cochar Crufe, her lover, to her. He challenged Cúchulainn and Cúchulainn slew him. In reparation Cúchulainn had to accept Cochar Crufe's duties as guardian of Dún Scáthach. Uathach became Cúchulainn's mistress.

Ugaine Mór. Sometimes give as Ugony Mór or 'The Great'. Said to have been High King in the sixth century BC. His rule extended not only to all of Ireland but to the Continental Celts of Gaul. He married a Gaulish princess named Cesair and their children were Laoghaire Lorc and Cobhthach. It is said that on his death Ireland was divided into twenty-five parts among his children and that this division of Ireland lasted three hundred years. The number twenty-five appears frequently in the myths; there are twenty-five battalions of the Fianna, and, according to Seathrún Céitinn, originally twenty-five dioceses in the country.

Uí Corra. Lochan, Emne and Silvester were three heroes of the clan Uí Corra who went on a voyage among strange and exotic islands. Scholars suggest that the composition of this story seems to date from the sixth century AD and that it was for Christian moral edification.

Uigreann. Sometimes Uirgriu. He was slain by Fionn Mac Cumhail. In one account the five sons of Uigreann revenged themselves on Fionn, each casting a spear at him so that it was said that all five killed him. It is also significant that Fionn was said to be one of the five masters of every art, the numeral having special significance.

Uillin. A grandson of Nuada who was said to have slain Manannán Mac Lir in Loch Corrib and given his name to Moycullin, Co. Galway.

Uisneach. 1. See **Usna**.

2. The Hill of Uisneach (formerly Balor's Hill), thought to be the 'navel of Ireland' or the exact centre of the country where the great Stone of Divisions (Aill na Mirenn) stands, marking the joining of the five provinces of Ireland. The actual site is near Ráthconrath, Co. Westmeath. Tuathal Teachtmhair built one of his four great palaces here and one of the three major festivals of Ireland was held here. Seathrún Céitinn says that the Feast of Bel (Bilé) was the prime ceremony at Uisneach. However, St. Patrick is said to have cursed the ancient stones there so they could not be heated by fire nor hiss when they were cooled by water. According to Geoffrey of Monmouth, Stonehenge in Britain was built by the druid Merlin who took the stones from 'Mount Killaraus' which is identified as Uisneach.

Ulaid. Dative form Ulaidh. Ulster. The ancient province and kingdom covers approximately the same geographical boundaries as the modern province, though this province must not be confused with the political province of Northern Ireland which only includes six out of the nine Ulster counties. These six counties (Antrim, Armagh, Down, Derry, Fermanagh and Tyrone) were partitioned from the rest of Ulster and Ireland in 1921. The Cos. Cavan, Monaghan and Donegal also comprise the province of Ulster. Rudraidhe, son of Partholón, was said to have founded the royal house of Ulster and the people were sometimes known as Clan Rudhraidhe and Rudricans. Its capital was at Emain Macha (Navan) two miles west of Armagh. The heroes of Ulster are more widely known than those of the other provinces thanks to the tremendous popularity of the Red Branch, or Ulster Cycle. Tradition has dated the decline of this kingdom as a significant power to the days of Cormac Mac Art (AD254–77). But some records show that the change in its fortunes was brought about by the northern expansion of the family of Niall of the Nine Hostages (*c*. AD379), that is the Uí Néill. See **Provinces**.

Ullan. Husband of Tuireann, the sister of Fionn Mac Cumhail. He had an affair with a druidess who became jealous of his wife Tuireann and changed her into a bitch-dog. In this form she gave birth to Sceolan and Bran who became Fionn's faithful hounds. Ullan promised the druidess that he would go with her if she turned his wife back into human shape.

Ulster. See **Ulaid**.

Ulster Cycle. See **Red Branch Cycle**.

Ultonia. Latin name for Ulster.

Uma. Son of Remanfissech. See **Remanfissech**.

Umal. One of the nine best pipers in the world.

Uman-sruth. The bronze stream. Cúchulainn possessed a spear named Cletiné with which he had slain many warriors and which Medb of Connacht coveted. She asked a bard to go to Cúchulainn and request the spear on the grounds that one must never refuse a gift demanded by a poet. The bard and Cúchulainn were standing by a stream when the bard requested the gift. Cúchulainn was so enraged that instead of handing the spear to the poet he flung it. With such strength did he fling it that it pierced the bard's head and the force broke the bronze (*umal*) of the spear which fell into the stream, giving it its name.

Underwater. There are several survival stories of human beings taken underwater by gods and able to return to the surface unharmed. In the Book of the Dun Cow there occurs the story of the flooding of Lough Neagh by Ecca. A woman survived the flooding and lived in her house for a year under the waves with her dog. Bored by this existence she changed into a salmon and lived three hundred years more until rescued by Congall who named her Muirgen 'born of the sea'. Ruadh and Mael Dúin both visited underwater kingdoms. The Cothulín Druith, placed on the head, enabled humans to live underwater. There appears a firm belief in the sea as the 'mother of all life'. Numerous submerged cities, fortresses and towns are a peculiar part of Celtic folklore.

Underworld. See **Otherworld**.

Undry. Sometimes Uinde (an act of beholding). The enchanted cauldron of the Dagda in which everyone found food in proportion to their merits and from which no one went away hungry.

Urias. Of the Noble Nature. He dwelt in the city of Gorias, one of the four fabulous cities from which the Dé Danaan originated. He was steeped in wisdom.

Úrscéal. Old Irish *ursgeul*. A saga or romance.

Usna. Variously given as Uisliu, Usnach, Uisneach and Usnagh. He was the husband of Ebhla. Ebhla was daughter of the druid Cathbad and of Maga, a daughter of the love-god Aonghus Óg. Usna and Maga had three sons, the Red Branch heroes Naoise, Ainlé and Ardan who feature in the tragic tale of '*Oidhe Cloinne Uisneach*' (The Exile of the Sons of Usna), the oldest of the famous *Trí Truagha na Scéaluidheachta*, The Three Sorrows of Story-telling. See **Deirdre** and **Naoise**.

Utherchair. Hornskin. Father of the Red Branch champion Celtchair.

Select Bibliography

IT would be an impossible task to attempt a comprehensive bibliography of Irish mythology in a work of this nature. The primary sources of Irish mythology are to be found in some five hundred or more manuscripts which date back to the eleventh century AD and which are mainly copies of older manuscripts which have not survived. A large proportion of these manuscripts have not been edited and there remains much work to be done in the field.

Among the principal sources are *Leabhar na hUidhre* (The Book of the Dun Cow), dating from the late eleventh century, and *Leabhar Laignech* (The Book of Leinster), a twelfth-century compilation, both of which are in the Royal Irish Academy. These have been edited by such scholars as R. I. Best, Oscar Bergin and M. A. O'Brien. The *Book of Ballymote*, which contains the famous 'Book of Rights', put together in 1391, is also held by the Royal Irish Academy. Its date of compilation was contemporary with the *Yellow Book of Lecan*, held by Trinity College, Dublin. This is not to be confused with the *Great Book of Lecan*, compiled about 1416, which is preserved by the Royal Irish Academy.

The main source book on these manuscripts remains R. I. Best's *Bibliography of Irish Philology and Manuscript Literature*, Dublin, 1913. An additional volume covering new materials found from 1913 to 1941 was published in Dublin in 1942.

It would be equally impossible to give an adequate listing of all the academic papers, essays and articles which have appeared over the years in the numerous scholastic journals such as *Eriu, Revue Celtique, Journal of Celtic Studies, Gadelica, Études Celtiques, Transactions of the Ossianic Society, Béaloideas* (Journal of the Folklore Society of Ireland) and so forth.

The purpose of this bibliography is, therefore, merely to give a selected general introduction to the many studies and interpretations that exist in book form, both academic and for the lay reader, together with a selection of re-tellings or fictional works based on the myths.

Academic studies

Atkinson, R., *The Book of Leinster*. Oxford, 1880.

Begin, Oscar, and Best, R. I., *Leabhar na hUidre* (Book of the Dun Cow). Dublin, 1929.

— *Tochmarc Étain*. Dublin, 1936.

Best, R. I. and O'Brien, M. A., *The Book of Leinster*. 5 vols. Dublin, 1954–67.

Binchy, Daniel A., *Críth Gablach*. Dublin, 1941.

Bjersby, Brigit M. H., *The Interpretation of the Cuchulain Legend in the Works of W. B. Yeats*, Uppsala Irish Studies No 1. Uppsala, 1950.

Byrne, F. J., *Irish Kings and High Kings*. London, 1973.

Campbell, J. J., *Legends of Ireland*. London, 1955.

Campbell, John G., *The Fions: Account of the Fenians in Scottish Tradition*. London, 1891.

Carmichael, A., *Carmina Gadelica*. Edinburgh, 1928.

Chadwick, H. M. and Nora, *The Growth of Literature*. 3 vols. Oxford, 1932.

Coghlan, Ronan, *Pocket Dictionary of Irish Myth and Legend*. Belfast, 1985.

Comyn, David, *Mac Gniomharta Fhinn* (The Youthful Exploits of Finn). Dublin, 1846.

Connellan, Owen, *The Annals of Ireland* (The Four Masters). Dublin, 1846.

Cross, Tom Peete, *Motif Index of Early Irish Literature*. Indiana University, 1919.

De Blácam, Aodh, *Gaelic Literature Surveyed*. Dublin, 1929.

— *A First Book of Irish Literature*. 1934.

De Jubainville, H. D'Arbois, *The Irish Mythological Cycle*. Dublin, 1903. (Translation of French original *L'Epopée Celtique en Irland*. Paris, 1884).

Delargy, J. H., *The Gaelic Storyteller*. London, 1947.

Dillon, Myles, *The Cycle of the Kings*. London, 1946.

— *Early Irish Literature*. Chicago, 1948.

— *Serglige Con Culainn*. Dublin, 1953.

— *Irish Sagas*. Dublin, 1954.

— *Lebor na Cert* (Book of Rights). London, 1962.

— See Sjoestedt, M. L.

Flower, Robin, *Byron and Ossian*. Oxford, 1928.

— *The Irish Tradition*. Oxford, 1947.

Gray, Elizabeth A., *Cath Maige Tuired: The Second Battle of Moytura*. London, 1983.

Greene, David, *Fingal Ronáin*. Dublin, 1955.

Gwynn, Edward John, *The Metrical Dinsenchas*. Dublin, 1903.

Henderson, George, *Fled Bricrend* (Bricriu's Feast). London, 1899.

Hennessy, William M. *Annála Uladh*. Dublin, 1887–1901.

— *Mesca Uladh* (Intoxication of Ulster). Dublin, 1889.

Hull, Eleanor, *The Cúchullin Saga in Irish Literature*, Grimm Library No. 8. London, 1898.

— *A Text Book of Irish Literature*. Dublin, 1906.

— *The Poem Book of the Gael*. Dublin, 1912.

Hull, Vernan E., *Longes Mac n-Uislenn*, Monograph of the Society of Modern Languages. New York, 1949.

Hyde, Douglas, *The Story of Early Gaelic Literature*, New Irish Library No.6. Dublin, 1893.

— *A Literary History of Ireland*. London, 1899.

Kavanagh, Peter, *Irish Mythology* (limited edition of 100). New York, 1958–59.

Keating, Geoffrey (Seathrún Céitinn), *Foras Feasa ar Éirinn* (History of Ireland), trs. David Comyn and Patrick Dineen. London 1902–14.

Kennedy, Patrick, *Legendary Fiction of the Irish Celts*. London, 1866.

— *The Bardic Stories of Ireland*. Dublin, 1871.

Knott, Eleanor, *Tógail Bruidne Da Derga*. Dublin, 1936.

— with Murphy, Gerard, *Early Irish Literature*. London, 1966.

Larmine, William, *Legends as Material for Literature*. Dublin, 1899.

Mac Alister, R. A. S. and Mac Neill, Eoin, *Leabhar Gabhála: The Book of Conquests*. London, 1917.

— *Lebor Gabál Erenn* (The Book of the Takings Of Ireland). 5 vols. London, 1938, 1939, 1940, 1941 and 1956.

— *Two (Irish) Arthurian Romances*. London, 1910.

Mac Cana, Proinsias, *Celtic Mythology*. London, 1970.

Mac Donogh, Thomas, *Literature in Ireland*. Dublin, 1916.

Mac Neill, Eoin, *Duanaire Finn* (Vol. 1). London, 1908.

— See Mac Alister, R. A. S.

Markle, Jean, *La Femme Celte*. Paris, 1972. Trs. *Women of the Celts*. London, 1975.

Meyer, Kuno, *Cath Finntragha or Battle of Ventry*. Oxford, 1885.
— *Aislinge Meic Conglinne*. London, 1892.
— *Liadin and Cuirithir: A love story*. London, 1900.
— *The Triads of Ireland*. Dublin, 1906.
— *The Instructions of Cormac Mac Art*. Dublin, 1909.
— *Fianairgreacht*. Dublin, 1913.
— *Death Tales of the Ulster Heroes*. Dublin, 1913.
— with Nutt, Alfred, *The Voyage of Bran*. 2 vols. London, 1895.
Murphy, Gerard. *Duanaire Finn*. Vol. 2, London, 1933; Vol. 3, London, 1954.
— *Saga and Myth in Ancient Ireland*. Dublin, 1961.
— *The Ossianic Lore and Romantic Tales of Medieval Ireland*. Dublin, 1955.
Nutt, Alfred, *Ossian and Ossianic Literature*. London, 1899.
— *Cúchulainn: The Irish Achilles*. London, 1900.
— See Meyer, Kuno.
Ní Sheaghdha, Nessa, *Tóruigheacht Dhiarmada agus Ghráinne*. Dublin, 1967.
O'Brennan, M. A., *Ancient Ireland*. Dublin, 1855.
Ó Cúiv, Brían, *Cath Muighe Tuireadh*. Dublin, 1945.
O'Curry, Eugene, *Cath Mhuige Leana*. Dublin, 1855.
O'Daly, M., *Cath Maige Macraime*. Dublin, 1975.
O'Donovan, John, *Annals of the Kingdom of Ireland*. Dublin, 1856.
— *Banquet of Dún na nGeid and the Battle of Mag Ráth*. Dublin, 1842.
Ó Fianneachta, Pádraig, *Táin Bó Cuailgne*. Dublin, 1966.
Ó Flannghaile, Tomás, *Laoi Oisín ar Thír na nÓg* (edited from the version of Micheál Coimín, c. 1750). Dublin, n.d.
O'Grady, Standish Hayes, *Tóruigheacht Dhiarmada agus Gráinne*. 3 vols. Dublin, 1854.
— *Silva Gadelica*. 2 vols. Dublin, 1893.
O'Grady, Standish James, *The History of Ireland: The Heroic Period*. Dublin, 1878–80.
— *Early Bardic Literature in Ireland*. London, 1879.
O'Keefe, J. G., *Buile Suibhne Geilt*. London, 1913.
Ó Suiochfhradha, Pádraig, *Cath Fionntragha*. Dublin, 1911.
— *Laoithe na Feinne*. Dublin, 1946.
Ossianic Society, *Imtheacht na Tromfhaimhe*. Dublin, 1960.
O'Rahilly, Cecile, *The Pursuit of Gruaidh Grian-Sholuis*. London, 1924.
— *Táin Bó Cuailgne* (from the Book of Leinster). Dublin, 1967.
— *Cath Finntragha*. Dublin, 1962.

— *Táin Bó Cualgne* (from the Book of the Dun Cow). Dublin, 1978.

O'Rahilly, Thomas F., *Early Irish History and Mythology.* Dublin, 1946.

Power, Patrick G., *A Literary History of Ireland.* Cork, 1969.

Rees, Alwyn and Brinley, *Celtic Heritage.* London, 1961.

Rolleston, T. W., *Myths and Legends of the Celtic Race.* London, 1912.

Russell, T. O., *An Bhóramha Laighean.* Dublin, 1901.

Saul, Charles B., *Traditional Irish Literature.* London, 1970.

Sjoestedt, M. L., *Gods and Heroes of the Celts.* Paris, 1949 (trs. by Myles Dillon, Dublin, 1949).

Spaan, D. B., *The Otherworld in Early Irish Literature.* Ann Arbor, USA, 1978.

Squire, Charles, *Celtic Myths and Legends.* London, 1901.

Thurneysen, Rudolf, *Scéla Mucce Meic Da Thó.* Dublin, 1935.

Ua h-Ogain, Seaghain and Laoide, Seosamh, *Teacht agus Imtheacht an Ghiolla Deacair, Tóriugheacht Chonáin agus Chudeachtaí.* Dublin, 1905.

Van Hamel, A. G., *Compert Con Culainn.* Dublin, 1933.

— *Myth en Historie in Het Oude Ireland.* Amsterdam, 1942.

Re-Tellings

Burc, Eamonn, *Eochair, a King's Son.* Dublin, 1982.

Byrne, Brian Oswald Donn, *The Island of Youth.* London, 1932.

— *The Hound of Ireland.* London, 1934.

Carleton, William, *Traits and Stories of the Irish Peasantry.* 1860.

— *Tales of Ireland.* 1834.

Colum, Padraic, *A Boy in Éirinn.* London, 1913.

— *Moytura: A Play.* Dublin, 1963.

— *A Treasury of Irish Folklore.* New York, 1963.

Cross, Tom Peete and Slover, Clark H., *Ancient Irish Tales.* London, 1936.

Curry, Jane Louise, *Beneath the Hills.* London, 1967.

Curtin, Jeremiah, *Hero Tales of Ireland.* Dublin, 1894.

— *Irish Folk-Tales.* Dublin, n.d.

De Blácam, Aodh, *The Druid's Cave.* Dublin, 1920.

De Vere, Aubrey, *The Foray of Queen Maeve.* London, 1882.

Donegan, Maureen, *Fables and Legends of Ireland.* 1976.

Duffy, Richard, *The Fate of the Children of Tuireann.* Dublin, 1901.

Dunbar, Aldis, *The Sons of O'Cormack.* London, 1904.

Dunn, Joseph, *The Ancient Irish Epic – Táin Bó Cuailgne*. London, 1914.

Fallon, Padraic, *Diarmuid and Gráinne*. Dublin, n.d.

— *The Vision of Mac Conglinne*. Dublin, 1953.

Faraday, (Lucy) Winifred, *The Cattle Raid of Cualgne*, Grimm Library No 16. London, 1904.

— *The Cuchullin Saga*. London, 1904.

Ferguson, Sir Samuel, *Congal*. London, 1872.

— *A Hibernian Night's Entertainment*. Dublin, 1887.

— *Lays of the Red Branch*. New York, 1893.

— *Aideen's Grave*. Dublin, 1925.

Fitzpatrick, Jim, *Celtia*. Dublin, 1975.

— *The Book of Conquests*. Dublin, 1978.

— *The Silver Arm*. Dublin, 1981.

— *Erinsaga* (introduced by Andrew M. Greeley). Dublin, 1985.

Flint, Kenneth, *Riders of the Sídhe*. New York, 1986.

Frost, Gregory, *Táin*. New York, 1986.

Gantz, Jeffrey, *Early Irish Myths and Sagas*. London, 1981.

Greeley, Andrew M., *The Magic Cup: An Irish Legend*. New York, 1979.

Gregory, Lady (Isabella) Augusta, *Cuchulain of Muirthemne*. London, 1902.

— *Gods and Fighting Men*. London, 1904.

Gwyne, Stephen Lucius, *A Lay of Ossian*. London, 1904.

Hazel, Paul, *The Finnbranch*. New York, 1986.

Hull, Eleanor, *Cuchulain – The Hound of Ulster*. London, 1909.

Hutton, Mary A., *The Táin – an epic told in English verse*. Dublin, 1978.

Hyde, Douglas, *The Three Sorrows of Storytelling*. London, 1895.

Ireland, Michael, *The Return of the Hero*. London, 1923.

Joyce, P. W., *Old Celtic Romances*. London, 1879.

Joyce, Robert Dwyer, *Blanid*. Boston, 1879.

—*Deirdre*. Boston, 1879.

Kinsella, Thomas, *The Táin*. Oxford, 1970.

Krape, Alexander Haggerty, *Balor with the Evil Eye*. New York, 1927.

Larmine, William, *Glanlua*. London, 1889.

— *Fand and other poems*. Dublin, 1892.

— *West Irish Folktales and Romances*. London, 1893.

Lawless, (Hon.) Emily, *Grania*. Dublin, 1892.

Leahy, Arthur Herbert, *The Courtship of Ferb*, Irish Saga Library No. 1. Dublin, 1902.

— *Heroic Romances of Ireland*, Irish Saga Library No 2. Dublin, 1905–6.

Leary, Edmund, *Irish Fairy Tales*. Dublin, 1889.

Levin, Betty, *The Sword of Culann*. London, 1973.

Lover, Samuel, *Legends and Stories of Ireland*. London, 1834.

Mac Leod, Fiona (pseud. of William Sharp), *The Washer of the Ford*. Portland, Maine, USA, 1896.

— *The Laughter of Peterkin*. Portland, 1897.

— *Deirdre and the sons of Usna*. Portland, 1903.

— *The House of Usna*. Portland, 1903.

— *The Isle of Dreams*. Portland, 1905.

— *The Immortal Hour: a drama*. Portland, 1907.

— *Ulad of Dreams*. Portland, 1907.

Mac Pherson, James, *Fragments of Ancient Poetry Collected in the Highlands*. 1760.

— *Fingal*. 1762.

— *Temora*. 1763. (Three volumes collectively known as Ossian.)

Martyn, Edward, *Maeve*. London, 1917. (Reprinted from *The Heath Field and Maeve*. Dublin, 1899.)

Milligan, Alice, *The Last Feast of the Fianna*. London, 1900.

— *Hero Lays*. Dublin 1908.

— *Oisín in Tír na nÓg (Oisín i dTir ná nÓg*, trs. *Tadhg Ua Dhonnchadha*. Dublin, 1944).

Neeson, Eoin, *The First Book of Irish Myths and Legends*. Cork, 1965.

— *The Second Book of Irish Myths and Legends*. Cork, 1966.

O'Connor, N. J., *Battles and Enchantments*. Dublin, 1924.

O' Faolain, Eileen, *Irish Sagas and Folk Tales*. London, 1954.

— *Children of the Salmon*. New York, 1965.

Offutt, Andrew, *Cormac Mac Art* (series vols 1–8). New York, 1979–86.

O'Grady, Standish James, *Fionn and His Companions*, Dublin, 1892.

— *The Coming of Cúchulain*. London, 1894.

— *Ulrick the Ready*. London, 1896.

— *The Departure of Dermot*. Dublin, 1917.

— *The Triumph and Passing of Cúchulain*. London, 1920.

Ó Laoire, Peadar, *Táin Bó Cuailgne*. Dublin, 1915.

Parsons, E. B., *Tales of Tara*. Dublin, 1933.

— *Dusk of the Druid*. London, 1935.

Perry, Mark C., *Morrigu: The Desecration*. New York, 1986.

Pilkington, Francis M., *Three Sorrowful Tales of Erin*. London, 1962.
— *Shamrock and Spear*. London, 1966.
Roberts, Keith, *Gráinne*. London, 1987.
Rolleston, T. W., *The High Deeds of Finn*. London, 1910.
Rush, Alison, *The Last of Danu's Children*. London, 1982.
Russell, Violet, *Heroes of the Dawn; The Fenian Cycle*. Dublin, 1913.
Scott, Michael, *The First Book of Irish Folk and Fairy Tales*. London, 1982.
— *The Second Book of Irish Folk and Fairy Tales*. London, 1983.
— *The Third Book of Irish Folk and Fairy Tales*. London, 1984.
— *A Celtic Odyssey: The Voyage of Maildun*. London, 1985.
— *The Children of Lir*. London, 1986.
— *Tales of the Bard: Magician's Law*. London, 1987.
Shaw, Francis, *The Dream of Oengus*. Dublin, 1934.
Sigerson, George, *The Saga of King Lir*. Dublin, 1911.
Squire, Charles, *The Boy Hero of Erin*. London, 1907.
Stephens, James, *Deirdre*. London, 1923.
— *In the Land of Youth*. London, 1924.
— *Irish Fairy Tales*. London, 1924.
Strachan, John, *Stories from the Táin*. London, 1908.
— *Táin Bó Cuailgne*. Edited by John Strachan and J. G. O'Keefe, revised by O. Bergin, Dublin, 1944.
Sullivan, T. D., *Blanaid*. Dublin, 1891.
Sutcliffe, Rosemary, *The Hound of Ulster*. London, 1963.
— *The High Deeds of Finn Mac Cool*. London, 1967.
Synge, J. M., *Deirdre of the Sorrows (a play)*. London, 1910.
Tannen, Mary, *The Wizard Children of Finn*. London, 1981.
Tennyson, Alfred, Lord, *The Voyage of Maeldune*, with analytical notes by J. Bennett. London, 1892.
Tremayne, Peter, *Raven of Destiny*. London, 1984.
— *My Lady of Hy-Brasil and other stories*. Kingston, Rhode Island, 1986.
— *Ravenmoon*. London, 1988.
Upton, W. C., *Cúchulainn: The story of his combat at the ford*. Dublin, 1887.
Wilde, Jane Francesca, *Ancient Legends of Ireland*. London, 1888.
Windisch, Ernest, *Der altirische Heldensage, Táin Bó Cuailgne*. Berlin, 1905.
Yeats, W. S. Plays: *On Baile Strand*, 1903; *Deirdre*, 1907; *The Golden Helmet*, 1908; *At the Hawk's Well*, 1917; *The Only Jealousy of Emer*,

1919; *A Vision*, 1926; *Fighting the Waves*, 1934; *The Death of Cúchulainn*, 1939.

— Poems: *The Wandering of Oisín*, 1889; *The Celtic Twilight*, 1893; *The Rose*, 1893; *The Wind Among the Reeds*, 1899.

— *Fairy and Folk Tales of Ireland*. Gerrards Cross, 1977.

— with Moore, George, *Diarmuid and Grania. Dublin Magazine*, April/June, 1951.

Young, Ella, *The Coming of Lugh*. Dublin, 1909.

— *Celtic Wonder Tales*. Dublin, 1910.

— *The Weird of Fionvara*. Dublin, 1922.

— *The Wondersmith*. Dublin, 1927.

— *The Tangle-Coated Horse*. Dublin, 1929.